Sequence and Space in Pompeii

EDITED BY SARA E. BON AND RICK JONES

Oxbow Monograph 77
1997

Published by
Oxbow Books, Park End Place, Oxford OX1 1HN

ISBN 1 900188 30 9

This book is available direct from
Oxbow Books, Park End Place, Oxford OX1 1HN
(Phone: 01865–241249; Fax: 01865–794449)
(E-mail: oxbow@patrol.i-way.co.uk)

and

The David Brown Book Company
PO Box 5111, Oakville, CT 06779, USA
(Phone: 860–945–9329; Fax: 860–945–9468)

Printed in Great Britain at
The Short Run Press, Exeter

Contents

List of Figures

List of Contributors

SARA E. BON
Research Laboratories of Anthropology
University of North Carolina
Chapel Hill, NC 27599–3120
USA

PAOLO CARAFA
Facoltà di Lettere – Dip. n. 40
Università di Roma "La Sapienza"
P.le A. Moro 5
00147 Roma
Italy

JOHN J. DOBBINS
Pompeii Forum Project
McIntire Department of Art
Fayerweather Hall
University of Virginia
Charlottesville, VA 22903
USA

STEPHEN L. DYSON
Department of Classics
712 Clemens Hall
SUNY Buffalo
Buffalo, NY 14260
USA

ANGELO GENOVESE
Dipartimento di Strutture, Funzioni e Tecnologie
  Biologiche
Università degli Studi di Napoli Federico II
Napoli
Italy

PIETRO GIOVANNI GUZZO
Soprintendenza Archeologica di Pompei
Via di Villa dei Misteri 2
80045 Pompei (NA)
Italy

GEMMA JANSEN
Vakgroep Klassieke Archeologie
Katholieke Universiteit Nijmegen
Erasmusplein 1
NL-6525 Nijmegen
The Netherlands

RICK JONES
Department of Archaeological Sciences
University of Bradford
Bradford BD7 1DP
UK

BERNICE KURCHIN
Department of Anthropology
Hunter College, CUNY
695 Park Avenue
New York, NY 10021
USA

ESTELLE LAZER
Department of Classical Archaeology
University of Sydney
Sydney, NSW 2006
Australia

ELEANOR WINSOR LEACH
Department of Classical Studies
547 Ballantine Hall
Indiana University
Bloomington, Indiana 47405
USA

JANE RICHARDSON
Department of Archaeology and Prehistory
University of Sheffield,
Northgate House
West Street
Sheffield S1 4ET
UK

DAMIAN J. ROBINSON
Department of Archaeological Sciences
University of Bradford
Bradford BD7 1DP
UK

GILL THOMPSON
Department of Archaeological Sciences
University of Bradford
Bradford BD7 1DP
UK

JANE K. WHITEHEAD
Classics Department, Colby College
Waterville, ME 04901
USA

1 Preface

Pietro Giovanni Guzzo

SPAZIO E TEMPO sono le due categorie di base per tentare di studiare la storia, fatta da eventi che si susseguono e si intrecciano su uno scacchiere le cui caselle hanno ognuna un proprio, e diverso, significato.

L'improvvisa interruzione che ha sofferto Pompei, e con lei Ercolano, Oplontis, Stabiae, ha indotto una consuetudine di conoscenze e studi a-temporali. La gigantesca evidenza della vita bloccata di un organismo complesso ne ha condizionato l'approccio. Il paradosso appena esposto ha, nella sua non verità, una verità di fondo, quasi inconscia. Si parla di Pompei 'romana': si passa sotto silenzio quella pre-'romana'.

Per quanto riguarda lo spazio, sembra che una concezione troppo modernista abbia viziato la valutazione dell'insieme urbanistico del centro. A sua volta, e a monte, una concezione del genere è condizionata della parziale valutazione della categoria tempo. Gli sviluppi spaziali di Pompei, così come sono generalmente ricostruiti, si adattano ad un modello meccanicistico: al quale manca, oltretutto, un comprovato collegamento con le generali dinamiche del popolamento territoriale circostante. Per impossibilità, derivante dalle coperture eruttive, e per un lungo disinteresse da parte della ricerca.

Non sarebbe impossibile per noi ergerci a giudici dei nostri precedessori: anche Fiorelli, nell'applicare un 'nuovo' modo di scavare per insulae, anzichè per cunicoli, muoveva un passo avanti rispetto al passato, in contrapposizione con i suoi predecessori. Ma, di certo, non è esercizio utile al progresso della conoscenza trinciare giudizi: anche perchè le domande che noi, oggi, ci poniamo discendono dalle risposte che hanno dato i nostri predecessori.

L'avanzamento delle esigenze scientifiche e culturali ha, parallelamente, conseguito un affinamento della tecnica d'indagine. Non tanto per ciò che riguarda l'applicazione e la integrazione con la tecniche chimiche, paleostologiche e paleobotaniche, quanto proprio per lo strumento principe della conoscenza archeologica: il modo di eserguire lo scavo e di annotarne i dati recuperati.

Anche se siamo ancora sulla linea di Fiorelli, l'attenzione maggiore alla categoria del tempo ha portato ad investigare, adesso, con maggiore sistematicità di quanto si fosse fatto in passato, il 'prima' di un medesimo spazio e, accanto al 'prima', anche il 'durante'.

È recente l'edizione degli Atti del Convegno Archäologie und Seismologie, ma già più di quindici anni fa Zanker aveva messo a frutto, con saporosi risultati, una lettura 'durante' il

1

tempo di uno stesso spazio. Nella breve durata, tra un sisma e l'altro, oppure nella lunga, dall'età del Ferro al 79 d.c., l'acquisizione controllata e sicura di dati materiali permette, ed unicamente giustifica, una rilettura delle vicende. Se le categorie, per loro natura, sono strumenti astratti del conoscere, è solamente dalla certezza dell'evidenza recuperata che esse possono divenire concretamente funzionali alla storia.

L'accumularsi di dati non dovrebbe, dal canto suo, risolversi in se stesso e così come l'applicazione di una severa metodologia di scavo non dovrebbe applicarsi al terreno, se non fosse stato prima espresso un problema da risolvere, o da chiarire. Le tecniche, quindi, ricondotte al loro ruolo strumentale: ma essenziali nella funzionalità di raggiungere gli obiettivi.

All'interno di questa cornice sistematica sono numerosi i temi e le attività da affrontare: la Soprintendenza ne sta redigendo l'inventario, che sarà, in breve termine, sottoposto all'attenzione ed alla critica degli studiosi interessati. Si vuole, con un concorso il più ampio possibile, arrivare ad uno sforzo congiunto finalizzato ad un'organica conoscenza storica di Pompei.

Dalla quale solamente si potrà derivare sia una giustificata metodologia di restauro sia razionali modalità di fruizione e valorizzazione. La responsabilità prima della Soprintendenza consiste nell'assicurare la conservazione delle documentazioni materiali della pregressa attività umana: affinchè esse possano essere investigate con ottica storica. L'applicarsi della responsibilità dev'essere consono alla natura delle cose da conservare: ed essendo esse cose documenti afferenti la Storia, la conservazione dovrà essere omogenea al metodo storico.

Pertanto, alla Soprintendenza, in quanto organo della Stato, incombe anche la responsabilità di realizzare condizioni di equità a disposizione di tutti coloro i quali, avendone titolo, si propongono come collaboratori all'interno del programma istituzionale. Il buon esito dei programma risiede nella qualità dei progetti: se alla base di essi saranno poste le categorie funzionali alla conoscenza storica, quelle dello spazio e del tempo, ci sarà buona probabilità che la scienza e la cultura riusciranno a sconfiggere la burocrazia e la superficialità.

2 Sequence and Space in Pompeii: An Introduction

Rick Jones and Sara E. Bon

POMPEII IS OBVIOUSLY a special site. Its catastrophic destruction left a monument which is unparalleled for its preservation of an ancient city at one point in time. It also presents remains of earlier occupations spanning the second half of the first millennium BC, and some vestiges from even earlier uses of the site. It has been a point of reference for much of Roman archaeology, but Pompeii's interest and importance transcend the Greco-Roman world. It is one of the best-preserved and most intensely studied of all ancient cities. It has the potential to contribute to discussions of pre-industrial urbanism in many disciplines and has much to offer to broader anthropological research on urbanism and complex societies. Researchers of Pompeii are thus called to recognize the importance of the site as a comparative study for other examples separated from Roman Italy by time and geography. In that recognition, it is hoped that the contribution that we make as a group is significant not only to the understanding of Roman Pompeii, but that beyond the boundaries of traditional classical archaeology it speaks to the interpretation of human societies in many contexts.

The study of Pompeii has included work on elaborate architecture, paintings, mosaics, and fine objects. These subjects have provided the bases for some of the most important and influential interpretive studies in Roman archaeology. The understanding of the occupation sequence and use of space at Pompeii itself has also been an asset to the perception of urban history in antiquity. The richness of the city's preservation has allowed a view of the ancient world which is vastly different from that afforded by other sites. The unusual preservation of structures and artifacts has inspired large-scale studies and secured the renown of the individuals who conducted them. Our understanding of Pompeii has been dominated by the authority of a series of great scholars such as Fiorelli, Mau, Spinazzola, Maiuri, Eschebach, and Van Der Poel, who laid the cornerstones for Pompeian research and whose work remains invaluable. This has sometimes given the impression that the major questions about Pompeii are well understood and that all that remains to be done is to add a few more details. Yet Pompeii is now enjoying an exciting phase of research, much of it employing new or more rigorous methods than those which have often been used to peruse the abundance of material remains there. The new works of scholars from many countries are linked by a consistent thread of the systematic study of detailed evidence, especially archaeological but also literary and artistic. These works are enhanced by the application of a wide range of modern archaeological methods, as well as by an increased consciousness of the need for more anthropologically aware theoretical considerations. We begin this discourse from the perspective of 'sequence and space at Pompeii,' keeping in mind that the goals of these studies are not sequence and space as an end. Rather they are the means to understanding Pompeian society and its manifestation throughout a long period of existence, and how its individuals carried out their lives within the context of a space that was increasingly urbanized in character.

The new research at Pompeii proposes a more productive examination of the first-century AD contexts (e.g. Allison 1992) and more attention to the early development of Pompeii. The systematic study of the earlier levels is currently at a greater intensity than ever before. Although studies of pre-Roman Pompeii are not new (cf. Maiuri 1973), the development of the urban environment at Pompeii has received less attention than the phase of the city preserved by Vesuvius in AD 79. However, significant work throughout this century has addressed some of the larger questions of Pompeii's own development and urban context. Many scholars, both Italian and international, have provided the rubric for our knowledge of when the settlement was defined by city walls and how the particular neighborhoods were filled in (e.g. De Caro 1985; 1986; Bonghi Jovino 1984; Chiaramonte Treré 1986; 1990; D'Ambrosio and De Caro 1989; Nappo 1988; Carocci et al. 1990; Arthur 1986). Without the work of all those who have already contributed to these discussions, we could never have come to the point of addressing the questions that we have arrived at now. We are fortunate to have the intellectual milieu created by these discussions of sequence and space into which to insert this volume.

Within the community of archaeological research at Pompeii, the ground has been prepared for the new phase of research which is sampled here in these collected papers. All these papers relate to issues of sequence and space. The analysis of space in Pompeii is something which has suggested itself to many authors. The extent of available knowledge of the layout of Pompeii has made it an obvious candidate for attention, from early discussions on its early urban planning (Haverfield 1913), to the first modern attempts at formal spatial analysis there (Raper 1977). The analysis of the use of space to reveal the dynamics of ancient urban society has underpinned recent research (Wallace-Hadrill 1994; Laurence 1994). These increasingly sophisticated studies have made significant advances in our understanding and posed new sets of questions. However, it has also been recognized for some time that it is impossible to fully understand the Pompeii of AD 79 without addressing the process of development which had created it. The layouts of individual buildings and the city as a whole were the products of complex processes of change: of design and redesign according to the changing needs of the people who lived in them. Therefore, an image of the city as a static entity pertaining to only one phase is an inherently limited view. The archaeological perspective allows a diachronic understanding which breaks through this limitation (cf. Dunbabin 1995, 390). Concern with the evolution of the city has been long established as part of Pompeian archaeological research, especially in the work of Amedeo Maiuri (1973), but it was emphatically advanced by the work of Roger Ling and his colleagues when they undertook the analysis of the Insula of the House of the Menander expressly to examine how the insula developed over time (Ling 1983). In short, space and sequence can only be understood properly in tandem. Together they form the key factors in analyzing the development of Pompeii's urban character.

From their different perspectives, the papers in this volume discuss either space or sequence, or both. As a whole they demonstrate the complementarity of the two themes, with the end result that the two reside within each other as essential components of the interpretation of Pompeian society. Some of the papers outline the principles behind excavation and survey programs and give their first results (Carafa; Bon et al.). Others consider specific aspects of the uses of urban space, both in specific loci and in a larger scope (Leach; Dobbins; Jansen; Robinson). Others again deal with the available information and future potential of method-ologies which are well established elsewhere, but are new to Pompeii (Richardson et al.; Lazer). This volume contains by no means all the new work being carried out at Pompeii. It presents some of the new approaches and research aims which are widely shared. Most of the papers are based on archaeological evidence, but the crucial contribution that the written evidence can make is well demonstrated in Leach's discussion of room names and functions. Many of the studies presented here are first steps toward a comprehensive view of an ancient society.

One of the stumbling blocks in the publication of Pompeian research has been the wealth of information. The quantity and richness of data have often been difficult to synthesize and present in single publications. This has at times slowed publication and thus hampered the sharing of research among the wider academic community. This volume presents the latest results of a number of studies. Many are early statements from projects that will continue for several more years before final reports are produced. Many research projects warrant multi-ple publications at various stages and of different orientations. It is hoped that this volume will address this problem by promptly disseminating results both from discrete studies (e.g. Leach; Jansen) and from investigations that will eventually result in large-scale publications of their own (e.g. Carafa; Dobbins; Bon et al.). In addition, we believe that it is important to make available the direction of current work at this point. It is of interest to demonstrate promptly how the preliminary results of new work are already challenging established inter-pretations. Perhaps it is even more worthwhile to expose new approaches to wide discussion at an early stage in order to stimulate further debate at a moment where it can contribute to the continuing projects. These papers all exhibit a commitment to the notion that academic debate on Pompeii is a lively and continuing process of developing ideas, rather than just a way of adding still more bits of knowledge to an established framework. This is especially apparent in those papers which argue the value of applying to Pompeii modern archaeologi-cal methods. These make pioneering studies of types of evidence which create whole new perspectives on the questions that can be addressed (Richardson et al.; Lazer). The methods presented in some of these papers (Dobbins; Bon et al.) are newly developed and may be built upon by the next wave of research projects. For this reason it is crucial that the experiences of these researchers be made available for the next researchers to learn from.

All students of Pompeii depend on each other's work. Sharing ideas and results benefits each of us, and the general progress of research. It is gratifying to acknowledge and enjoy a collaborative spirit among the contributors to this volume. Several of these papers were pre-sented in a Colloquium under the same title held at the Annual Meeting of the Archaeological Institute of America in San Diego in December 1995 (Bon; Carafa; Bon et al.; Dobbins; Richardson et al.; Robinson). Andrew Wallace-Hadrill presented a paper there on the work of the British School at Rome-University of Reading project in Insula I, 9. We regret that due to publication commitments elsewhere, that project is not represented here. We are grateful to all the scholars who participated in a fruitful discussion in San Diego, to the contributors to the original session, and to those who have added their work to extend the scope of this volume. The authors of these papers have made great efforts to meet tight deadlines in order to produce promptly a volume of current research.

It is a special pleasure that the Soprintendente alle Antichità di Pompei, Prof. Pietro Giovanni Guzzo has contributed the preface to the volume. This volume has enjoyed the welcoming support and encouragement of the Soprintendenza Archeologica di Pompei. A special debt is due from all scholars who come to study Pompeii to Prof. Guzzo and his colleagues in the Soprintendenza, especially Dott. Antonio D'Ambrosio, Dott. Antonio Varone and Dott.ssa Annamaria Ciarallo.

ACKNOWLEDGEMENT

At critical moments in the editing of the volume in Bradford Sally Fox, Mary Lewis, Nicoletta Momigliano and Armin Schmidt provided much-appreciated help.

References
Allison, P.M. 1992. Artefact assemblages: not 'the Pompeii Premise', in E. Herring, R. Whitehouse and J. Wilkins (eds.), *Papers of the Fourth Conference of Italian Archaeology* (Accordia Research Centre: London): 49–56.
Arthur, P., 1986. Problems of the urbanization of Pompeii: excavations 1980–1, *Antiquaries Journal* 66: 29–44.
Bonghi Jovino, M., 1984. *Ricerche a Pompei. L'Insula 5 della Regio VI dalle origini al 79 d.c.* (Università degli Studi di Milano, Istituto di Archeologia, Biblioteca Archaeologica 5. Bretschneider: Rome).
Carocci, F., de Albentiis, E., Gargiulo, M., and Pesando, F., 1990. *Le Insulae 3 e 4 della Regio VI a Pompei. Un analisi storico-urbanistica* (Archaeolgia Perusina 5. Bretschneider: Rome).
Chiaramonte Treré, C., 1986. *Nuovi Contributi sulle Fortificazioni Pompeiane* (Quaderni di Acme 6, Università degli Studi di Milano: Milan).
Chiaramonte Treré, C., 1990. Sull'origine e lo sviluppo dell'architettura residenziale di Pompei sannitica, *Acme* 43,3: 5–34.
D'Ambrosio, A., and De Caro, S., 1989. Un contributo all'architettura e all'urbanistica i Pompei in età ellenistica. I saggi nella casa VII, 4 , 62, *Annali dell'Istituto Orientale di Napoli* 11: 173–215.
De Caro, S., 1985. Nuovi indagini sulle fortificazioni di Pompei, *Annali dell'Istituto Orientale di Napoli* 7: 75–114.
De Caro, S., 1986. *Saggi nell'area del Tempio di Apollo a Pompei* (Istituto Universitario Orientale di Napoli, Quaderni 3: Naples).
Dunbabin, K.M.D., 1995. Houses and households of Pompeii, *Journal of Roman Archaeology* 8: 387–390.
Haverfield, F. 1913. *Ancient Town Planning* (Clarendon Press: Oxford).
Laurence, R. 1994. *Roman Pompeii: Space and Society* (Routledge: London).
Ling, R., 1983. The Insula of the Menander at Pompeii: interim report, *Antiquaries Journal* 63: 34–57.
Maiuri, A., 1973. *Alla ricerca di Pompei preromana* (Società Editrice Napoletana: Naples).
Nappo, S.C., 1988. Regio I, Insula 2, *Rivista di Studi Pompeiani* 2: 186–192.
Raper, R. 1977. The analysis of the urban structure of Pompeii: a sociological examination of land-use (semi-micro), in D.L. Clarke (ed.) *Spatial Archaeology* (Academic Press, London): 189–221.
Wallace-Hadrill, A. 1994. *Houses and Society in Pompeii and Herculaneum* (Princeton University Press: Princeton).

3 A City Frozen in Time or a Site in Perpetual Motion? Formation Processes at Pompeii

Sara E. Bon

INTRODUCTION

The magic of Pompeii comes from the image it creates as a city frozen at a moment in time, when all activity was stopped in the middle of busy lives involving plates of food, households full of possessions, and the workings of ancient life preserved as in an archaeologist's dream. It cannot be denied that the preservation of Pompeii in the midst of occupation created archaeological contexts of rare quality. However, those preserved by volcanic deposits comprise only a portion of the archaeological contexts which exist at Pompeii. Both before and after AD 79, human and natural activity have affected archaeological remains there. These formation processes are analogous to those found at other ancient sites, with deposition and replacement providing the gradual movement of artifacts and structures from their use-contexts into archaeological contexts, and post-deposition cultural and non-cultural influences affecting both artifacts and architecture.

Pompeii had a long history prior to the first century AD; its final urban form so famously preserved was produced during centuries of development. The remains of the earlier periods are not Pompeii's most spectacular, and consequently have received much less attention. Recent research has recognized the archaeological importance of the early phases (e.g. Arthur 1986; Bonghi Jovino 1984), and current work is providing more evidence for early use of the site (Carafa, this volume). With more and more attention devoted to the evidence of Pompeii's pre-Roman period, a picture of those events is emerging. Remains from earlier than the fourth century BC are still unconnected with one another, but it is clear that there was some activity at the site as early as the eighth or even ninth centuries BC (Carafa, this volume). There is a definite case for a walled sixth century settlement of considerable size, encompassing what may have been an agricultural and mercantile populace and two temples (Arthur 1986, 40). Continually more evidence produces a view of considerable construction during the fourth century BC (Carafa, this volume), with significant development of public and private spheres in the second century BC.

This second-century reconfiguration may have produced the urban layout that we see in the first-century AD plan of Pompeii. However, what we do see in the preserved plan and occupation contexts is not an untouched glimpse of ancient assemblages and architecture.

7

Considerable intervention occurred before modern archaeology took responsibility for Pompeii's riches, and changes occur even today in the standing remains. In the volcanic deposits, for example, there may have been property recovery and looting in antiquity which robbed these contexts of objects with monetary, personal, or art-historical value. Since then, looting has been commonplace, and early excavation was primitive enough to have not vastly different effects. Currently earthquakes, vegetation, water, tourist wear, atmospheric pollution, excavation, vandalism, and re-building for maintenance threaten the monument and alter its condition.

It is the combination of these influences before and after AD 79 which provide the contrasting diachronic view of the city, so different from the synchronic frozen moment for which Pompeii is known. A great deal of the research newly undertaken at Pompeii is aimed either at investigating pre-AD 79 development or post-AD 79 change, or incorporates a more thorough and critical use of the rich data from the volcanic contexts.

STILL CHANGING AFTER ALL THESE YEARS

Some of the forces presently altering the city are specific and identifiable events. For example, the last half century alone has seen serious earthquake damage (Adam 1983) as well as bomb damage during World War II (Descoeudres 1994, 48–49), both of which had considerable impact on the city. Much of the current change in the monument occurs on a daily basis and is considerably less dramatic than earthquakes or bombings. Millions of visitors a year walk through the ruins, and the exposed structures succumb to the pressures of gravity, millions, of feet, and an occasional act of vandalism. In the wake of all this, maintenance and reconstruction present significant demands at Pompeii. As walls and floors crumble, teams of workers rebuild. When possible, ancient materials are re-used and are employed following ancient building styles. The repairs themselves are at times necessary for structural stability or visitor safety, and equally important is an interest in presenting a historically accurate interpretation. Retaining authenticity, however, can lead to trouble discerning ancient from modern constructions. In some cases there are indications which signal modern reconstruction, but where these markers do not occur, the modern components blend with ancient phases of building and modification.

Sometimes destruction is immediately addressed; more obvious signs of weathering and disrepair are often remedied promptly, and the bomb impact was quickly assessed, with repairs implemented in the following years (Laidlaw 1993, 217). But much of the damage done to masonry structures, floor surfaces, and wall decoration has been incorporated into the general state of crumbling which seems inevitable in the extensive unearthed areas of the monument. Building episodes imitating ancient architectural events and unaddressed deterioration are both types of change which contribute to a dynamic monument. Pompeii, rather than being a city frozen in time, is in a constant state of flux. Upon recognizing the perpetual state of change in the monument, one of the important tasks currently facing research at Pompeii is the documentation of the existing state of the site. This forms an archive necessary for identifying future changes, and is the basis for interpreting the building sequences in antiquity and their differentiation from those which have occurred since the first excavations.

RECOGNIZING THE FORMATION PROCESSES

Documenting the changes in the city since burial and then during and since excavation has been a significant task (Adam 1983; Laidlaw 1993; Pagano 1991–2). Adam produced a definitive review of current deterioration at Pompeii which also proposed recommendations for repair of structural damage of many kinds, including earthquake damage from 1980. However, even assessments of visible damage may not be complete inventories of present change. It is likely that for some events such as World War II bombardments, we know only a portion of their true impact. While some of the visible bomb damage was recorded and repairs made (Descoeudres 1994; Laidlaw 1993), little is known of bomb damage to buried remains. The Anglo-American Pompeii Project has unearthed a bomb crater of considerable size in the House of the Vestals (Bon et al. 1995, 8; Bon et al. this volume), and it is likely that explosions elsewhere in the city also reached the levels of earlier occupation phases. Clearly at a site of the magnitude of Pompeii, documenting modern modifications to standing structures and buried remains is a phenomenal undertaking. It is nearly impossible to track changes in all parts of the exposed city.

The manipulation of artifact assemblages during excavation has also been significant, revealed most resoundingly by the work of Allison (cf. Allison 1992). There is an assumption that due to Pompeii's simultaneous catastrophic abandonment and preservation, the artifacts which exist there presently, or are known from excavation, are ideal assemblages. That is, it is presumed that the archaeological inventories approximately equal the materials that were in use there at the time of the eruption, or the systemic inventories (Schiffer 1972). Pompeii appears to be a site where all human activity was halted at a moment in time, thus producing artifact assemblages reflecting their inventories in daily use. According to archaeological theory, the cessation of Pompeian habitation within one catastrophic event created an unusual preservation of artifact assemblages and structures. Short of such catastrophic destruction, objects and buildings do not become abandoned and preserved as whole sets. Had occupation not terminated as it did, walls would have been knocked down and rebuilt to accommodate changing needs for space; decoration would have been altered as styles evolved, and household items would have been replaced as they were either discarded, lost, worn out, or broken. Even though most durable goods are eventually a part of an archaeological assemblage (Ascher 1961, 324), they do not become a part of an archaeological assemblage as a complete set, as they had been utilized together in their functional use-lives (Schiffer 1972). Rather, they do so as individual elements when their functional lives end. At Pompeii, the material goods which were preserved were put out of use at a specific point in time, creating a more homogenous temporal input into the archaeological assemblage. The presumed lack of re-use, scavenging, and exportation of objects created an archaeological inventory which closely resembled the systemic inventory. Artifacts and buildings were not re-used, replaced, or modified by later needs or styles. The material goods of first century AD Pompeii differ from those belonging to other abandoned settlements in that for the most part they were not removed either by their owners or by scavengers for re-use or recycling.

The problems with the assumption of an ideal assemblage are two: the first is that even in the AD 79 contexts, there was in fact much interference with structures and assemblages after the inhabitants of Pompeii left and before modern archaeological documentation occurred. The second fault in the assumption of Pompeii as a site of ideal assemblages is that the discussion centers solely on the single context of AD 79. This synchronic view of the city ignores the earlier contexts which hold the remains of many centuries of occupation and which are necessarily a part of understanding the whole of Pompeii, both its sequence and space.

Even the occupation levels of the first century AD which are so renowned for their sealed contexts present a more complex picture than has been assumed. It has been correctly pointed out (Allison 1992) that in spite of the preservation which makes Pompeii known as an extraordinary site, there were intervening events between the moment of abandonment and destruction and the arrival of modern archaeologists who have also complicated the artifact assemblages by removing and re-positioning artifacts (cf. Allison 1992; Binford 1981; Schiffer 1972; 1985).

The creation of archaeological contexts in the first century AD was probably less uniform than presumed, as abandonment of some buildings probably occurred prior to the eruption. While occupation of the city as a whole ceased on 24–25 August of AD 79 (Sigurdsson et al. 1982), life at the city before this point was disrupted by one or more damaging earthquakes. And after the eruption people continued to interfere with the remains in ways that affect the current archaeological inventories.

The last decades of Pompeian occupation were characterized by reconstruction due to reconfiguration of property ownership and repair stemming from the seismic activities beginning with the earthquake of AD 62 (Nappo 1995; Allison 1992). During this time, some buildings may have been abandoned and some occupied or reoccupied with secondary, temporary, or multiple usages. There may have been looting during the final decades of occupation, and perhaps again soon after burial. The discussion of post-eruption looting or property recovery has not been answered for all of the city, although there was probably little chance that the owners of particular properties came back to their houses to recover their own belongings (Descoeudres 1993).

Looting in various formats occurred for centuries before rigorous archaeological research was established at Pompeii. Early archaeological clearing of volcanic fill engaged no more careful planning than following the ancient streets. There were no records kept to speak of, and at best recovered material goods appear in the National Archaeological Museum at Naples, rarely with reliable records of context or provenience. At worst, the material goods retrieved disappeared into private homes and collections and lost any historic or archaeological value. During some of the early excavations of Pompeii, artifacts were often re-positioned to accommodate interpretations (Allison 1992). Allison concludes that 'archaeological remains have been corrected to fit preconceived ideas of how the record should have looked in Pompeii'

(1992, 52). Not only were there scanty and unreliable records of these excavations, but artifacts were moved from room to room, re-oriented, or placed where they were thought to have belonged.

CONSIDERING POMPEII'S DEVELOPMENT

The current condition of Pompeian assemblages and structures was created by influences altering the city's remains since its volcanic burial, but was also formed by a long occupation prior to AD 79. Interest in the city however, has traditionally concentrated on Roman Pompeii, the last phase of occupation of the ancient city. The emphasis on the richly preserved phases of Pompeian occupation is more than understandable, and is to a large extent appropriate considering that in few other places is such a quality of data available. It is also true that the earlier phases of Pompeii have often been neglected. Centuries of occupation preceded the last phase which was sealed, however imperfectly, by the volcano. The preservation of these earlier phases more closely resembles other sites with long histories of occupation than the first century deposits of Pompeii. The pre-Roman components of Pompeii are the contexts in which the first century AD city was formed.

Known as a spectacular Roman site, Pompeii was only politically Roman for a short period of its history. Roman authority was notable at Pompeii from the end of the fourth century BC. However it was not until the first century BC that Roman citizenship was given to the inhabitants of Pompeii, followed closely by the establishment of a veterans' colony there. By the time Pompeii was politically Roman, it had seen nearly a millennium of occupation under the spheres of non-Roman political, economic, and cultural influence. It is difficult to say at what point Pompeii became culturally Roman, since it was certainly incorporated into the Roman realm of trade, government, architecture, and aesthetics long before its denizens had rights of Roman citizenship. Because of this, the nature of what is culturally Roman – or architecturally, or aesthetically Roman – is complicated. Pompeii's richly preserved Roman remains have drawn attention to that phase of habitation. To understand even the last phase, though, and perhaps more abstractly the meaning and development of Roman-ness at Pompeii, it is valuable to investigate the context in which it developed.

CONCLUSIONS

Excavation combined with detailed structural recording and analysis is providing the data necessary to reconstruct a long and complicated history of human presence in Pompeii, including the final phase of Roman occupation, but stretching to incorporate the often neglected prehistoric phases (Bon et al. 1995). It is necessary to understand these earlier phases in order to appreciate the spectacularly preserved first century component of Pompeii. The buildings that existed at the time of the eruption, and in fact of the society which lived at Pompeii then, were the product of a development during centuries of occupation. To consider only the product of this process is to start at the end of the story.

The richness of Pompeii can be most advantageously considered within its chronological context, which is a long sequence beginning early in the first millennium BC. It is only the final phase of Pompeian occupation which belongs to the richly preserved site with its intact structures and nearly complete artifact assemblages. As we have seen, even this extraordinarily preserved monument presents a complicated network of formative events, both in its development during antiquity, the several centuries of modern archaeological and antiquarian interest in the city, and in salvage and looting in the intervening time. This same richness creates particular demands of recording for archival purposes, for public interpretation and greater academic understanding, and for the maintenance and preservation of the physical remains themselves. It is hoped that the new phase of Pompeian research is one of more resourceful use of archaeological remains of all phases.

Acknowledgment

I would like to thank the Archaeological Institute of America for its generous support in the form of a Graduate Student Travel Award which allowed me to present a version of this paper at its 1995 Annual Meeting in San Diego.

References

Adam, J.-P., 1983. *Dégradation et Restauration de l'Architecture Pompéienne* (CNRS: Paris).

Allison, P., 1992. Artefact assemblages: not 'the Pompeii Premise', in E. Herring, R. Whitehouse, and J. Wilkins (eds.), *Papers of the Fourth Conference of Italian Archaeology* (Accordia Research Centre: London): 49–56.

Arthur, P., 1986. Problems of the urbanization of Pompeii: excavations 1980–81. *Antiquaries Journal* 66: 29–44.

Ascher, R., 1961. Analogy in archaeological interpretation, *Southwestern Journal of Anthropology* 17 (4): 317–325.

Binford, L.R. 1981. Behavioral archaeology and the 'Pompeii Premise', *Journal of Anthropological Research* 37 (2): 195–208.

Bon, S.E., Jones, R., Kurchin, B., and Robinson, D.J, 1995. *Anglo-American Research at Pompeii, 1995* (Bradford Archaeological Sciences Research 1: Bradford).

Bonghi Jovino, Maria, (ed.), 1984. *Ricerche a Pompei: L'Insula 5 della Regio VI dalle origini al 70 d.C.* (L'Erma di Bretschneider: Rome).

Descoeudres, J.-P., 1993. Did some Pompeians return to their city after the eruption of Mt. Vesuvius in AD 79? Observations in the House of the Coloured Capitals, in L. Franchi dell'Orto (ed.), *Ercolano 1738–1988. 250 Anni di Ricerca Archeologica*. Soprintendenza Archeologica di Pompei, Monografie 6 (L'Erma di Bretschneider: Rome): 165–178.

Descoeudres, J.-P., 1994. *Pompeii Revisited: The Life and Death of a Roman Town* (Meditarch: Sydney).

Laidlaw, A., 1993. Excavations in the Casa di Sallustio, Pompeii: a preliminary assessment, in R.T. Scott and A.R. Scott (eds.), *Eius Virtutits Studiosi: Classical and Postclassical Studies in Memory of Frank Edward Brown (1908–1988)*. (National Gallery of Art, Washington D.C.: Hanover and London): 217–233.

Nappo, S.C. 1993. Evidenze di danni strutturali, restauri, e rifacimenti nelle insulae gravitanti su Via Nocera a Pompei, in T. Fröhlich and L. Jacobelli (eds.), *Archäologie und Seismologie* (Verlag Biering & Brinkmann: Munich).

Pagano, M., 1991–2. Metodologia dei restauri borbonici a Pompei ed Ercolano, *Rivista di Studi Pompeiani* V: 169–191.

Schiffer, M.B., 1972. Archaeological context and systemic context, *American Antiquity* 37 (2): 156–165.

Schiffer, M.B., 1985. Is there a 'Pompeii Premise' in archaeology? *Journal of Anthropological Research* 41 (1): 18–41.

Sigurdsson, H., Cashdollar, S., and Sparks, S.R.J., 1982. The eruption of Vesuvius in A.D. 79: Reconstruction from historical and volcanological evidence, *American Journal of Archaeology* 86 (1):39–51.

4 What was Pompeii before 200 BC?
Excavations in the House of Joseph II, in the Triangular Forum and in the House of the Wedding of Hercules[1]

Paolo Carafa

INTRODUCTION

One of the most debated problems in Pompeian studies relates to the origins of the settlement and its urban development (De Caro 1992). Several aspects of important historical themes connected to this issue still need to be fully explained (Lepore 1992). Consider, for example, the ongoing discussion on the structure of the oldest indigenous communities of Campania (Cristofani 1992); on the dynamics of the Samnite take over of the region (Zanker 1993); on how and at what point Greek and Roman cultural influences reached the Campanian centers (Zanker 1993) and when their definitive romanization finally occurred (Zanker 1993, 71–83). Nonetheless it is generally accepted that the city of Pompeii was founded at the beginning of the sixth century BC. In this early phase, the inhabited area was probably restricted to the southwest corner of the lava plateau, the so called *Altstadt*, even if the circuit of the fortification wall enclosed already an area sixty-six hectares wide. At the end of the fourth century BC, after the final defeat of the Samnite league and the victory of the Roman armies, the layout of the settlement changed. A number of blocks were built in the wide open areas within the fortification wall, creating the town plan which has been preserved for us by the eruption in 79 (De Caro 1992).

In the course of the debate many have pointed out how the lack of reliable archaeological data accentuates the problem of limited literary documentation. Yet, so far, the need for new data has not led to specific investigations on the issue. As a result, the oldest phases of Pompeii have received, in general, little attention. Therefore the dating of the initial site occupation and the layout of the settlement during the centuries preceding the Roman take over of

[1] This paper is a preliminary report on the 1994 and 1995 excavations in Pompeii directed by Andrea Carandini and completed with the collaboration of Maria Teresa D'Alessio and Angelo Amoroso. I wish to thank former Soprintendente alle Antichità Baldassarre Conticello for encouraging the beginning of this research project and the present Soprintendente Pier Giovanni Guzzo for insisting that the project develop on an even larger scale. I also wish to thank Antonio D'Ambrosio, Direttore degli Scavi di Pompei, for helping us throughout the excavation; Caterina Cicirelli for being present on the excavation; all the Soprintendenza staff members who directly or indirectly contributed to the project. I am grateful to Clementina Panella for examining some of the pottery used to establish the chronologies presented here; and to Gianni Ponti for translating the text into English. I am of course responsible for any errors or inaccuracies that remain.

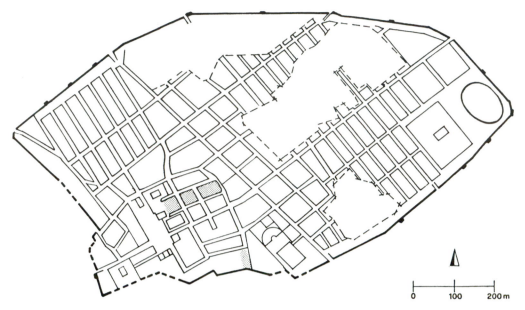

Fig. 4.1 *Plan of Pompeii: the investigated areas in gray.*

Campania and the Punic Wars could be considered still problematic and to some extent unresolved issues.

For these reasons, thanks to the good will of the Soprintendenza Archeologica, we pre-pared a detailed research plan to investigate the topographic and urban development of the Vesuvian city (Fig. 4.1). One of the project's main objectives was to excavate a large enough area of the so-called *Altstadt* to obtain a clear reading of any early phases predating the Hel-lenistic layout of the city. Excavation began in the summer of 1994: during the first campaign work was limited to a confined area of Regio VIII, while later archaeological investigation focused on part of Regio VII, between the Forum and the Stabian Baths.

Choosing sites for the excavation:

The oldest settlement and a sanctuary on the acropolis

In Regio VIII we chose the area between house VIII, 2, 38–39 and the court of the Triangular Forum. The house, also known as the House of Joseph II or the House of Fuscus, is well known as a result of F. Lehmann Hartleben's publication of the entire Insula (Lehmann Hartleben 1936). In terms of the present research these two monuments are of interest for their topographical location. The insula that includes the house falls completely within the supposed boundaries of the *Altstadt* and one of its sides seems to correspond to the presumed southern boundary of the hypothetical older settlement. The insula is not only the possible

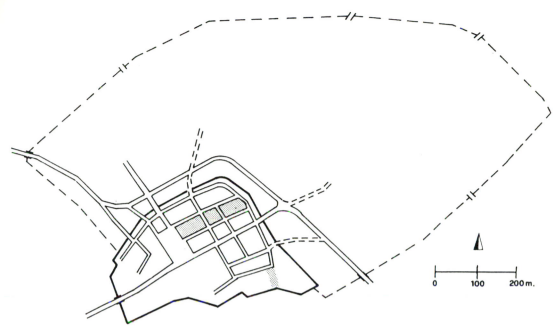

Fig. 4.2   *The investigated areas related to the lay-out of the supposed Altstadt. (after Eschebach 1970)*

boundary between the inner and outer sections of the settlement. It also represents the limit between a residential area and a public area of the town, namely the court of the Triangular Forum with the adjacent sanctuary of the Doric Temple (de Waele 1993). The reconstruction of the original sacred precinct and its relation to the Archaic settlement are still unresolved issues. Assuming that the limits of the sanctuary and other unknown features of the sacred area had in fact survived, we hoped to identify them by stratigraphic investigation.

The area selected in Regio VII is also entirely contained within the *Altstadt* (Fig. 4.2). We investigated its two extremities: taberna VII, 11, 16–17 and house VII, 9, 47, also known as the House of the Wedding of Hercules, due to a fresco which represented the hero's nuptial ceremony. These two virtually unpublished monuments are significant because of their location: the house is right next to the Forum and lies at the center of the presumed Archaic settlement. The taberna, on the other hand, lies in what could have been a peripheral area.

THE EXCAVATION

The House of Joseph II – VIII, 2, 38–39

Excavation in the House of Joseph II included the atrium proper (Fig. 4.3) and parts of the three eastern rooms (Carafa-d'Alessio, forthcoming). All excavation reached virgin soil except in one trench.

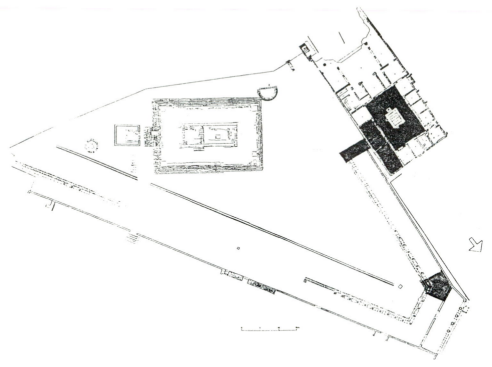

Fig. 4.3 *Plan of the House of Joseph II and the Triangular Forum. (after Lehmann Hartleben 1936)*
The excavated area in gray.

The different elevations of Insula 2, the Triangular Forum and the Great Theater with the so called 'barracks of the gladiators' show that the plateau where Regio VIII subsequently developed, had a terraced eastern slope. This natural configuration of the terrain was artificially increased before the construction of the Insula, possibly when a sanctuary was first inaugurated in the area of the Triangular Forum. The short slope which marks the difference in level between the two upper terraces was in fact regularized. The separation between the upper and lower area was emphasized by the excavation of two parallel ditches on the plateau of the Doric Temple. The ditches, five metres apart, can be interpreted as the sides of an ancient road. Probably during this phase a hut was built on top of the hill: it was a small rectangular structure with rounded corners, located near the edge of the terrace which set it apart from the sanctuary. Unfortunately the stratigraphy related to the occupation period of the hut has not survived. The oldest finds associated with the structure suggest a construction date for the hut ranging between the Iron Age and the middle of the seventh century BC.[2]

At some point between the middle of the fourth and the end of the third century BC a small

---

[2]   The finds consist of some fragments of coarse impasto and good quality bucchero. For the ditch closer to the Doric Temple we have a good *terminus ante quem*: the ditch was in fact cut by a pit whose fill yielded part of a bucchero *kantharos* of the first half of the sixth century BC.

Fig. 4.4 *The remains of the rectangular building. In the foreground the foundation trench of the eastern wall filled with fragments of limestone blocks. Note the post holes of the earlier hut cut by the trench. (photo by the author)*

rectangular masonry building replaced the hut[3] (Fig. 4.4). The foundations of small limestone blocks of the south, east and north walls are preserved. The structure, possibly a house, was not particularly sophisticated in terms of its construction techniques, but was probably decorated with architectural terracottas and painted plaster. In the following century the two ditches were filled with a series of clay layers and subsequently covered by a thick layer of backfill that lies against the artificial cut into the hill. The backfill, which reaches the level of the upper terrace, was not completed as a single event: we noted at least two interruptions within it. The first consists of five post-holes which can be identified as the remains of a palisade that preserved the orientation of the underlying ditches. The second is a channel with the usual north-south orientation, cutting directly into in the layers of the backfill. In the first half of the second century BC two small pilasters in lava and limestone blocks sealed the last layer of the backfill, marking for the last time the original orientation of the ditches.

During the third quarter of the second century BC the house was built (Figs. 4.5–6). The

---

[3] The date for the structure is based on sherds found within the foundation and in related layers. If we accept the proposed chronology for the hut we have the problem of explaining why we do not have any stratification that relates to four centuries of occupation of the structure. Either the hut was not occupied for a prolonged period of time or occupation in the area of the plateau continued in alternating phases.

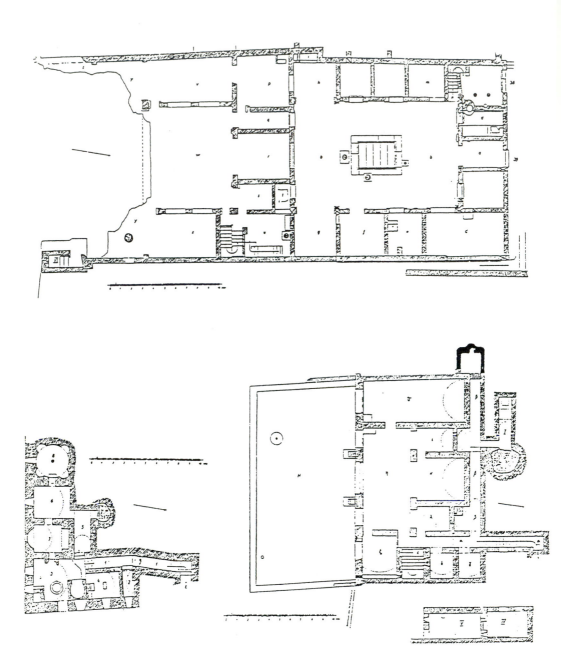

Fig. 4.5 *The House of Joseph II. (after Lehmann Hartleben 1936)*

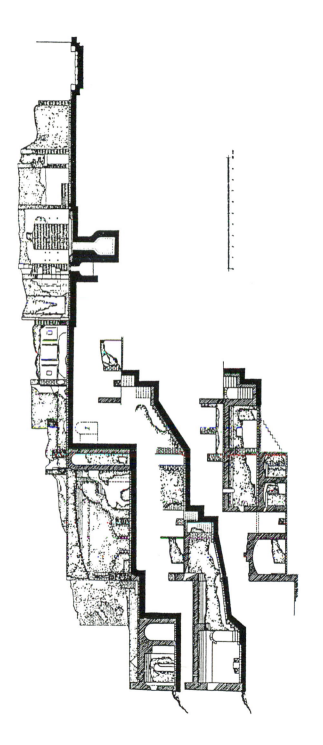

Fig. 4.6 The House of Joseph II: architectural sections. (after Lehmann Hartleben 1936)

original layout already featured a tablinum in axis with the fauces, a Tuscan atrium with alae and four Corinthian semicolumns in Nocera tufa to embellish the corners, two lower floors with terraces and a small bath complex. The impluvium, also built in Nocera tufa, is located at the center of the atrium and is flanked by two cisterns. A small limestone drain in opus incertum runs under the vestibule and fauces, discharging directly into the street.

The western porticus of the Triangular Forum

In the western porticus of the Triangular Forum we opened two test trenches: a rather small one, in the vicinity of the House of Joseph II, to obtain a revealing section of the area between the presumed *Altstadt* and the sanctuary court below; the other in the northern corner of the portico to verify information recovered in the smaller trench.

We have already mentioned the two ditches that marked the original boundaries of the sanctuary. In this area we also uncovered two post-holes cut into virgin soil, showing the presence of a wooden structure of uncertain date. During the second century BC a building whose overall plan is yet to be defined was erected. The excavation brought to light the remains of some foundation walls, built in extremely compact *opus caementitium* (Fig. 4.7). These foundations were subsequently robbed and partially destroyed by the construction of the porticus. A small rectangular basin, coated with mortar and filled with the building's destruc-

Fig. 4.7 *The Triangular Forum: trench excavated in 1995. (photo by the author)*

tion debris, was cut in one of the foundations. There is not enough evidence to determine the original character and function of the building. The location and the range of architectural terracottas, figurines (Fig. 4.8) and pottery that were recovered out of context in levels associated with the building's destruction, suggest that the structure was somehow related to the sanctuary. These finds can be dated between the sixth and first centuries BC and seem to belong to a votive deposit. The construction of the porticus followed the destruction of the building.

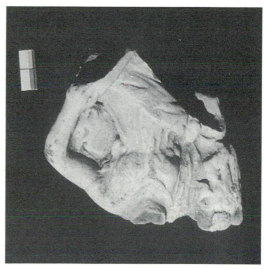

Fig. 4.8 Terracotta figurine from the Triangular Forum. (photo courtesy of the Soprintendenza Archeologica di Pompei)

Taberna VII, 11, 16–17

We decided to investigate this limited area to obtain a complete stratigraphic sequence down to virgin soil in a relatively short amount of time – something which would not have been possible had we opened a trench in a larger area like the atrium of a domus. Unfortunately most of the stratigraphy had already been removed by a wide pit which marked the definitive destruction of the taberna in the Julio-Claudian period. It was possible to establish, however, that the taberna was built in the second half of the second century BC[4] in what had been previously an undeveloped area. Under the room floors we identified a sequence of sterile layers, cut by pits of varying size and depth (Fig. 4.9). Analysis of soil samples is currently underway in the laboratories of the Soprintendenza Archeologica di Pompei to establish if the soils were used for agricultural activity and possibly to identify crop types.

Also in this case the oldest activities cannot be precisely dated. Nonetheless the Hellenistic and Imperial layers yielded quantities of sherds that range between the Iron Age and the sixth century BC, confirming the existence of protohistoric and archaic occupation.

The House of the Wedding of Hercules

The House of the Wedding of Hercules is a typical Pompeian *Kalksteinhaus* with a Tuscan atrium, two alae, a tablinum in axis with the fauces, and a peristyle (Fig. 4.10). As in the House of Joseph II, excavation focused on the atrium and on the surrounding rooms. In this neighbourhood stratigraphic accumulation is more substantial than in the three areas we have already discussed. Even though we have not yet reached virgin soil, the segment of stratigraphy which we have finished investigating has already confirmed data recovered in the other areas.

---

4   The latest sherds recovered in the context of construction activity of the building are Dressel 1 amphora.

Fig. 4.9 *Taberna VII, 11, 16–17. Note the pits filled with fragments of stones and pottery visible in the section.*
(photo by the author)

The House of the Wedding of Hercules was built during the second half of the second century BC and the original layout of the building already featured an open, or partially open area behind the tablinum. Here, before the construction of the house, there was a small building with foundations of limestone fragments supporting wooden and clay walls (Fig. 4.11). A vaguely circular arrangement of post-holes that we uncovered around the later impluvium shows that part of this structure was built entirely of wood. The remains are badly preserved and it is difficult to reconstruct the original plan. We can probably recognize two rectangular rooms looking out onto an open court, and possibly the main entrance to the building (Fig. 4.12). The materials from the layers cut by the foundations are few and hardly significant: however, sherds of Campanian black painted ware do not allow us to date these layers before the fourth century BC.

This structure was preceded by two other buildings which are only partially visible. The oldest one, with soft lava walls, is still undated. The later structure was built in limestone fragments: excavation of the fill of one of the foundation trenches yielded more sherds of Campanian black painted ware.

Since these structures lie directly over each other and maintain the same orientation, it would seem that we are dealing with successive reconstructions of the same building which developed over a long period of time. By widening the excavation we hope to establish if the first

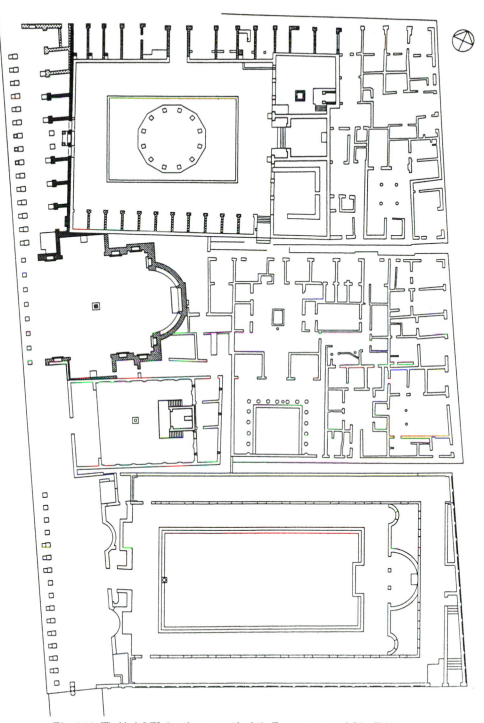

Fig. 4.10 *The block VII, 9 at the eastern side of the Forum. (courtesy of John Dobbins)*

Fig. 4.11 *House of the Wedding of Hercules: the excavated atrium. (photo by the author)*

Fig. 4.12 *House of the Wedding of Hercules: the remains of the earlier building. (photo by the author)*

building was surrounded by other structures and, if so, of what type. Up to now excavation below other rooms of the House of the Wedding of Hercules has not uncovered remains of earlier structures.

INTERPRETATION

We can thus summarize the data gathered so far. Excavation has identified remains of a permanent settlement of the second half of the seventh century BC, characterized so far only by wooden or soft lava structures. The first obvious changes of this settlement occurred in the fourth century BC when the older buildings were substituted by new ones, structurally more solid yet still elementary in plan. After approximately two centuries the Insulae in regions VIII and VII were built. This sequence of events clearly differs from generally accepted theories on the historical and urban development of Pompeii. Continuing research will certainly have to reconstruct the nature and the overall appearance of this earlier settlement which was completely rebuilt in the second century BC. Even though the present research project is just completing its initial stage, we would like to propose some hypotheses by considering our data in relation to other archaeological evidence from Pompeii.

a) One of the principal problems in reconstructing the history of the Vesuvian city lies in the difficulties one encounters in trying to determine when the plateau was first occupied on a permanent basis, before Pompeii actually developed as a city. If on one hand there are no structures securely dated to the sixth century BC (Cristofani 1991, 13ff.; De Caro 1985, 107ff.), we do know of ceramic and bronze materials of the protohistoric period. These finds are indeed scarce, but nonetheless indispensable for proper dating of initial site occupation. Other than the eneolithic stone axe found outside Porta Nocera (De Caro 1985, 107), the oldest objects found within the city or just outside the perimeter of the fortification walls are limited to about a dozen sherds that date to the Early and Late Bronze Age.[5]

We also have evidence from the IX and VIII centuries BC.[6] The distribution of these finds includes areas of the city beyond the theoretical boundaries of the *Altstadt* (Fig. 4.13), so that

---

[5]   Early Bronze Age sherds, of the Palma Campania facies come from soundings in the House of M. Lucretius Fronto (Brunsting and Wynia 1993, 329–331). More material comes from sounding 4 of the city walls, to the east of Tower III (De Caro 1985, 101–103, Fig. 28, 102–115). The state of preservation of the sherds is such that one cannot establish to which phase of the Bronze Age they belong. Only one sherd (De Caro 1985, Fig. 28.115) could tentatively be dated to the Late Bronze Age because of grooves on the exterior surface. I would like to thank Marco Bettelli for dating the sherd. Among the finds from the deepest levels identified under the House of M. Lucretius Fronto (V, 4, a) H. Brunsting (1975, 199) mentions 'prähistorische Scherben, die wir auf den ersten Blick nicht datieren konntenn' and hypothetically relates them to known Bronze Age tombs in the territory around Pompeii. For these finds also see Brunsting and Wynia 1993, 15.

[6]   For materials of the ninth century BC see Varone 1989, 231 (impasto sherds from stratigraphic soundings in the Temple of Isis), Brunsting and Wynia 1993, 15 (impasto sherds from the House of M. Lucretius Fronto), Reusser 1982, 355ff., Abb. 1 and 2, Taf. 134.1–2 (ceramic and bronze materials from the House of Ganimede). The fragment of a bronze belt found in the House of the Clay Molds could also date to the Iron Age (D'Ambrosio and De Caro 1989, 205 Fig. 48.FC 2074). For materials of the eighth century BC see De Caro 1986, 112 n.90 tav. L (bronze fibula from the Apollo sanctuary) and also note 48. Along with the coarse wares found in our excavations of the House of Joseph II and of taberna VII, 11, 16–17, some sherds of the same type were found in the excavations of the University of Reading in Insula 9 of Regio I (Wallace-Hadrill pers. comm.).

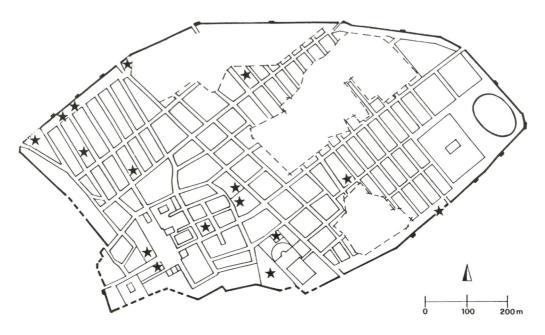

Fig. 4.13 *Pompeii: distribution of proto-historic and archaic finds.*

it is legitimate to presume that the entire area within the walls was in fact inhabited as early as the Iron Age. The overall extent of the settlement could have already reached the 66 hectares covered by the city in historical times. Compared to contemporary Campanian or Italic settlements in central Italy it must have been a settlement of remarkable size,[7] a fact which seems to indicate that Pompeii always was the major center of the Sarno valley. The existence of at least one public cult within the settlement, as shown from late Iron Age materials found in the votive deposits of the sanctuary of Apollo,[8] seems to confirm the high level of political and social organization reached by the first community in Pompeii.

b) Recent research has established that settlements along the Sarno valley, known from the famous cemeteries of S. Marzano sul Sarno, Sarno, San Valentino Torio and Striano[8] (Fig. 4.14),

---

[7]   See the figure proposed by Cornell 1995, 23.

[8]   Note the bronze fibula mentioned above (De Caro 1986, 112 n.909) and an impasto cup, unfortunately lost, dated to the Iron Age (De Caro 1986, 110). A jug and a jug with geometric decoration can be dated to the Orientalizing Period, possibly to the eighth century BC (De Caro 1986, 66, tav. XXXXIII, LXI, 361 and 362). Beyond parallels mentioned here, see Johannowsky 1984, 181ff. and 188, tav. 25a and 28 bis, for a jug from St. Angelo in Formis; 274ff. and tav. 61b for jug from Sessula. See also Lupo 1992, 512, tav. 5/3 and 13/1 for a jug from Boscoreale.

[8] Gastaldi 1979, Varone 1988, 195ff. with bibliography, D'Ambrosio 1990. The possibility of dating the first settlement before the end of the seventh century BC had already been proposed by Riemann 1979, 326. For the most recent overview of the Sarno territory in the Iron Age see Colonna 1991, 42 and Cerchiai 1995, 26–33 with bibliography.

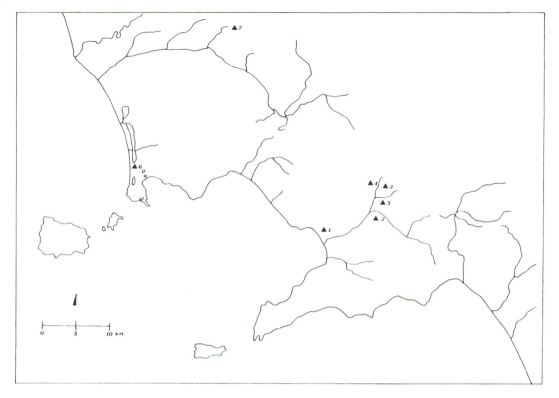

Fig. 4.14 *Northern Campania and the Sarno Valley with major centers in proto-historic and archaic times (after Cristofani 1992). (1: Pompeii, 2: S. Marzano sul Sarno, 3: Sarno, 4: Striano, 5: S. Valentino Torio, 6: Cuma, 7: Capua.)*

were not abandoned during the sixth century BC. If evidence from Stabia[10] seems to point towards significant political turmoil in the area during this period, it is clear, nonetheless, that the cemeteries continued to be used without interruption at least until the fifth century BC (Arthur 1986, 40). This evidence suggests that it will be necessary to reconsider the widely accepted synchronism between the end of the Sarno settlements and the founding of Pompeii (Arthur 1986, 40). The Archaic Period was, undoubtedly, an extremely important phase in the history of the city, leading to the construction of the first fortification wall and to the monumentalization of the sanctuaries of Apollo and of the Triangular Forum. These developments have been considered by most scholars as formative events, representing the foundation of the urban settlement.[11] But if we consider that for at least two centuries there had

---

[10] It is a known fact that the countryside around Stabia was suddenly abandoned in the middle of the sixth century BC. See Cerchiai 1987, 46 and Miniero 1993.

[11] See De Caro 1992 especially 69 and 72, where the author believes that the Temple of Apollo was the civic temple of the emerging community.

already been a settlement with at least one major cult area,[12] these building activities, including the construction of the fortification walls, cannot be considered events which determined the foundation of the city. In this earlier phase, however, Pompeii is still a settlement with open, undeveloped spaces with occasional wooden structures and some soft lava masonry buildings.[13]

c) In Pompeii, we now have firm archaeological evidence that allows us to date confidently to the second century BC both the limestone building techniques and the house type with Tuscan atrium, alae and tablinum in alignment with the entrance.[14] It is therefore impossible to associate these buildings with the Samnite period.[15] In fact, as research develops, there is an increase in the number of structures that precede the second century BC house and that can be dated between the fourth and third centuries BC.[16] As we gradually come to identify some of the fundamental components of the settlement, we realize that the landscape must have been quite similar to the mixed urban and rural landscapes of the Archaic Period.[17] The buildings are indeed elementary in character, yet they have precise parallels with some con- temporary buildings in the Abruzzo or Molise areas.[18] I believe that useful comparanda for settlements of this type should in fact be available in the Sannio hinterland: settlements with incomplete urban development, enclosed by fortification walls that surround a broad area

---

[12]   The presence of cult areas in the vicinity of the House of the Etruscan Column and the House of Ganimede, often emphasized by several authors (most recently Cristofani 1991, 16), still needs to be confirmed. The hypotheses derive from the discovery of an antefix both in the House of the Etruscan Column (Bonghi Jovino 1984, 249ff., tav. 140.2) and in the House of Ganimede (Reusser 1982, 264ff., Abb.16–18, Taf.136. 1–2).

[13]   Besides the hut we uncovered, a series of channels, post-holes, pits and different kinds of structures cut into bedrock have been brought to light around the Forum area (Arthur 1986, 61ff.), in the House of the Clay Molds (D'Ambrosio and De Caro 1989, 191), in the Calcidicum of the Basilica (Maiuri 1973, 209 and 211), and in the House of Ganimede (Eschebach 1982, 278–297 and 310). Soft lava structures have been uncovered in house VIII, 5, nos. 2, 9 and 28; in houses VI, 8, 22 and VI, 10, 6; in house VI, 6, 1 (most recently De Caro 1992, 17); in the area of the Calcidicum and of the Basilica (Maiuri 1973, 208 and 212–216). One has to note however that dating of these structures to the Archaic Period is almost always inferred indirectly, without supporting stratigraphic evidence.

[14]   Besides the data we present here see Zevi 1992b, 52 and 56 especially for the House of the Faun; Eschebach 1982, 310ff. for the House of Ganimede; Bonghi Jovino 1984, 378–385 for the House of the Etruscan Column; Descoeudres-Sear 1987, 28ff. for the House of the Painted Capitals; Franklin 1990, 45–50 for the House of The Sailor; De Caro 1992, 88 for the houses in limestone opus quadratum in Regio I and II; D'Ambrosio and De Caro 1989, 180 for the House of the Clay Molds; Hoffmann 1990 for the houses with monumental façade in opus quadratum in the Regiones VI and VII; Strocka 1991, for the House of the Labyrinth.

[15]   A separate chronological problem exists for the date of the House of the Surgeon and the House of Sallust. If it were possible to confirm that these buildings date to the III century BC, they would be the only two houses predating the second century BC, and would thus be related to the new urban layout (see Nappo, forthcoming).

[16]   See remains found under the House of the Faun (Zanker 1993, 42–44); house VIII, 2, 13 (unpublished excavations of I. Dall'Osso of 1905, Archivio Soprintendenza Archeologica di Pompei, Cartella VI); the House of the Clay Molds (D'Ambrosio and De Caro 1989, 189–194); the Temple of Isis (Varone 1989) and the small Hellenistic houses we discovered (Carafa and D'Alessio, forthcoming).

[17]   The relation between these buildings and the layout of the area within the walls, recently examined by Stefano De Caro (1992, 76–78, tav. V.2), needs further clarification. Established practice in the Archaic Period suggests that in Pompeii the fortifications do not represent a break in the subdivision of the area around the inhabited nucleus (Zevi 1982, 354–356; De Caro 1992; Nappo, forthcoming).

[18]   At Alfedena (Mariani 1902, 519) and Monte Vairano near Campobasso (De Benedittis 1991, 52–55).

which is in fact larger than the area occupied by dwelling structures; and with enough open space available for agriculture or for herd gathering in times of threatening unrest (Franchi dell'Orto and La Regina 1978, 401–431; La Regina 1989, tavv. VII-XXXII).

CONCLUSIONS

It would seem that we can now have some evidence to suggest that Pompeii's first, proper urban development was completed within the second century BC. I wish to emphasize that this seems to have been a new development in the history of a pre-existing settlement, which radically transformed the appearance of the inhabited area. Until today we believed that the Etruscans and the Romans were the main protagonists in Pompeii's development: the former, toward the end of the seventh century BC, by actually causing the birth of the settlement; the latter by creating the necessary conditions for the first monumental development after the destruction of the Nocera League in the aftermath of the second Samnite war (Cerchiai 1995). The archaeological record suggests that a settlement with an even older history gradually evolved into a complete, structured city without needing military conquests or violent upheavals (Eschebach and Eschebach 1995, 72). Continuing research will aid us in reconstructing the different aspects of this gradual transformation.

References

Arthur, P., 1986. Problems of the urbanization of Pompeii: excavations 1980–1981, *Antiquaries Journal* 61.1: 29–44.

Bonghi Jovino, M., 1984. *Ricerche a Pompei. L'insula 5 della Regio VI dalle origini al 79 d.C.* (Università degli Studi di Milano, Istituto di Archeologia, Biblioteca Archaeologica 5, Bretschneider: Rome).

Brunsting, H., 1975. Forschungen im Garten des Marcus Lucretius Fronto, in B. Andreae and H. Kyrieleis (eds.), *Neue Forschungen in Pompeji* (Recklinghausen 1975): 198–199.

Brunsting, H., Wynia, S.L., 1993. I mobilia, in Peters, W. J. Th., (ed.), *La casa di Marcus Lucretius Fronto a Pompei e le sue pitture* (Scrinium 5. Thesis: Amsterdam): 15–37.

Carafa, P., d'Alessio M. T., forthcoming. Lo sviluppo urbanistico di Pompei alla luce delle recenti scoperte. Considerazioni preliminari in margine alle nuove ricerche nelle *Regiones* VIII e VII, *Rivista di Studi Pompeiani*.

Cerchiai, L., 1987. Il processo di strutturazione del politico: i Campani, *Annali dell'Istituto Orientale di Napoli* 9: 41–54.

Cerchiai, L., 1995. *I Campani* (Longanesi: Milano).

Colonna, G., 1991. Le genti anelleniche, in G. Pugliese Carratelli (ed.), *Storia e civiltà della Campania. L'evo antico*, (Electa: Napoli): 25–67.

Cornell, T., J., 1995. *The Beginnings of Rome. Italy from the Bronze Age to the Punic Wars (c. 1000–264 BC)* (Routledge: London and New York).

Cristofani, M., 1992. La fase etrusca di Pompei, in Zevi 1992a: 9–22.

D'Agostino, B., 1987. Il processo di strutturazione del politico nel mondo osco-lucano. La protostoria, *Annali dell'Istituto Orientale di Napoli* 9: 23–40.

D'Agostino, B., 1992. Greci, Campani e Sanniti: città e campagna nella regione campana, in *La Campania fra il VI e il III secolo a.C. Atti del XIV Convegno di Studi Etruschi e Italici*. Benevento 1981 (Congedo Editore: Galatina): 74–83.

D'Ambrosio, A., 1990. Ricerche archeologiche a Striano. Lo scavo di via Poggio Marino, *Rivista di Studi Pompeiani* 4: 7–44.

D'Ambrosio, A., De Caro, S., 1989. Un contributo all'urbanistica e all'architettura di Pompei in età ellenistica. I saggi nella casa VII, 4, 62, *Annali dell'Istituto Orientale di Napoli* 11: 173–215.

De Benedittis, G., 1991. Monte Vairano, in *La Romanisation du Samnium aux IIe et Ière siècles av. J. C.* (Centre Jean Bérard 4, Bibliothèque de l'Institut Française de Neaples, série 2, vol. 9: Napoli): 47–55.

De Caro, S., 1985. Nuove indagini sulle fortificazioni di Pompei, *Annali dell'Istituto Orientale di Napoli* 7: 75–114.

De Caro, S., 1986. *Saggi nell'area del Tempio di Apollo* (Istituto Universitario Orientale di Napoli, Quaderni 3: Napoli).

De Caro, S., 1992. Lo sviluppo urbanistico di Pompei, *Atti della Società della Magna Grecia*: 67–90.

De Waele, J. A. K. E., 1993. The 'Doric' Temple on the Forum Triangulare in Pompeii, *Opuscula Pompeiana* 3: 105.118.

Descoeudres, J. P., Sear, F., 1987. The Australian expedition to Pompeii, *Rivista di Studi Pompeiani* 1: 11–36.

Dobbins, J. J., 1994. Problems of chronology, decoration and urban design in the Forum at Pompeii, *American Journal of Archaeology* 98: 629–694.

Eschebach, H., 1970. Die städtebauliche Entwicklung des antiken Pompeji, *Mitteilungen des Deutsches Archäologisches Instituts*. Römische Abteilung, Supplementband 17.

Eschebach, H., 1982. Ausgrabungen und Baugeschichte, *Mitteilungen des Deutsches Archäologisches Instituts*. Römische Abteilung 89: 219–313.

Eschebach, H., and Eschebach, L., 1995. *Pompeji von 7. Jahrhundert v. Chr. bis 79 n. Chr.* (Böhlau Verlag: Köln, Weimar, Wien).

Franchi Dell'Orto, L., and La Regina, A., 1978. *Culture adriatiche antiche d'Abruzzo e di Molise* (De Luca: Roma).

Franklin, J. L., 1990. *Pompeii: The 'Casa del Marinaio' and its History* (Soprintendenza Archeologica di Pompei, Monografie 3. L'Erma di Bretschneider: Roma).

Gastaldi, P., 1979. Le necropoli della valle del Sarno. Proposte per una suddivisione in fasi, *Annali dell'Istituto Orientale di Napoli* 1: pp. 13–57.

Hoffmann, A., 1990. Elemente Bürgerliche Räpresentation eine spätellenistische Hausfassade in Pompeji, in *Akten des XIII. Internationalen Kongresses für Klassische Archäologie*. Berlin 1988 (von Zabern: Mainz am Rhein): 490–495.

Johannowsky, W., 1984. *Materiali di età arcaica dalla Campania* (Gaetano Macchiaroli Editore: Napoli).

Kockel, V., 1986. Archäologische Funde und Forschungen in den Vesuvstädten 2, *Archäologische Anzeiger*: 443–579.

La Regina, A., 1989. I Sanniti, in *Italia omnium terrarum parens* (Garzanti-Schweiller: Milano): 301–432.

Lehmann Hartleben, K., 1936. *Baugeschichtliche Untersuchungen am Stadtrand von Pompeji* (De Gruyter: Berlin & Leipzig).

Lepore, E., 1992. Le strutture economiche e sociali, in *La Campania fra il VI e il III secolo a.C. Atti del XIV Convegno di Studi Etruschi e Italici*. Benevento 1981 (Galatina): 175–185.

Lupo, I., 1992. Materiali archeologici di età preromana nella biblioteca comunale di Boscoreale, *Rendiconti dell'Accademia di Lettere e Belle Arti di Napoli* 63: 499–560.

Maiuri, A., 1973. *Alla ricerca di Pompei preromana* (Società Editrice Napoletana: Napoli).

Mariani, L., 1902. Scavi nell'acropoli dell'antica Alfedena, *Notizie degli Scavi di Antichità*: 516–520.

Miniero, P., 1993. Insediamenti e trasformazioni nell'Ager Stabianus tra VII secolo a. C. e I secolo d. C., in L. Franchi dell'Orto (ed.), *Ercolano 1738–1988, 250 anni di ricerca archeologia* (Soprintendenza Archeologica di Pompei, Monografie 6. L'Erma di Bretschneider: Roma): 581–594.

Musti, D., 1992. Per una valutazione delle fonti sulla storia della Campania, in *La Campania fra il VI e il III secolo a C. Atti del XIV Convegno di Studi Etruschi e Italici*. Benevento 1981 (Galatina): 31–41.

Nappo, C. S., forthcoming. Alcuni esempi di tipologie di case popolari di fine III inizio II ec. a. C. a Pompei, in R. Laurence and A. Wallace-Hadrill (eds.), *Domestic Space in the Roman World* (Journal of Roman Archaeology Supplement: Ann Arbor).

Peroni, R., 1994. *Introduzione alla protostoria italiana* (Laterza: Roma & Bari).

Reusser, C., 1982. Archäische Funde, *Mitteilungen des Deutsches Archäologisches Instituts*. Römische Abteilung 89: 353–372.

Richardson, L., 1989. *Pompeii. An Architectural History* (Johns Hopkins University Press: Baltimore).

Riemann, H., 1975. Die vorsammnitische Pompeji, in B. Andreae and H. Kyrieleis (eds.), *Neue Forschungen in Pompeji* (Recklinghausen): 225–233.

Sogliano, A., 1925. Il foro di Pompei, *Memorie dell'Accademia dei Lincei* 1, f. III: 221–272.

Strocka, V. M., 1991. *Casa del Labirinto (VI, 11, 8–10)* Häuser in Pompeji 4 (Hirmer: München).

Varone, A, 1988, Note di archeologia sarnese: i cippi funerari a stilizzazione antropomorfa, *Apollo* 6: 195–260.

Varone, A., 1989. Attività dell'Ufficio Scavi: 1989, *Rivista di Studi Pompeiani* 3:-225–238.

Varone, A., 1990. Attività dell'Ufficio Scavi: 1990, *Rivista di Studi Pompeiani* 4:-225–238.

Zanker, P., 1993. *Pompei* (Einaudi: Torino).

Zevi, F., 1982. Urbanistica di Pompei, in *La regione sotterrata dal Vesuvio. Studi e prospettive* (Francesco Giannini e figli Editore: Napoli): 353–365.

Zevi, F., ed. 1992a. *Pompei 1* (Guida Editore: Napoli).

Zevi, F., 1992b. L'edilizia privata e la Casa del Fauno, in Zevi 1992a.: 47–74.

5 The Context of the House of the Surgeon: Investigations in Insula VI,1 at Pompeii

Sara E. Bon, Rick Jones, Bernice Kurchin and Damian J. Robinson

APPROACHES

Our project[1] is committed to the comprehensive study of a complete insula of Pompeii. We are recording its above- and below-ground archaeological remains in close detail in order better to understand the spatial and chronological contexts in which the city developed. Insula VI,1 contains the House of the Surgeon. In 1926 this property was the subject of Amedeo Maiuri's first stratigraphic excavations in the cleared area of Pompeii. Maiuri conducted excavations in the foundations and gave the house a probable date in the third century BC (Maiuri 1973, 8). The House of the Surgeon is often cited as important because of this widely accepted early date which places it among the earliest houses still standing in the first century AD. Even though this house overshadows its neighboring properties in discussions of Insula VI,1, our research program treats this property as only one element in the development of the whole insula. By establishing the contexts in which the House of the Surgeon was originally built and then modified, we will improve our understanding not only of the house itself, but also of the broader processes of urban development at Pompeii. Our work employs excavation, with a significant emphasis on the examination of environmental data, combined with the stratigraphic analysis of standing structures. We have begun these procedures on several properties in the insula, and by the end of the project's fieldwork which is envisaged as including at least six seasons, will have reconstructed the evolution of a city block during a lengthy pre-Roman period and the final phase of intense urbanism. The context of the so-called House of the Surgeon will provide a narrative of the evolution of one portion of Pompeii, and will enrich our understanding of the long sequence which created the celebrated city of the first-century AD.

Pompeii is usually studied as a single-phase site, with an unsurprising concentration on the city as it stood at the moment it was buried. This emphasis belies the fact that the city and the community that lived in it had evolved during a long period of occupation prior to Vesuvius'

[1] The Anglo-American Pompeii Project is substantially supported by and organized from the Department of Archaeological Sciences of the University of Bradford. The field program is based on a Field School accredited by Hunter College of the City University of New York. We have also enjoyed the enthusiastic encouragement and continual assistance of the Soprintendenza Archeologica di Pompei, especially Prof. Pietro Giovanni Guzzo, and his colleagues Dott. Antonio D'Ambrosio, Dott. Antonio Varone, and Dott.ssa Annamaria Ciarallo.

eruption in AD 79. To understand the physical remains with the intent of interpreting the social dynamics of Pompeii in any phase, including that which ended in AD 79, it is essential to consider the development into that form. The archaeological remains at Pompeii provide unrivaled opportunities to examine both the public and private spheres of a society throughout the city's long occupation. The great potential for a diachronic understanding of Pompeii has not been fully investigated. Current research re-expresses an interest in investigating the early phases there as well as the more thorough examination of the first century AD contexts. Much of this research employs innovative methods to gain new information from both the much-studied first century AD contexts and earlier occupations.

The development of Pompeii has been discussed in many pioneering studies, but firm evidence for the earliest Pompeian settlements has remained limited (cf. Maiuri 1973; Ling 1983; Bonghi Jovino 1984; Arthur 1986; De Caro 1985; 1986; Chiaramonte Treré 1986; D'Ambrosio and De Caro 1989; Nappo 1988; Carocci et al 1990; Carafa this vol.). There is some consensus that the occupation originated early in the first millennium BC, with significant activity dating to the sixth century (cf. Arthur 1986; Bonghi Jovino 1984); most authors agree that the intensely built-up pattern of the later city was created several centuries later. This schema raises questions concerning the point at which Pompeii can be first described as an urban community, and how the changes leading to and stemming from that urban development created the city that was destroyed and preserved in AD 79. Elements of urbanism can be traced in the pre-history of Pompeii as its concentration of population and intensity of occupation increased, its urban layout appeared, and economic activities, both productive and redistributive, took on urban configurations. The archaeological record provides direct evidence for these characteristics, and careful study furnishes information for the nature of social differentiation during the course of Pompeian occupation as well as the centralization of power, both religious and civic. Our research on a complete Pompeian insula produces data which will eventually contribute to a discussion of these issues.

Detailed examination of building sequences is the most effective method of studying changes in the city over time. This is evident in the pioneering work in the Insula of the House of the Menander (Insula I,10) and now in Insula I,9 (Ling 1983; DeLaine et al. 1995). Other projects have analyzed individual properties, such as the House of Sallust in Insula 2 of Regio VI (Laidlaw 1993). Intensive studies of selected areas of the city can only provide direct evidence for these areas themselves, yet the necessary level of detailed work cannot practically be conducted across the whole city at once. Individual studies provide samples which may be drawn together to create new interpretations of the city's development. The study of a complete insula rather than a single house provides the additional benefits of incorporating the contexts of individual properties and the relationships between them, both of which are crucial to interpreting the changes in any single property. To take on the detailed examination of the diachronic and spatial contexts of a complete insula – its sequence and space – requires a major commitment from a large multidisciplinary team, both in terms of fieldwork and analysis. All of these projects have or will be conducted over numerous seasons, and their publication is a considerable undertaking.

Stratigraphic excavation is a well-established technique in the research of the early contexts at Pompeii. Although the number of cases where this has been done in Pompeii is limited, early-phase test units have consistently provided new results which allow more securely established interpretations of the city's structural history (discussion in Carafa, this vol.). The systematic sampling of stratified deposits for the recovery of environmental evidence is adding an extra dimension to ideas of how the settlement developed (Richardson et al., this vol.).

Methods of recording and analysis of non-art historical architecture at Pompeii are less evident than those of stratigraphic excavation of early contexts. Our project considers standing remains both in terms of our intent to elucidate the structural history of Insula VI,1 and in terms of the documentation of a monument which is currently in a state of change (cf. Bon, this volume). The two views overlap but present different perspectives on method and interpretation.

Efficient and accurate documentation is the first step in comprehending the evolution of the insula. We tried drawing walls in the traditional manner of drawing stratigraphic profiles. We found that it is too slow for recording each of the walls in Insula VI,1 at the desired level of detail during the proposed duration of the project. We experimented with several photographic methods and selected a method which allows speedy and accurate recording with the results usable for interpretation within the same field season (Bon et al. 1996). We use a still-video camera, computer and software which are all readily available commercially. With the still-video camera we record a digital image of each of the standing walls and use a computer-generated version of this image as a template for a scale drawing of the wall. This drawing is based on the same premises of recording and interpretation as the drawing of stratigraphic profiles. It is a document which identifies all the events, both ancient and modern, which appear in the wall – plastering, mortaring, the blocking of windows and doorways, reconstruction and repairs – and their relative sequence. The benefits derived from the application of digital technology are that it eliminates the need for manually measuring each stone, or each element of a wall, and that a computer and paper archive is created of the insula in its current condition. There has been inconsistent documentation of the changes in the standing structures of Pompeii that have taken place since they began to be first uncovered over two centuries ago. The archive created by digital imaging serves both as a record from which future observations of change may be based, and as a source for interpreting the evolution of the insula. It is critical at this moment to create an archived record of the walls before further events change their condition.

Insula VI,1

Insula 1 of Regio VI lies at the north-west corner of the city next to the Herculaneum Gate. It was first uncovered in the late eighteenth century. The insula contains a mélange of properties typical of Pompeii. In its immediately pre-eruption form the insula contained two large residences (the House of the Surgeon and the House of the Vestals), a shrine, and commercial properties (a probable inn, bars, and a workshop). In earlier phases patterns of land use and the statuses and uses of the properties differed from their first century AD configurations. Over the last two hundred years the decoration of the walls has deteriorated badly. The very limited records from the original excavation summarized by Fiorelli (1875, 76–82) fail to inform us of the details of decoration on walls throughout the insula, where the plaster is now largely lost or very badly degraded. One example of what could have been recorded can be found in the publication of the painting on a single wall in the peristyle of the House of the Vestals. Mau's drawing shows an elaborate decoration with fruit, plants, fish and birds (Mau 1874, tav. III). Now a century afterwards that has almost completely faded away. In contrast, the basic fabrics of the structures survive well, apart from damage sustained in World War II (Descoeudres 1994, 48–49). Our recording emphasizes the stratigraphic and architectural rather than the art historical, appropriate for this insula perhaps more so than for others.

Our systematic analysis of standing structures will include the House of the Surgeon (VI,1,10) whose façade of Sarno blocks (Fig. 5.1) has been regarded as a characteristically early style of architecture, broadly of the Samnite period (Adam 1994, 293; Peterse 1993). Much of the chronological interpretation of the house, primarily that by Maiuri in 1926 (Maiuri 1930) and including the earliest dating, is disputed (Chiaramonte Treré 1990). In plan the House of the Surgeon appears quite easy to understand (Fig. 5.2). It seems to have begun as a substan-

Fig. 5.1 *House of the Surgeon (VI,1 10): the frontage on Via Consolare. (Anglo-American Pompeii Project)*

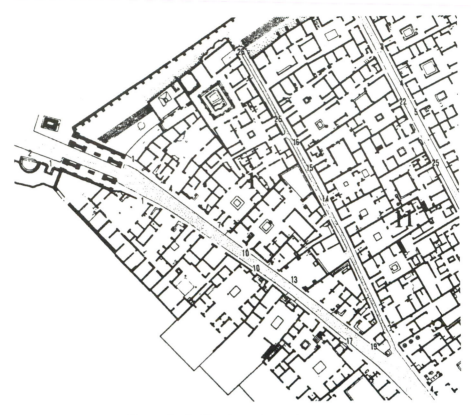

Fig. 5.2 Insula VI,1: plan. (After Van Der Poel 1984)

tial atrium house, with some later modifications and extensions providing service rooms and two separate properties to the south. This scheme of development fits the orthodox view of the history of Pompeian houses (cf. Laidlaw 1993). Yet the complexity of structural changes in this house is easily visible, even before we have begun systematic analysis within it (Fig. 5.3). The House of the Surgeon demonstrates the need to take a comprehensive and contextual view of a single house. The changes there closely involve its neighboring properties, extending the necessary unit of study to the whole insula.

Workshops and Bars

Our 1995 season included detailed work in the block of workshops and bars which form the southern end of the triangular plan of the insula (Fig. 5.4). These were laid out initially as a single building unit. The northernmost property of this group contains a row of tanks (Fig. 5.5). It was long ago given the name of the 'soap factory', which has stuck with the property despite being rejected by Fiorelli (1875, 81). Work so far has concentrated on this workshop, where there were potential areas for extensive excavation. It was hoped that excavation there

Fig. 5.3. *House of the Surgeon (VI,1, 10): south-east side. (Anglo-American Pompeii Project)*

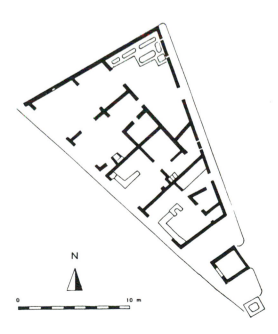

N

0   10 m

Fig. 5.4. *Workshops and bars (VI,1, 14–18, 20– 21): plan. (Anglo-American Pompeii Project)*

Fig. 5.5.   *Tanks in VI,1, 14/21. (Anglo-American Pompeii Project)*

Fig. 5.6   *Workshop VI,1, 14/ 21: raised threshold on Via Consolare. (Anglo-American Pompeii Project)*

Fig. 5.7 *Workshop VI,1, 14/ 21: industrial features. (Anglo-American Pompeii Project)*

would yield evidence for the functions of the tanks, for whatever production processes were associated with the tanks, and for the origins of this groups of properties.

Excavation at the street frontage of the workshop showed that there was an earlier industrial phase inside the building. The ground surface at this time was considerably lower than that of AD 79. It was raised by the accumulation of deposits associated with a group of small industrial hearths which were probably used for some kind of metalworking (Figs. 5.6–7). It is likely that at least some of the tanks were in use in this primary industrial phase. Also near them at the rear of the workshop was a flush toilet (Fig. 5.8; cf. Jansen, this vol.). This drained into a large sump or cesspit, and then away beneath the back wall of the property. It may also have been used to dispose of waste liquids from the nearby tanks. The pit was covered with some kind of wooden floor, supported by a pair of joists set across the corner of the back room of the workshop. Later these industrial features were radically changed. The cesspit was filled in, a new mortar floor was laid above the hearths, and the street threshold was raised. A new doorway faced in brick was added, opening to the back street. Most significantly a floor was put in for an upper storey.

Fig. 5.8   *Workshop VI,1, 14 / 21: flush toilet*
chute. (Anglo-American Pompeii Project)

Thus far we only have a partial history of this portion of the block. Nonetheless it is clear that it began as and remained a commercial place, even though the nature of what was being done in the workshop changed. The reorganization involved with adding an upper floor presumably provided a lot more useable space, perhaps for some residential rooms. As yet it is not possible to give a secure date for the construction of this part of the insula. However some Italian *terra sigillata* was associated with the industrial hearths, suggesting that they were used at least as late as the first century BC. We may therefore suggest that this block at the south end of the insula was built relatively late in the history of Pompeii. It was always commercial, and it was significantly remodeled at least once.

HOUSE OF THE VESTALS

Excavation and wall analysis in 1995 in the House of the Vestals presents a different picture. The house's final form had been created by the amalgamation of pre-existing houses into a large sprawling property immediately to the north of the House of the Surgeon. It included

Fig. 5.9   House of the Vestals (VI,1 6–8): the entrance from Via Consolare. (Anglo-American Pompeii Project)

at one end an elaborate peristyle and at the other a grand entrance (Fig. 5.9), but its plan shows no real coherence to connect these two parts which had once been separate atrium houses (Fig. 5.10). The house which eventually formed the southern end of the House of the Vestals opened from the Via Consolare into a wide atrium (Fig. 5.11). A variety of rooms lay on the north side of the house. In the middle was a small garden (Fig. 5.12). In its later form this contained a fountain, with the garden framed by four brick pillars. Preceding the fountain in that spot there was a shrine within a small garden space. The garden was created as a device to link together into this single southern house what had been two houses. These had each been thoroughly remodeled, though parts of the earlier buildings survived, such as walls of *terre pisé* construction. The earlier arrangement had seen two small houses (probably with atria), one opening on each of the streets, the Via Consolare and the Vicolo di Narciso, and therefore on different alignments (Fig. 5.13).

Work in this property shows that this area had a long and complex structural history, of which we have as yet examined only a portion. It is likely that the earliest structures there are no longer extant. For example in the foundations for the tablinum of the house on the Via Consolare were re-used stones that had already been faced in white plaster. This suggests that

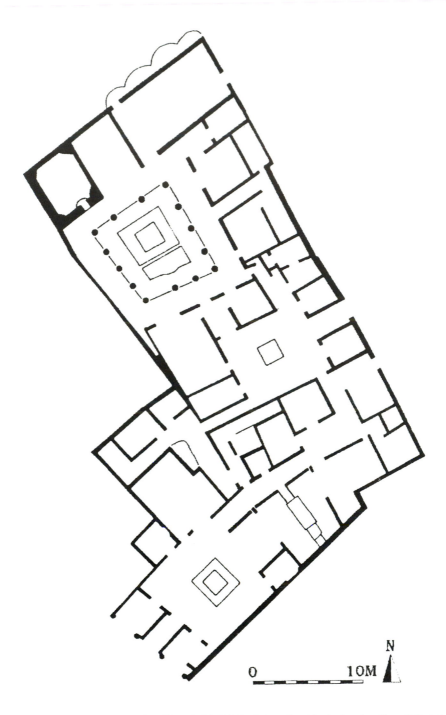

Fig. 5.10   *House of the Vestals (VI,1 6–8, 24–26): final phase plan. (Anglo-American Pompeii Project)*

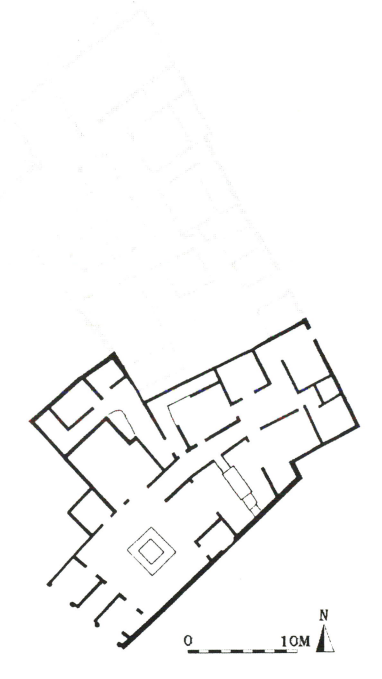

Fig. 5.11 *House of the Vestals (VI,1 6–8, 24): plan of the southern end as a single house. (Anglo-American Pompeii Project)*

Fig. 5.12 *House of the Vestals (VI,1 6–8, 24–26): the small garden, view from the north-west. (Anglo-American Pompeii Project)*

they came from another earlier masonry building which had existed somewhere in the vicinity. Maiuri records similarly re-used stones in the House of the Surgeon (Maiuri 1973, 11). Below this tablinum, probably cut concurrently with its construction, was a large pit. There was no domestic rubbish in its fill (Fig. 5.14), but there was a group of six votive cups (Fig. 5.15) associated with bones of juvenile pig (cf. Richardson et al., this vol.). The upper part of the pit was badly disturbed by a World War II bomb which made a direct hit on the ancient pit. Other cups and pig bones were found in the disturbed fill of the bomb crater. It would seem clear that the purpose of the pit was ritual. Its date is hard to determine. The votive cups are generally given dates from the fourth to second centuries BC, similar to Campanian black gloss wares which were also found in the pit fill (cf. Bonghi Jovino 1984, 175–6, 191, tav. 111).

The southern wall of the House of the Vestals seems to have existed as a-free-standing wall before the houses were built alongside it. It formed the common wall with the House of the Surgeon, but it seems not to have been part of any primary version of that house either. It is more probable that it was a property wall around the plot later occupied by the House of the Surgeon. Both it and the wall on the south side of the House of the Surgeon's plot of land were penetrated by wide doorways or gateways that were later blocked. They show that

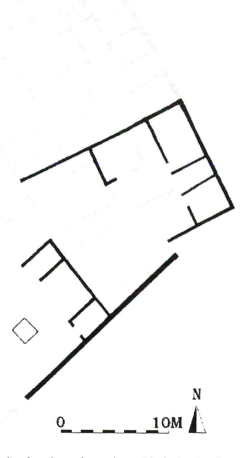

Fig. 5.13 *House of the Vestals (VI,1 6–8, 24): plan of southern end as two houses. (Anglo-American Pompeii Project)*

Fig. 5.14 *House of the Vestals (VI,1 6–8, 24–26): the early pit. (Anglo-American Pompeii Project)*

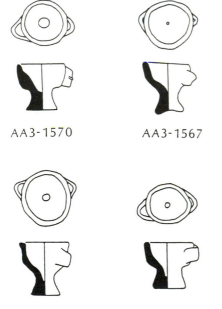

AA3-1570   AA3-1567

AA3-1568   AA3-1571

Fig. 5.15 *House of the Vestals (VI,1 6–8, 24–26): votive cups from the early pit. (Anglo-American Pompeii Project)*

at an early stage in the block's history there was lateral movement across the lines of what became the later property divisions. We cannot yet identify the character of the occupation of the land at that point, but the walls and the entrances through them do show that the basic arrangements of property allocations were changed from the early dispositions. These observations in themselves confirm Maiuri's argument that the layout of the House of the Surgeon which is now visible did not belong to the earliest building phase to have existed in the insula (1973, 11). Another indication of the same conclusion comes from the back door of the house. It is clear that what was later a standard, quite narrow service entrance, had originally been a wide doorway looking very much like the entrance to a house in its own right (Fig. 5.16). An early house, presumably a small atrium-style house, would have underlain some of the service rooms that were later added to the rear of

Fig. 5.16 *House of the Surgeon: rear door (VI,1,23).*
(Anglo-American Pompeii Project)

the House of the Surgeon. This structure would have also occupied at least part of the area of what became one of the House of the Surgeon's large reception rooms (cf. Fig. 5.2). The best interpretation for these observations is that this presumed early house had been one of a row of small atrium houses along the east side of insula VI,1 which preceded the layout of the House of the Surgeon, the house usually claimed to represent the early stages of Pompeii.

CONCLUSIONS

The project of understanding Insula VI,1 has made a promising start. The integration of very detailed stratigraphic recording of the standing walls and selective excavation is proving especially powerful. Our chosen methodology has been justified especially through its revealing the full complexity of the structural histories of the standing remains and by its recovery of stratified groups of artifacts which will give direct dates for the sequence. We can show that the workshops and bars were in use during the first century BC. They were probably built not long before that, and certainly as a separate unit post-dating the construction of the properties to the north. For the earliest occupation of the insula we can support Maiuri's argument that there were phases preceding the visible structures of the House of the Surgeon. The pottery from the ritual pit beneath the earliest buildings found in the House of the Vestals sequence can at present only be given a broad date somewhere between the fourth and second centuries BC. The current lack of precision is clearly unsatisfactory. We must hope that further research on the pottery will refine the dating in order to relate the early phases of this part of the city to the new evidence now presented from elsewhere in Pompeii (e.g. Carafa this vol.), and that further excavations in the foundations of the House of the Vestals and in the rest of the insula will provide a more precise set of dates for the earlier sequence.

Our results already suggest a number of themes that have relevance beyond the insula in question. In our work to date, there is clear evidence for two processes taking place: there are changes in economic activities, and the use of space became more intensified. The number of properties involved in commerce and production increased, as seen in the construction of the block of bars and the workshop, as well as the addition of bars at the north end of the insula. Upper storeys were added late to the workshop and bars, as well as to parts of the House of the Vestals. This process parallels the infilling of the space in the southern part of the House of the Surgeon's plot. The ground area of the insula was completely filled, with large areas of upper storeys built above. Although some researchers have linked increases in commercial activity with declines in social status, here the aggrandizement of élite houses happened at the same time as the commercialization of the streets.

A growing inequality of property sizes is clearly demonstrated within the House of the Vestals in the step by step combining of properties from perhaps five original houses into two, and then one property. The re-structuring of rooms there indicates the parsimonious use of space to meet changing needs. New rooms were added both for elegant purposes and for service functions. The changes in the workshop area leave the same impression. In Insula VI,1 space was increasingly valuable. This makes it more likely that the growing inequalities we observe in the insula were not just in the size of buildings, and that the architectural changes related to a real process of increasing social inequalities, reflecting changes in social hierarchy, shifts of power, and the ways in which power was expressed. It is important to consider whether architectural changes reflected substantive increases in social differentiation, or simply changes in how existing differences were expressed though architecture. These issues will demand further examination related to the role of the commercial premises attached to the House of the Surgeon and adjacent to the House of the Vestals. Future research will investigate the way in which these buildings were altered, and their relationships to other changes in the large residences. The analysis of the tanks and metal-working hearths in the workshop inform our knowledge of production in the city and contribute to broader technological and economic studies. The documentation of how properties were combined opens questions of social hierarchy and intensity of use. Such new research will help to understand Pompeii's development in terms of the dynamic interplay of political, social and economic relationships within an urban community and with its environment, both natural and cultural.

References

Adam, J.P., 1994. *Roman Building. Materials and Techniques* (Batsford: London and Indiana University Press: Bloomington).

Arthur, P., 1986. Problems of the urbanization of Pompeii: excavations 1980–1, *Antiquaries Journal* 66: 29–44.

Bon, S.E., Jones, R., Kurchin, B., and Robinson, D., 1995. *Anglo-American Research at Pompeii 1995. Preliminary Report.* (Bradford Archaeological Sciences Research 1: Bradford).

Bon, S.E., Jones, R., Kurchin, B., and Robinson, D., 1996. Digital imaging of standing buildings in Insula VI,1 at Pompeii, *Archeologia e Calcolatori* 7.

Bonghi Jovino, M., 1984. *Ricerche a Pompei. L'Insula 5 della Regio VI dalle origini al 79 d.c.* (Università degli Studi di Milano, Istituto di Archeologia, Biblioteca Archaeologica 5, Bretschneider: Rome).

Carocci, F., de Albentiis, E., Gargiulo, M., and Pesando, F., 1990. *Le Insulae 3 e 4 della Regio VI a Pompei. Un analisi storico-urbanistica* (Archaeolgia Perusina 5, Bretschneider: Rome).

Chiaramonte Treré, C., 1986. *Nuovi Contributi sulle Fortificazioni Pompeiane* (Quaderni di Acme 6, Università degli Studi di Milano: Milan).

Chiaramonte Treré, C., 1990. Sull'origine e lo sviluppo dell'architettura residenziale di Pompei sannitica, *Acme* 43,3: 5–34.

D'Ambrosio, A., and De Caro, S., 1989. Un contributo all'architettura e all'urbanistica di Pompei in età ellenistica. I saggi nella casa VII, 4 , 62, *Annali dell'Istituto Orientale di Napoli* 11: 173–215.

De Caro, S., 1985. Nuovi indagini sulle fortificazioni di Pompei, *Annali dell'Istituto Orientale di Napoli* 7: 75–114.

De Caro, S., 1986. *Saggi nell'area del Tempio di Apollo* (Istituto Universitario Orientale di Napoli, Quaderni 3: Naples).

DeLaine, J., Fulford, M., and Wallace-Hadrill, A., 1995. *Urban Development at Pompeii. Regio I, Insula 9 excavation and survey in 1995* (British School at Rome, University of Reading: Reading).

Descoeudres, J.-P., 1994. *Pompeii Revisited: The Life and Death of a Roman Town* (Meditarch: Sydney).

Fiorelli, G., 1875. *Descrizione di Pompei* (Tipografia Italiana: Naples).

Laidlaw, A., 1993. Excavations in the Casa di Sallustio, Pompeii: a preliminary assessment, in R.T. Scott and A.R. Scott eds., *Eius Virtutis Studiosi: Classical and Post-Classical Studies in memory of Frank Edward Brown, 1908–1988* (National Gallery of Art: Washington D.C.): 217–233.

Ling, R., 1983. The Insula of the Menander at Pompeii: interim report, *Antiquaries Journal* 63: 34–57.

Maiuri, A., 1930. Saggi nella 'Casa del Chirurgo', *Notizie degli Scavi di Antichità* (1930): 381–395. (Reprinted in Maiuri 1973).

Maiuri, A., 1973. *Alla ricerca di Pompei preromana* (Società Editrice Napoletana: Naples).

Mau, A., 1874. Parete dipinta della Casa delle Vestali, *Giornale degli Scavi di Pompei*, nuova serie, vol.3 (Naples): 107–130.

Nappo, S.C., 1988. Regio I, Insula 2, *Rivista di Studi Pompeiani* 2: 186–192.

Peterse, C.L.J., 1993. *Bouwkundige Studies van Huizen in Pompeii. Muurwerk, Maatvoering en Ontwerp* (Indagationes Noviomagenses IX, Katholieke Universiteit Nijmegen: Nijmegen).

Van Der Poel, H.B., 1984. *Corpus Topographicum Pompeianum, III The RICA Maps of Pompeii* (University of Texas at Austin: Rome).

6 Oecus on Ibycus:
Investigating the Vocabulary of the Roman House

Eleanor Winsor Leach

A NUMBER OF PAPERS in this group have protested the dominance of literary evidence in interpreting the function of domestic spaces in Pompeii. There are many good reason to sympathize with this point of view and to entertain the modifications of conventional wisdom that it urges. Since the preponderance of literary evidence is Roman either in origin or in reference or in both, its application to Pompeii all too easily results in consideration of the city as an adjunct or analogy to Rome. In cultural and political terms this is not only to overlook the origins and development of Pompeii as an Italic city before its colonial appropriation, but also to ignore the differences between the political operations of the two cities during the Empire. Although it is often mentioned how the magistrate systems of *municipia* echo in miniature that of Rome, it should also be remembered that *municipia* preserved their systems substantially unchanged long after imperial restructuring had altered the nature of elections and the conduct of patronage at Rome.

Finally one must look critically at the nature of the sources commonly invoked as literary evidence. The greater part of information derives from Vitruvius' prescriptive manual of Augustan date *De Architectura*. Although some Pompeian scholars realistically observe that the measurements and proportions Vitruvius recommends often differ from the mass of Pompeian evidence (Evans 1978, 175), so canonical is the ancient authority that the notion persists of its being the norm from which actual practice deviates (Clarke 1992, 14).

Granting all these points, it remains that Pompeian houses comprise the principal body of evidence for the study of Roman domestic space from the Republic through the early Empire, and also that our second repository of evidence for this period is in fact literary. Beyond this, certain rudimentary correspondences exist between these two bodies of evidence that cannot be discarded or ignored. For a person with my own interest in the significance of mural decoration to its patrons within the institutional dynamic that shapes their daily program of activities, it is necessary to populate the spaces of the Roman house with activities, and this repopulation must take place at hypothetical points of inter-section between Roman words and Pompeian rooms. But the inevitability of using literary evidence does not correspondingly necessitate mere repetition of familiar sources and formulas. It is one thing for Vitruvius or for a Roman lexicographer such as Varro to mention something in a prescriptive or explanatory manner and another for persons in ordinary discourse to mention items that they and their readers take for granted. My interest is in the kind of dialogue that can result from bringing lived experience into confrontation with the supposed codes of definition.

Working through language I am investigating the frequency and function of nomenclature in actual dramatic contexts to ascertain what such indirect evidence can reveal about the functions of domestic spaces. The tool of my investigation is the computer program, Ibycus, that searches Latin and Greek texts on CD Rom for words or even combinations of words. Unlike the (still incomplete) *Thesaurus Linguae Latinae* or other lexical compilations Ibycus stores words by author alphabetically and thus exposes them in an unsorted, semantically unprejudicial order. I have turned to this program with the double aim of learning more about such familiar names for domestic spaces as the *atrium*, the *triclinium*, and also of investigating less familiar names. I might call this project an archaeology of nomenclature. I am looking for literary material that works in the same manner as material evidence in archaeology to refine and qualify what we think we already know. The aspect of my investigation that I will discuss in this paper is the discrepancies it has brought to light between some of the terms generally applied to the archaeology of the Roman house and some of the vocabulary of Roman everyday usage.

That the inter-relationship of architecture and spatial function is culturally formed is axiomatic. For Pompeian studies, Rapoport's observation that systems of activities occur within systems of settings is productive (Rapoport 1990, 9–11). Currently two modes of conceptualizing the axis of function in the Roman house exist: the one Greek and Roman; the other public and private. Speaking historically, the Greco-Roman axis is a product of late nineteenth century interpretation. The German archaeologist August Mau described Pompeian/Roman space by means of this schematized diagram he termed an 'ideal plan' representing no one house exactly, but features common to many (Fig. 6.1; Mau 1904, 247). From his chronological perspective the plan represents a cumulative stage in an evolution that had begun with a

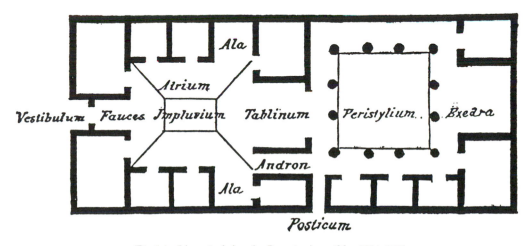

Fig. 6.1 Schematized plan of a Pompeian house (Mau 1904, 247).

simple and basic dwelling progressively amplified by a variety of appendages. Mau's matured house comprises two conjoined architectural centers, the *cavum aedium* complex, preserving the original Roman domestic core and a peristyle complex developed on a Greek model. Drawing his nomenclature from Vitruvius who designates a set of canonical proportions for the rooms, Mau describes a complex of *atrium, tablinum, alae,* and *fauces/ vestibulum,* with side rooms called *cubicula.* The House of the Surgeon and the House of Sallust in its early phases come closest to this plan. This is the formal reception area and scholars following Mau's lead have noticed that the disposition of rooms on the 'ideal plan' is both axial and symmetrical; this formality of design now colors standard views of the way in which the *atrium* complex served as staging for the rituals of patronage (Brown 1961, 21–22; Bek 1980; followed esp. by Clarke 1992,1–29). Beginning in the second century BC the owners of most large houses expanded their spatial dominance by the addition of a colonnaded open courtyard with surrounding chambers. Mau posits the deliberately Hellenic aura of such quarters by pointing out the Greek derivation of the names, including not only *peristylium* but also the rooms surrounding it: *triclinium, oecus, exedra* as opposed to the Latin words *atrium, tablinum, alae* and *vestibulum* designating the reception spaces.

As anyone familiar with Pompeii can recognize, the simplification of the ideal plan falls short of encompassing the idiosyncratic complexities of actual dwellings. To mediate between general principles and specific embodiments, the consideration of public vs. private space enters in, but one may notice how the prevailing definitions of public and private have changed over recent years. Building upon Mau's Greco-Roman axis the architectural historian Frank Brown linked private life with a new strain of phil-Hellenic self-cultivation that opposed expansive leisure to the stiffness of political ceremony (Brown 1961, 21). The more recent tendency is to allow for Roman aristocratic integration of public activities into the residential sphere by reference to the Vitruvian idea of distinguishing the public and private areas of the house on the basis of controlled social access (Wallace-Hadrill 1988, 43–97). Cicero's advice that an impressive house can advance its owner's political fortunes is often cited (*De Officiis* 1.139–140), along with Vitruvius' prescription that the houses of important personages must include spaces such as *vestibula* and *cava aedium* that make a grand impression on visitors (*De Architectura* 6.5.1– 2). These are public space, so to speak into which even uninvited persons may enter, while others that he calls *propria patribus familiarum* (belonging to the heads of families) require an invitation. By classing the peristyle among public rooms, Vitruvius does create some confusion about spatial boundaries. He makes an important distinction between the Greek and the Roman house when he says that the Greeks have no use for *atria* which, in consequence, they do not build (6.7.1) and gives information about the nature of Greek peristyles that allows us to distinguish them clearly from Roman.

What happens, however, when we check Mau's series of rooms on Ibycus? Surprisingly we discover little reinforcement for the seemingly authoritative descriptions of *tablinum* and *alae* in Vitruvius. The first of these occurs only in antiquarianizing contexts. Pliny speaks of the *tablinum* as a family record room containing *codices* and *monumenta* of deeds accomplished in office (35.2.7: *rerum in magistratu gestarum*). The importance of the *tablinum* to the official life of the patron is corroborated only by the lexicographer Festus who supplies that it is a '*proxime atrium locus*' called *tablinum* because the former magistrates (*antiquii magistratus*) kept there on tablets their reckonings of public accounts. Another lexicographer, Nonus (83M) attributes to Varro (*Vita Pop. Rom.* 28.2) a different explanation of the *tablinum* as a spacious place (*locus propatulus*) used for summer dining in country houses. Nonus preserves Varro's characteristic penchant for etymology in the deriving of the name from boards (*tabulae*) used in building the structure. But why is there almost no mention of this area in actual use?

As for *alae* within the *cavum aedium* complex no writer other than Vitruvius mentions these. His description of the ideal proportions of domestic *alae* in relationship with those of contiguous spaces does ostensibly point to the symmetrical recesses frequently found at the inward end of many *atria*. Although he also says that *alae*, along with *tablina*, should be useful, even Mau in coordinating spaces and written description (1904, 258–259) was puzzled as to the functional character of these spatial extensions which he rationalized as a survival from an earlier period when different conditions of life prevailed. Records of material finds give little assistance, as Penelope Allison has concluded from her study of domestic assemblages that reveal *alae* either empty or else used for storage of random, eclectic combinations of objects and building material (1994, 52–53).

Granted that the use of these spaces is uncertain, the absence of literary usage corroborating Vitruvius makes one wonder whether *alae* was their accustomed name. Since Vitruvius similarly refers to extensions at the rear of the cella in Etruscan and other Etruscan derived temples as *alae* (*De Architectura* 4.7.2) it is quite possible that he borrowed this term as a metaphor from public architecture. When Quintilian in laying out visual frameworks for memory exercises mentions spaces opening onto the *atrium*, he names these either *cubicula* or *exedrae*, the difference clearly being that *exedrae*, like our putative *alae* are spaces open along their full length. Recesses screened by columns symmetrically facing the *impluvium* in the grandiose *atrium* of the House of Epidius Sabinus that archaeologists commonly call *alae* (Richardson 1988, 112–114) were probably considered as *exedrae* by the house owner on the analogy of equivalent spaces in the public world (Fig. 6.2) and similar examples of centrally located recesses shaping a cruciform *atrium* occur periodically as in Region IX, 5, 6.

Lexical investigation of the word *fauces* commonly used to describe the long narrow entrance passage leading into the *atrium* of many Pompeian houses casts doubt upon its use as a standard Roman term of reference. Again Vitruvius stands alone. He specifies suitable breadths for the *fauces* of large and small *atria* in proportions relative to those of the *tablinum* but indicates no volumetric conformation of the space (*De Architectura* 6.3.6). By any definition the name is metaphorical. Although *fauces* is frequently employed in narrative passages to signify an entrance or exit the contexts are virtually never architecturally defined but rather involve natural conformations, mountains, caverns or rivers where the metaphorical implications of jaws and devouring have their full force. Such a comparison is operative when Vergil in three instances places *fauces* at the entrance of the underworld kingdom (*Georgics* 4.467; *Aeneid* 6. 201; 6.273). It is the efforts of Aulus Gellius (*Noctes Atticae*, 16.5.1–2) to explain Vergil's description in *Aeneid* 6.273 of phantoms clustered at the entrance of Hades (*vestibulum ante*

Fig. 6.2 *House of Epidius Sabinus (IX,1, 20): atrium with colonnaded recesses. (photo by the author)*

ipsum primisque in faucibus Orci) that gives rise to our popular identification of the feature as a narrow passage (Greenough 1890, 1–12). Attempting to reconstruct practices already out of use, Gellius seems to contradict his own information when he places the *vestibulum* before the doorway (*ante ianuam*), but then calls Vergil's *fauces* an '*angustum iter per quod ad vestibulum adiretur*' instead of the reverse. Macrobius (*Saturnalia* 6.8.8–22) does not correct the error but corroborates it in specifying that the *fauces* leads into the vestibule from the street ('*per quod ad vestibulum de via flectitur*'). That the entrances to many Pompeian atria were long and narrow is self-evident, and the same appears true of early houses in Rome (Wallace-Hadrill 1991, 263), yet the phenomenon we call *fauces* fits best with Vitruvius' description (6.7.1) of the Greek entranceway as a long narrow corridor (*iter*) with a room on one side for the *ostiarius* and a stable on the other.

Rather than the dubious *fauces*, Roman literary sources present strong evidence for a reception area called the *vestibulum* to accommodate clients waiting to enter the house as when Cicero (*De Oratore* 1.45 200) has Crassus remark how the doorway *ianua* and *vestibulum* of the venerable jurisconsult Quintus Mucius are thronged every day. In Republican Rome and thereafter, as frequent mentions indicate, the *vestibulum* is often an architecturally defined space, enclosed or semi-enclosed, that separates the house from the street and provides a gathering place or shelter (Wiseman 1987, 393–413). Here is an apparent difference from general Pompeian custom, where most doorways opened directly onto the sidewalk and exterior benches were the primary provision for clients. One must observe that these cannot have accommodated large numbers, but perhaps the Pompeians were less attuned to early arrivals and waiting. All the same we can recognize vestibules in a few Pompeian houses. Sometimes they are built over as Mau recognized in the House of the Vestals where the original covered entrance way had matched the *atrium* in breadth but was later subdivided (cf. Fig. 6.3; Mau 1904, 248). Others are token spaces but elegant as in the House of the Faun with its three dimensional frieze decoration of colonnaded façades, and the House of the Silver Vessels (VI, 7, 20) on the Via di Mercurio, where a separate pair of columns separates entrance from atrium. The largest of Pompeian *vestibula* in the House of Julius Polibius stressed its public affiliations in being decorated with a loggia reminiscent of the Pompeian basilica itself (Fig. 6.4; Leach 1993, 23–28).

If *vestibula* in literary sources are crowded, likewise the crowded *atrium, atrium frequens* in Seneca's words (*Ep. Mor.* 76.11.6), is proverbial. Sometimes the two spaces are named together as when Seneca describes a typical aristocrat's *atrium* as being so full that even the *vestibulum* outside is packed with those still awaiting entry (*ad Marc.* 6.10.1). Similarly Ovid, with a reflection of the senatorial houses of the late Republic that lined the streets leading up the Palatine, pictures the *atria* of the Olympian gods overflowing crowds from their lofty wide-flung doors (*Met.* 1.168). Such references dramatize Vitruvius' designation of the forecourt as ceremonial space. Seneca speaks of receiving visitors in three categories, some privately, some in com-

Fig. 6.3 *House of the Vestals (VI,1, 6–8): subdivided entrance space. (photo by the author)*

Fig. 6.4 *House of Julius Polibius (IX,13, 3): entrance room. (photo by Christopher Parslow)*

pany with select others, and some en masse (*De Ben.* 6.34.1–5). *Turba* and *caterva* are the words he uses to describe the throng, characterizing the *atrium* as a place that is *hominibus plenum, amicos vacuum*. Conversely, he pictures an 'empty *atrium*' and an 'unaccompanied litter' as the condition of those who have forsaken the ambitious life (*Ep. Mor.* 22.9 1). Status has its obligations and the epitome of self-indulgent decadence is the man who avoids crossing his own packed *atrium* (*atrium refertum*) and deceives the waiting crowd by leaving through a secret rear door (*De Brev. Vitae* 14.10.4).

Under these conditions it is worth asking whether the familiar conceptualization of the *atrium / tablinum* axis as a succession of visually framing spaces was so obvious as it seems to us. The impressions perpetuated in scholarly literature are unconsciously shaped by experience of the vast empty spaces we see now in visiting Pompeii. Realistically these spaces will afford a fairer approximation of the lively scene that Roman clients will have encountered in paying their daily visits when we think of them overflowing with tourists. A packed *atrium* gave the ordinary visitor little chance of a view from one to the other side of the space. In fact this may explain why atrium decorations such as those in the House of the Menander, the House of M. Lucretius Fronto or the House of Modestus (VI, 5, 13) display no center of interest paintings at eye level. If an *atrium* is distinguished by special figured decorations these are generally placed in the frieze zone where they will be visible over the heads of the crowd. Furthermore the *tablinum* was often screened from the *atrium*. In one instance in Herculaneum the carbonized wooden screens are in place, but a large number of instances show holes for door posts.

Several further questions may be asked about the *atrium* within the dynamics of the house; one concerns the regularity with which it was reserved for the ceremony of political patronage, another the extent to which it is employed in houses outside municipal centers, and the third its historical persistence as the primary high status area of the house. If the location of the *atrium* does certify its designation as ceremonial space, all the same the notion that it was exclusively ceremonial reflects the generally male oriented disposition of archaeological interpretation.

It is interesting that Varro (*LL* 5.160) defines the *cavum aedium* as a covered space (*locus tectus*) left vacant to be used by the household in common. Although this definition may be antiquarianizing, it is not out of keeping with Allison's recent questioning of the exclusively ceremonial use of *atria* on the basis of material finds indicating common household storage in these rooms (Allison 1993, 4–7). In the same passage mentioned, Varro also names *cellae* as storage spaces surrounding the *cavum aedium*. In fact the absence of any specifically designated women's quarters in Roman houses is an indirect argument for multiple users of common space. Given that activities outside the house occupied male aristocrats from the second to the ninth hours of the ordinary Roman day, Ray Laurence has recently suggested a temporal gendering of spaces in place of the structural gendering reputedly built into Greek houses (Wallace-Hadrill 1988, 51; Laurence 1994, 122–129), but Greek archaeologists have recently called even this canonical idea into question on the grounds that it is not reflected in archaeological evidence (Jameson 1990; Nevett 1994). One might add that the depictions both in Lucretius and in Vergil of children's games in *atria* suggest that the space, when devoid of clients, was scarcely off limits to family members. In Lucretius' picture (*DRN* 4.400–404) the child stops short in his dizzy motion to see the room continue turning about him with columns spinning above his head. Vergil pictures the great halls empty as boys persistently drive their spinning tops in great circles through the space (*Aeneid* 7.377–389).

To address the second question, Vitruvius prescribes a plan for agricultural villas that is an inversion of the town house plan, with the major entrance leading into the peristyle so that crops from the country might be brought in directly, while the *atrium* stood further within. The Villa of the Mysteries, as Richardson has shown, exemplifies this plan perfectly (1988, 171–176), and I believe it was also the original plan for the Villa of the Papyri (Wojcik 1986, 36). But not every country villa observed the full formality of an *atrium*. For all the elegant decoration of a peristyle fully accommodated as a center for hospitality, the second style Boscoreale has no *atrium* (Richardson 1988, 176–180). Cicero counsels his brother Quintus against introducing an *atriolum* into the colonnade of a villa he was having remodeled at Arcanum, on the grounds that these are not customary unless a greater *atrium* also exists (*QF* 3.1.2.1–3). But over a century later Pliny gives prominent mention to the *atria* in both his villas. At Laurentium the space is modest, but not mean (*sordidum*) and it opens onto a fashionable 'D-formed' porticus (2.17). The Tuscanum has *atrium etiam ex more veterum* (5.6). In my opinion Pliny does not mean that the simple fact of having an *atrium* conforms with antique custom, but rather that this *atrium* is structured in the 'ancient manner' without columns, whether this means Tuscan or even testudinate.

Pliny's remark is not, I believe reliable evidence for the declining importance of the *atrium* in the Empire. The reason it has been cited in this capacity is because certain Pompeian houses of the later period do appear to have moved the *atrium* off the earlier axis and or even displaced it in favor of other rooms. This is true of some Pompeian town houses, such as the House of the Golden Cupids, and also of what Richardson calls garden houses, like the House of Loreius Tiburtinus with its terraced arrangement of dining areas and fountains (Richardson 1988, 309–317). In Herculaneum the House of the Stags subordinates the *atrium* to a large room opening upon the garden. Yet at the same period Seneca writing about Roman rituals and status gives a picture of the traditional room filled with clients and decorated with ancestral masks, while Martial, looking backwards at a slightly later date, sketches a comparable picture of *atria* with all their *stemmata* belonging to the Pisones contemporary with Seneca (4.40.1–4) not to mention those of the Seneca family themselves. In general Martial's *Epigrams* give every impression that the *atria potentum* are places of influence in his day (5.20.5). As a potential patron in Spain, he directs a client seeking legal aid to cultivate *atria ambitiosa* (12.68.1–2). From a personal point of view his poems rate *atria* on the basis of their hospitality to verse (1.70). In contrast with the elitist standpoints previously cited, Martial supplies pictures of clientship from the participant's point of view stressing the often futile expense of energy in the hopes of getting ahead (3.38.12–13; 9.100–1–2). Juvenal, too, from his podium of intellectual superiority, compares ancestors with their modern descendants in *Satire* 8.19–20, and derides the belief that the *nobilitas* attested by an *atrium* decorated with ancient 'waxes' can substitute for nobility of virtue. Such invocations by Imperial authors of the crowded *atrium* to stand for the politically active urban life is reasonable evidence that the ceremonies of clientship had by no means declined with the consolidation of power. In Pompeii where, in fact, the forms of municipal government continued unaffected by the Empire, they were even less likely to have altered (Franklin 1980; Mouritsen 1988, 90–9). One may imagine what an assemblage of morning visitors the influential M. Holconius Rufus with his Augustan accolade of *tribunus militaris ex populo* must have drawn (D'Arms 1989, 51–68).

A brief glance at the extensive poetic history of *atria* yields impressions of grandeur, especially in epic where regal spaces are common. Vergil anachronistically places *atria* in Dido's Carthaginian palace and also in the palace of Priam at Troy. Yet the greater number of his *atria* are not populated but empty, with small children or circling swallows. Clearly the euphonic melancholy of *vacua atria* appealed. The most celebrated *atria* of Ovid's *Metamorphoses* are those of the Olympian deities ranged along the Milky Way, a celestial Palatine, as the poet calls it with an irreverent glance at his contemporary world (1.171–172). The *atria* of Circe are filled with wild animals (14.10–11), but in other places *atria* serve as settings for dramatic scenes, especially the ill-omened weddings of Andromeda (5.2.4), Perithoos (12.215) and Eurydice (10). In epic Statius also attributes *atria* to deities and princes (*Thebaid* 1.197; 2.49; 2.214; *Achilleid* 1.755–57), but in the wedding poem for L. Arruntius Stella in the *Silvae* it is crowded with human guests (1.2.48–49).

Turning to the Greek nomenclature that Mau assigns to rooms in the peristyle complex yields even more challenges to traditional assumptions, including the canonical naming of the space itself, since Roman writers seldom mention peristyles by that name, preferring either the functional Latin terms *porticus* and *ambulatio* or else more specialized words with honorifically Greek associations such as *xystus* (Cicero *Brutus* 9.3; *Lucullus* 9.15; *Att.* 1.8.27) or *palaestra* (Cicero *De Oratore* 2.20; *Ad Fam.* 7.23.13; *Att.* 1.10.2). Vitruvius, whose writing most frequently mentions peristyles, both in public and in private contexts, classes this space among the public areas that can be entered without invitation. This categorization is not difficult to understand if we consider that its influential Greek model was not the covered domestic peristyle, but actually the open public space of the *gymnasium* so often mentioned in philosophical contexts for its associations with the intellectual life (Sauron 1980, 277–301). Practically speaking the Roman peristyle stands as a zone of transition between public and invitational, giving access to quarters that included dining areas, baths and libraries. We do not know who inaugurated the fashion, but the aristocrat most often cited for provoking competition in luxurious villa building is L. Licinius Lucullus, who commanded in the Mithridatic Wars before Pompey. Plutarch's life has much to say about dispositions in his villa that were considered unusual in his time, including apartments facing on open air porticoes (*Lucullus* 39.3).

In their distribution of surrounding spaces, as well as their structure and decoration, no two Pompeian peristyles are alike. The critical question is how these surrounding rooms possess identity. Is it because of their location? Because of their specific shapes? Because of their intentions for use? Because of the kind of furniture placed in them? Or in fact, do they only have identity from the kind of action in progress in them? Beyond this, does one kind of room witness more than one activity?

If functional identifications of these spaces are difficult, they are also important in the study of wall painting because of a widespread tendency to interpret the paintings on the basis of their appropriateness to one or the other activity of sleeping or dining (Lehmann 1953, 118–123; Ling 1991, 48–51). In attempting to clarify these identities I have found Ibycus most useful because the first thing I discovered was that two classes of nomenclature apply to such rooms: on the one hand those which describe the furnishing or the activity that takes place within the room, such as *triclinium, cenatio, cubiculum* or *bibliotheca*; on the other hand words that designate structure or form such as *oecus, exedra, camera* or *conclave*. The two classes are by no means mutually exclusive; as I shall show there are cases in which literary reference gives both a structural and a functional identity to a room. No evidence indicates that Romans observed Mau's distinction between Latin *vs.* Greek nomenclature in the placement of rooms. But the employment of structural terms is of particular interest to wall painting because it points to the fact that some rooms of unremarkable size or shape but advantageous location will have been specifically intended for variable use. Depending what furnishings were placed within them, they could serve multiple purposes: sleeping, dining, study and private conference in accordance with the dictates of weather and need. The portable nature of Roman furniture, consisting primarily of couches and small tables, easily permitted transfer from one to another space as desired.

Two types of room that Mau assigns to the peristyle are *oecus* and *exedra*. Vitruvius speaks of square *oeci* and on this basis the archaeologists have identified an *oecus* in virtually every large Pompeian house. Richardson (1988, 432) calls it a large reception room used often for dining but without the characteristic shape of the *triclinium* (Fig. 6.5). A review of its actual currency shows that *oecus* occurs in only one Latin author other than Vitruvius. The Elder Pliny (*NH* 36.25.60) refers to a kind of mosaic pattern, the *oecus asaroticus* that visually proclaimed its associations with dining by being decorated with scraps and refuse from the table (*purgamentum cenae*). In Greek of course the word *oecus* means house in the inclusive sense and less often a specific room. Cicero does in his letters use the Greek word *oikeion* to focus on domestic affairs and within the specific context of purchasing decorations of sculpture and tablets. For Vitruvius *oecus* appears to be a sub-category of dining space but perhaps with architectural styles reflecting foreign associations. Four specific types of *oecus* he describes have names that carry an international flavor: tetrastyle, Corinthian, Egyptian and Cyzicene.

The exotic character of these Vitruvian *oeci* caught the imagination of the Italian 17th century architect Palladio who reconstructed them from descriptions for use in his own designs, and in turn these elegant interpretations inspired Amedeo Maiuri to document the existence of three types of Vitruvian *oecus* in Pompeii (Maiuri 1952, 1–8). The tetrastyle *oecus* whose vault is carried on four columns appears as part of the second style decoration (reconstructed) in the House of the Silver Wedding in Pompeii (Fig. 6.6), but also in the House of Augustus on

Fig. 6.5 *House of the Dioscuri (VI,9, 6–7): room at the east end of the peristyle. (photo by the author)*

Fig. 6.6 *House of the Silver Wedding (V, 2): tetrastyle oecus east of peristyle. (photo by the author)*

the Palatine in Rome (Carettoni 1983, 52–60). The single existing example of the Egyptian *oecus* is a good one. 'A basilica like room with a clerestory' is just what we see in place of the conventional tablinum-box in the House of the Mosaic Atrium in Herculaneum. For the Corinthian *oecus* we have two excellent examples, one early, one late, the first in the Pompeian House of the Labyrinth and the other in the House of Meleager. Both illustrate Vitruvius' prescription for the room as having a single file of columns surmounted by an architrave. These were specifically intended for dining. All three of these rooms, as Vitruvius prescribes, should be of the proportions of *triclinia* save that their columns make them more spacious.

The *exedra* is another spatial designation named in Greek. Although rarely employed, it is more frequent than *oecus* and carries more specific connotations. I believe we can find a complete agreement in its uses and applications. In the Greek world an *exedra* is a recess with benches; it is uncovered and generally associated with the porticoes of *gymnasia* as the setting for philosophical discussions. Vitruvius (5.11.2) describes these spaces designed for philosophers, rhetors and others dedicated to learning. Cicero (*De Finibus* 5.4.8) also mentions an Athenian *exedra* set within the groves of the Academy. Piso speaks of the sentimental associations with the *exedra* where Carneades was accustomed to sit. The public usage carries over into the scenarios for his dialogues *De Natura Deorum* and *De Oratore*. In both cases Cicero presents himself as a visitor who finds his friends in an *exedra*. In a letter (*ad Fam.* 7.23.3) commissioning purchase of various art objects Cicero requests some *tabellae* to decorate the *exhedriae* he has just created in his small *porticus* at Tusculum. Pliny names no *exedrae* in either of his villas, but he does in a letter to Trajan mention that he has honored him by the dedication of an *exedra* within a *porticus* in Bithynia (10.70.3). Thus like the *xystus* which both Cicero and Pliny mention we may assume that the *exedra* as a domestic feature is meant to stress affinities with the public world.

Vitruvius explicitly indicates that *exedrae* are open. In one place (7.3.3) he says they are not exposed to smoke, and in another he compares (7.9.2) them with peristyles. His discussion of painting (7.5.2) contains a passage on decorating *exedrae* with *scenae frons* designs that has caused confusion in the field of Roman wall painting because the examples of stage fronts that we know do not really seem to occur in *exedra*-like rooms. Mau (1904, 261) places *exedrae* in peristyles on axis with the *atrium* in a position paralleling that of the *tablinum* but in actual fact their locations are much more various. Whatever the custom in Greek architecture, the Roman also classed interior rooms as *exedrae*. Quintilian makes this clear in his recommendations on the use of domestic interiors as the setting for a memory exercise (11.7.2). The practitioner is told to arrange his artificial images beginning with the *vestibulum*, then surrounding the *impluvium*, not only in the *cubicula* and *exedrae* but also attached to statues and images. Thus such a recess as that opening onto the *atrium* of the House of the Menander decorated with a collection of three Trojan War paintings can accurately be called an *exedra*.

The majority of the rooms bordering peristyles are of modest proportions lacking the distinctive features of Vitruvius' *oeci* or *exedrae* and their identities must be sought under other names, some familiar and others unfamiliar. I will begin by taking up certain functionally neutral terms employed in a variety of contexts with sufficient frequency to suggest that the Romans themselves tended to think of rooms as spatial containers that took their real identity from action.

The word *camera* has a specific technical meaning and is frequently used. Derived, as the Romans see it, from the word for curve, it designates a ceiling vault or a vaulted room. This form of construction is by no means limited to domestic spaces. Sallust (*Cat.* 55.4.1–3) describes the noisome underground chamber of the Mamertine prison as a *camera* joined to arches of stone. It is commonly used with reference to the vaulted chambers of baths (Vitruvius 5.11.5). Thus *camera* is a term associated both with public and with private architecture.

Looking at some appearances of *camera* in Latin texts gives the impression that form often preceded function in the designer's or patron's thinking. Letters that Cicero wrote to his brother Quintus in Gaul describe building operations at Quintus' villas and his Roman house which Clodius had wrecked during Cicero's exile. These are useful descriptions of work in progress from a quasi-technical point of view. At Arcanum where an extensive renovation campaign was in progress under the direction of a slow-moving architect named Diphilus, Cicero found certain vaulted rooms (*camerae*) unsatisfactory and ordered them to be redone (3.1.1). These rooms form their own class that appears to be categorically different from the *cubicula* since those are located on another side of the peristyle in proximity to the baths (3.1.2). Vitruvius, also concerned with *camerae* in domestic contexts (7.3.1–11), gives instructions for building

Fig. 6.7 House of the Silver Wedding (V, 2): twinned camera south of peristyle. (photo by the author)

frames, pouring the cement and finishing the stuccoed surfaces of the vaults and cornice moldings.

A great many Roman and Campanian rooms come into the category of *camerae*. Apart from the elegant but rare tetrastyle *oeci*, we find barrel vaulted chambers of every period most often opening on peristyles (Fig. 6.7). In the Roman House of the Griffins on the Palatine three such rooms were decorated in the early first century BC (Rizzo 1936, 3–7). Primarily within the second style period a kind of room with two vaulted alcoves and prominent cornices was popular. Well known examples are in the Villa Oplontis and Villa of the Mysteries. All three Pompeian bathing establishments have vaulted *apodyteria* (Fig. 6.8). Writers from the Republic to the Empire – Varro, Propertius, elder Pliny, Seneca, Statius – mention *camerae* in a luxury context, with ivory marble, glass or gilded decorations, but Varro also uses it to describe the niches in a dovecote and also the best kind of chamber for storing fruit (*DRR* 1.59.2–3). Some people, as he remarks, like to spread their dining tables in such chambers, since they are coated with marble to keep them cool: 'Why not enjoy a *spectaculum naturae*?'

Frequently as it may recur in description, all the same *camera* does not occur as a setting or background for narrative or dramatic action in the same manner as the other words I shall discuss, except when technical information is important. For instance, Phaedrus (*Fab.* 4.26.23), when retelling the well known story of Simonides and the collapsed ceiling gives the story an

Fig. 6.8 *Suburban Baths: camera leading to natatio. (photo by the author)*

anachronistic Roman coloring by calling the fatal accident the *ruina camerae* of a *triclinium*. No doubt he was aware of the potential precariousness of plastered vaults. Valerius Maximus (6.7.2) recounts the anecdote of the Roman matron Turia who concealed her proscribed husband between the vault (*camera*) and roof (*tectum*) of the couple's *cubiculum*, keeping him both safe from execution and available to her embrace. One exception to the rule of technical informa- tion may be of interest. References to the doorway and ceiling of the room where the elabo- rate feast of Petronius' *Cena Trimalchionis* is staged suggest that this dining room had an arched entrance and was vaulted itself.

The most general and neutral word in the technical vocabulary of the house is one seldom mentioned by students of Roman architecture: the word *conclave*. This word first roused my curiosity when I saw it in a passage of Suetonius concerning the Emperor Augustus' domes- tic unpretentiousness: he had no splendid *conclavia* or showy pavements (*Vita Augusti* 72). Festus explains *conclave* as a room to be closed with one key. This technical specification is overlooked by Boethius and Ward-Perkins (1970, 155–156) who do make mention of *conclavia* as 'living rooms' around the peristyle. Ibycus has brought out the frequency with which *conclavia* occur and in what a variety of contexts in Roman writing from Plautus to the Bible. To this the *Thesaurus Linguae Latinae* adds that *conclave* is not used by poets save for the comic playwrights, Horace in the *Satires*, Martial, all the more to mark it as a down-to-earth, everyday word.

Technical allusions carry no specific determination of shape or size and the range of occurrences indicates its independence of trends and fashions. In actual practice a *conclave* can be decorated as elaborately or as simply as the owner desires, and may serve alternatively as a dining chamber or bedroom.

Several sources attest to the use of *conclave* as a builders' word. One is Cicero's correspondence with Quintus where, as already mentioned, the chambers appear to be designated by technical names. At the Roman house a roof has just been completed over a series of *conclavia* which slopes down to a lower colonnade (3.1.14; 3.9.7). Quintus did not want this roof gabled; it has accordingly been made with a slope. Cicero mentions this twice reassuring his brother that the *conclavia* are right. This passage suggests that *conclavia* are to be associated with peristyles, a suggestion borne out by Suetonius' mention in the Life of Augustus of those located near the peristyle. The generalization here seems to include that one and the same *cubiculum* in which Augustus slept for forty years of his life.

Vitruvius also frequently uses *conclavia* in writing of domestic architecture. For him it seems to be a generic word that encompasses various species. In 6.8.1 the classification *conclavia* includes both oblong *triclinia* and squared *oeci*; in another passage he links the words *triclinia* and other forms of *conclavia*. In 7.2.2 we find vaulted *camerae* classed as a species of *conclavia*. In other passages he speaks of their proper orientations and decoration. In 7.3.3 we see that they can be either summer or winter rooms since he mentions that some of them must be artificially heated and lighted. In the same category we can place a remark Varro makes in *LL*. 8.32 that twin (*gemina*) *conclavia* may be dissimilarly furnished.

In some contexts where activities are associated with *conclavia*, a completely neutral denotation provides no indication of specific use. So in Plautus' *Mostellaria* the word is used to gesture towards the rooms of the house being inspected on the assumption that it has been offered for sale. In other cases where the use is indefinite there is all the same a connotation of privacy. In *Aulularia* 434 the suspicious miser Euclio angrily accuses Congrio, the hired cook, of having invaded every corner of his *aedes* and *conclavia* instead of tending to his offices by the hearth. Privacy also obtains in Plautus' *Miles Gloriosus* where a *conclave* figures in the plot. Pyrgopolynices has assigned one such room (*unum conclave*) to Philocomasium as her private space (141: *quas nemo nisi eapse inferret pedem*), and this is the room which is dug through to facilitate Philcomasium's meeting with her lover Pleusicles. Notably this must be situated near a party wall. Finally in Terence's *Eunuchus*, we hear that the virgin whom Chaerea will soon ravish is sitting in a *conclave* decorated with a picture showing Jupiter's descent to Danae in a shower of gold. Both these women's rooms might be assumed to be bedrooms, however the usage is even more definite in some cases. In *Pro Roscio Amerino* 23.64 Cicero cites the example of Titus Cloelius, a well-known citizen of Tarracina who was murdered while sleeping in a *conclave* with his two adult sons. Here the fact of the room's having only one door was important to the defense of the young men, found still sleeping when the door was opened (*Tamen, cum planum iudicibus esset factum aperto ostio dormientis eos repertos esse...*). Cicero (*De Div.* 2.20) tells a story about a prophetic omen that prevented King Dioterius from a journey where he would have slept in a *conclave* that collapsed in ruins next day. Nepos (*Life of Dion* 8.5.2) mentions sleeping in a *conclave*. Celsus refers more than once to the *conclave* used as a sickroom, while Justinian mentions it as a birthing chamber.

Varro's reference to two differently decorated *conclavia* includes different kinds of couches with the implication that those used for dining might be of a higher grade of material than those for sleeping. The distinction suggests that he associates the name both with bedrooms and with dining rooms. For indication of a *conclave* as dining room Cicero in *Verrines* 2.4.58 testifies to the governor's megalomania by claiming that he owns individual *conclavia* in which he can dress three hundred dining couches not only in Rome but also in all of his villas. The name certainly signifies a dining room when Cicero (*Philippics* 2.28) remarks on Antony's tenancy of the house of Pompey that he has set up stables in the *cubicula* and cookshops where *conclavia* used to be (*Pro conclavibus popinae sunt*). Last, but scarcely least, the room within which Horace's town mouse introduces his country visitor to the advantages of city dining is a *conclave* (*Satires* 2.6.113).

On the basis of common usage of the word and its and application to diverse dramatic situations, one may suspect that Pompeian householders may have spoken of many rooms in their houses as *conclavia*. Such closed chambers occur in all quarters of the house from corridors of the peristyle to interior corners of the *atrium* (Fig. 6.9). Their condition ranges from undecorated to some of the most elegant in the city, and the decorations themselves are

Fig. 6.9 *House of the Ceii (I,6, 11): conclave in south-east corner of atrium. (photo by the author)*

generally symmetrical in composition. The nature of their decoration is to be considered in terms of their place in the hierarchy of the program based upon their location within the house plan rather than by their exclusive dedication to the activities of sleeping or dining. Thus one might also explain why in August when Vesuvius erupted, the majority of such rooms located within the core of the house were either empty or utilized for storage while some of the more open rooms, especially those around the peristyle housed a certain number of dining or bed couches (Allison 1994, 62–65).

Another word of Greek derivation that may be used to designate spaces of variable function is *diaeta*, but unlike *conclave* and *camera* which refer to single spaces, those of the *diaeta*, properly speaking, are plural, a point that some (e.g. Elia 1934, 217–219), but not all who describe Pompeian houses have recognized. In the Greek world *diaita* is a word of multiple significance whose occurrences go back to the fourth century. From its designation of a regimen, it gravitates to a life-style and seemingly from thence to an apartment, but this can be either public or private. In Pompeian studies *diaeta* has commonly been used to designate a room for day-time, as opposed to night-time, use but literary references suggest that the word is properly applied to nuclei formed of two or three adjacent rooms.

A survey of uses indicates that the word enters into Latin vocabulary in the early Empire. Vitruvius does not use it, but Pliny uses it several times as does Justinian. It is the word Plutarch employs to describe the interior arrangements of Lucullus' magnificent villas, both the coastal villas and the Tusculan, where the *diaitai* are located by open porticoes (*Lucullus* 39.3). Other aspects of the biography indicate that these rooms are primarily intended for dining. Because the word does not appear among Cicero's Greek adaptations, I propose that Plutarch has adopted this term from the common store of contemporary vocabulary to describe a phenomenon that earlier writers had called by other names. Pliny seems well accustomed to the term. It is from him that we can discover the multiplex composition of *diaetae* since he often details the subordinate chambers making up the complex: *cubicula, triclinia,* etc. He gives this name to the apartment in Pomponius' house at Stabiae where his uncle was housed on the night of Vesuvius' eruption (6.16.3). It was close to an open area where ashes threatened to block access, and the elder Pliny was sleeping in a *cubiculum*. In his own villas Pliny has several *diaetae*. His favorite, in the Laurentian villa, comprises three rooms each receiving a different exposure of sunlight. One may be reminded of the similarly compounded suites that Vitruvius terms *hospitalia* in the Greek house, that afforded privacy to guests, yet for the most part Pliny's suites appear to have been designed and reserved for his personal use and their great asset is their removal from noise. In Justinian also one notes that *diaetae* as quarters are essentially separate and probably contain multiple rooms. By this token a perfect *diaeta* is the small complex of rooms on an interior corridor with their own garden in the House of the Vettii.

Predictably the spatial terms most frequently mentioned and also most specifically characterized by activity in literary sources are *triclinia* and *cubicula*. Their real life embodiments also present the most difficult problems of distinction, although many persons differentiate them on the basis of the markings in mosaic pavements indicating where couches are placed. Naturally such questions arise only in the case of unfurnished *triclinia*, since the permanent variety with fixed stone couches are intended exclusively for dining. Unfurnished *triclinia* are not restricted to any given location. However all the architectural references make it clear that such rooms are designed for different seasons. Varro notes that both doors and windows differ with the season (*LL*. 8.28.4). Vitruvius uses *triclinia* with four seasonal adjectives: *hiberna, aestiva, verna* and *autumnalia,* the latter two having similar eastern exposures.

Size is another question to be asked about *triclinia*; it is of particular interest when one is confronted with a large chamber that lacks identifying characteristics. The name itself suggests a room to be furnished with a canonical three couches, but since many dinners exceeded nine persons, one wonders whether these rooms might accommodate more or whether rooms of larger size go officially by different names. Vitruvius calls *triclinia* oblong, and includes them within a general class of *conclavia*. Several passages I have examined suggest that large parties use multiple *triclinia*. Suetonius mentions that Julius Caesar when traveling in the provinces was accustomed to entertain in two *triclinia*, one for ethnics and the other for local officials and his own retinue (*Vita Julii* 48). But when he called in 45 BC with 200 soldiers at Cicero's Puteolan villa, in a sojourn 'more like a billeting than a visit', the host could barely find a *triclinium* empty for Caesar himself to dine. Three *triclinia* were copiously filled by the company with freedmen and slaves spilling over (*Att.* 13.52.1–3). At a time like this, it seems likely that rooms had to be used irrespective of their seasonal orientation.

In contrast to *triclinium* which suggests close association among guests with emphasis upon the sociable aspects of dining, I believe that *cenatio* generally designates a larger room. Suetonius uses this word for the opulent dining room in Nero's *Domus Aurea* reputed to have a ceiling of movable ivory panels. Seneca may well refer to the same in *Ep. M.* 90.14 when he mentions *cenationes* with movable ceiling panels. Seneca also uses *cenatio* (*Ep.M.* 115) although in a generic designation when he speaks of a room with marble columns that is *capax populi* surely intending more than the traditional nine guests. The elder Pliny uses it to refer to a grandiose dining room with 30 onyx columns built by the freedman Callistus – perhaps a Corinthian *oecus*. All these rooms would seem larger than the normal Pompeian dining room, but one must recall than even in Pompeii there are rooms of very large dimensions such as one in the peristyle of the House of the Menander. Trimalchio, when he boasts of the assets of his house, counts four *cenationes*, but with a character so prone to misusage we cannot be certain whether the term is rightly or mistakenly applied. Even so a *cenatio* is not invariably large because Pliny (*Ep.* 2.17.10) speaks of a room can be considered either a generously sized *cubiculum* or a modest *cenatio*. His letters appear to differentiate rather precisely between *triclinia* and *cenationes*, but context does not supply a clear rationale for the distinction. Perhaps the *triclinia* are the kind with fixed couches, but several possess windows and views.

The Roman vocabulary for sleeping chambers includes also words of Greek and Roman derivation: *thalamus* and *cubiculum*, but the distinctions between these seem rather different from those for dining chambers since, in this case, the Greek word, instead of designating a grander room or one of distinctive design seems infrequent in everyday use, but is common in poetic vocabulary where it often conveys a certain formality appropriate to royal apartments or else may underscore the institutional sanctity of marriage chambers. Beyond this, a *thalamus* is always a bed-chamber, while the spaces denoted by the Roman word *cubiculum* may witness a variety of personal activities.

Of all the words I have been investigating, *cubiculum* figures most frequently both in narrative and in description. Because of the divers uses this name appears to encompass and its semantic range from technical to symbolic, I have reserved it for the final item of discussion. One point to note is the extent to which the location of a given room does influence the nature of the activities staged within it. In the Greek house bedchambers appear to have canonical places, perhaps in relationship to the gender axis of the house. In Roman houses there are many possible locations. Although the *cubiculum* may be private in the sense that entrance to it is invitational, in another sense it is semi-public. Especially it is the rooms of variable identity that are most likely to function as *cubicula* for private interviews. Additionally, one or more *cubicula* may be included in the *diaetae* commonly used as guest apartments. Even discounting possible invitations, however, Wallace-Hadrill has done well to remind us how little privacy will ever have obtained in a large Roman house with its multitudinous *familia* (1988, 78–79).

Cubicula figure frequently in historical and biographical writing as settings for adultery (Seneca *Cont.* 1.4.11.5; 2.1.34.3–10; 2.4.5.10; 7.6.48; Suetonius *Augustus* 69.1.2.) death (Tacitus *Annales* 15.63.18; 16.11.5; 16.35.4) and murder (Seneca, *Cont.* 7.5.pr.4; Quintilian 4.72.3). For the first and last of these activities, one assumes that a degree of seclusion is requisite; such events cannot easily have taken place in the little rooms around the *atrium* that are commonly called *cubicula* and identified as sleeping chambers. Two sources attest to the nomenclature, but not necessarily the function of these rooms. Cicero writes to Quintus about the *cubicula* and other *membra* surrounding the *atrium*; while Quintilian, as earlier noted, mentions *cubicula* and *exedrae* along with statues and portrait representations (*similibus*) as points of reference for the practice of artificial memory (11.2.20). Presumably such rooms were once sleeping chambers, but Dr. Allison's investigation of excavation records found that the interior *cubicula* in Pompeii were being used in large part for storage to suggest that bedrooms had migrated into other quarters of the house. One may recall the majority of Pompeian houses did have upper stories. That in the House of Julius Polibius is among the best preserved. Unfortunately our literary references seldom locate a chamber upstairs. About location near peristyles they say more. The villa of Quintus Cicero at Arcanum has two *cubicula* in the *ambulatio* near the baths. They are large and the one for winter is also high (3.1.2) The single chamber in which Augustus was reported to have slept for forty years was located, for its healthful advantages, near a peristyle. Trimalchio brags that he has twenty *cubicula,* and also one in which he himself sleeps. No doubt he imitates Augustus yet many narrative references suggest that the use of a single bedroom was fairly common.

Another class of room called *cubicula*, although personal, was not designed exclusively for sleeping. Cicero (*Fam.*7.1.5) pictures his friend Marius, the owner of a Pompeian villa, spending his mornings with light reading in a *cubiculum* which he has pierced to lay open the entire Bay of Stabiae (*ex quo tibi Stabianum perforando patefecisti sinum*). Pliny (1.31), in praising the villa of a friend on Lake Como speaks of day and night *cubicula*; later he speaks of his own villa so close to a lake that he can drop in a fish-hook from the couch in his *cubiculum* (9.7.3). His more extensive and detailed descriptions of his Laurentian and Tuscan villas indicate that he uses their numerous, well-situated *cubicula* as studies for reading and writing. Many of these have window views. But also he consults with his closest friends in a *cubiculum* (5.1.4), or summons them there for a reading of his verses (5.3.10).

Whatever the real degree of privacy in *cubicula* they are certainly as much symbols for the private life as is the *atrium* for the public profile of the house. When Cicero is prosecuting Verres, he represents the conduct of judicial business in a *cubiculum* as a decadent abuse of power. But writing to his brother Quintus in Gaul, he praises such accessibility beyond the call of duty (*ad QF* 1.1.59). Pliny's *Panegyric* utilizes a similar ethic in stressing that Trajan as Emperor has brought government out of the *cubiculum* into the public eye. Most striking, however is the contrast posed by two books of the Republic and Empire. At the opening of the *De Re Publica*, Scipio dresses and walks out of his *cubiculum* into the *porticus* to begin his discussion of the state. At the beginning of Tacitus' *Dialogus* Julius Maternus receives his callers in his *cubiculum* where they remain conversing about the decline of oratory as the powerful discourse of public life. Whatever the status of space in the Roman house and its employment, Tacitus' symbolic scene setting aims to signify that the temper of public life has suffered change.

Returning from political drama to technicalities, this survey of names and spaces leads me to two conclusions. The first is simply a recommendation that the functional unprejudicial names of *camera* and *conclave* should be introduced into descriptive vocabulary with application to qualified spaces suited for variable use. The second point with a bearing on the decoration of such spaces involves principles that will be familiar to anyone acquainted with current trends in the study of Roman painting. First of these is the observation advanced by an Italian scholar that the decoration of spaces is coordinated with the kind of traffic or passages that they are intended to facilitate. Corridors and ante-chambers tends to receive continuous, paratactic decoration that does not delay the spectator's attention or in some cases actually moves him along; rooms planned as settings for stationary activity – dining, resting or reading – are framed by more elaborate and usually symmetrical decoration with figured centers of interest (Scagliarini Corlaita 1974–76, 3–44). To this may be added the concept of hierarchy in decorative programs: that the most significant rooms no matter whether they are located in the quarters we have been calling public or private receive the most complex and opulent decoration (Barbet 1985, 55–77). These two principles work together to correct earlier notions that the degree of complexity or simplicity of walls was entirely a matter of stylistic evolution, which is to say that a wall decorated with a closed panel system must be earlier than one with an illusionistic opening of the wall. Consider two rooms in the Villa of the Mysteries both attributed to the second style, yet to different moments of stylistic evolution. Now in a house like this instead of a succession of decorative periods one can see synchronic components of a complete program or plan.

At the present moment, however, application of the principles of hierarchy remains based upon prior determinations concerning the functional identity of rooms, which is to say that a *triclinium* must outrank a *cubiculum* (Barbet 1985; Wallace-Hadrill 1988). If however we regard these uses as variable, we can understand a far higher degree of flexibility within the parameters of decorative mural programs.

ACKNOWLEDGMENT

An earlier version of this paper was written during the period of my Fellowship at the National Humanities Center with additional support from an ACLS Senior Research Fellowship. I can scarcely overstate my appreciation of the ideal conditions for research and colleagueship that the Center provides. I owe thanks to Professor Gerhard Koeppel, President of the Research Triangle Society of the Archaeological Institute of America for the invitation that resulted in this paper and to my hosts on other occasions, Professor Robert Sutton President of the Central Indiana Society and Dr. Rick Jones of the University of Bradford. Additionally I wish to thank Prof. Kent Rigsbee of the Duke University Classics Department for his kindness in providing access to the department's Ibycus program and facilities, and to Prof. Lawrence Richardson Jr., as ever, for conversation and correspondence concerning all things Pompeian.

References

Allison, P.M., 1993. How do we identify the use of space in Roman houses?, in E.M. Moorman (ed.), *Functional and Spatial Analysis of Ancient Wall Painting*, Proceedings of the Fifth International Congress on Ancient Wall Painting, Amsterdam, 8–12 September 1992. Publications of the Dutch Institute in Rome 3 (Stichting BABESCH: Leiden): 1–8.

Allison, P.M., 1994. *The Distribution of Pompeian House Contents and its Significance* Vols. I and II. (UMI: Ann Arbor).

Barbet, A., 1985. *La Peinture Romaine: Les Styles Décoratifs Pompéiens* (Picard: Paris).

Bek, Lise, 1980. *Towards Paradise on Earth: Modern Space Conception in Architecture: A Creation of Renaissance Humanism*. Analecta Romana Instituti Danici, supplement 9. (Accademia di Danimarca: Rome).

Bek, Lise, 1983. *Questiones conviviales*: the idea of the triclinium and the staging of convivial ceremony from Rome to Byzantium, *Analecta Romana Instituti Danici* 12: 81–107.

Boethius, Axel, and Ward Perkins, John, 1970. *Etruscan and Roman Architecture* (Pelican History of Art: Harmondsworth).

Brown, Frank, 1961. *Roman Architecture* (Studio Vista: London).

Carettoni, Gian Filippo, 1983. *Das Haus des Augustus auf dem Palatin* (P. von Zabern: Mainz).

Castrén, Paavo, 1975. *Ordo Populusque Pompeianus: Polity and Society in Roman Pompeii* (Acta Instituti Romani Finlandiae, 8: Rome).

Clarke, J.R. 1992. *The Houses of Roman Italy 100 B. C. – A. D. 200: Ritual, Space and Decoration* (University of California Press: Berkeley).

D'Arms, John H. 1989. Pompeii and Rome in the Augustan Age and beyond: the eminence of the *Gens Holconius*, in Robert I. Curtis (ed.), *Studia Pompeiana & Classica in Honor of Wilhelmina F. Jashemski*, I *Pompeiana* (Caratzas Brothers: New Rochelle, New York): 51–68 and figs. 1–5.

Elia, Olga, 1934. La casa di un Augustiano a Pompei, *Atti del III Congresso di Studi Romani* 1: 215–226.

Evans, Edith, 1978. A group of Atrium houses without side rooms in Pompeii, in H.McK. Blake, T.W. Potter, D.B. Whitehouse (eds.), *Recent Research in Prehistoric, Classical and Medieval Archaeology: Papers in Italian Archaeology I: The Lancaster Seminar* (BAR Supplementary Series 41(I); Oxford):-175–191.

Franklin, James L. Jr., 1980. *Pompeii: The Electoral Programmata, Campaigns and Politics, A.D. 71–79*. Papers and Monographs of the American Academy in Rome, 28. (American Academy in Rome: Rome).

Greenough, J.B., 1890. The *fauces* of the Roman house, *Harvard Studies in Classical Philology* 1: 1–12.

Jameson, M.H., 1990. Domestic space in the Greek city-state, in Susan Kent (ed.), *Domestic Architecture and the Use of Space: An Interdisciplinary Cross-cultural Study* (Cambridge University Press, Cambridge): 92–113.

Laurence, Ray, 1994. *Roman Pompeii: Space and Society* (Routledge, London/New York).

Leach, E.W., 1993. The entrance room in the House of Julius Polibius and the nature of the Roman vestibulum, in E.M. Moorman (ed.), *Functional and Spatial Analysis of Ancient Wall Painting,* Proceedings of the Fifth International Congress on Ancient Wall Painting, Amsterdam, 8–12 September 1992. Publications of the Dutch Institute in Rome 3 (Stichting BABESCH: Leiden): 23–28.

Lehmann, P. W., 1953. *Roman Wall Paintings from Boscoreale in the Metropolitan Museum of Art* Monographs in Archaeology and the Fine Arts 5 (Archaeological Institute of America: Cambridge, Mass.).

Ling, Roger, 1991. *Roman Painting* (Cambridge University Press: Cambridge).

Mau, August, 1904. *Pompeii: Its Life and Art*, F. Kelsey trans. (Macmillan: New York).

Maiuri, Amedeo, 1952. Gli 'Oeci' Vitruviani in Palladio e nella casa pompeiana ed ercolenese, *Palladio* 2:1–8.

Mouritsen, Henrik, 1988. *Elections, Magistrates and Municipal Élite: Studies in Pompeian Epigraphy* Analecta Romana Instituti Danici. Supp. 15 (Accademia di Danimarca: Rome).

Nevett, Lisa, 1994. Separation or seclusion: towards and archaeological approach to investigating women in the Greek household in the fifth to third centuries B.C., in M.P. Pearson and Colin Richards (eds.), *Architecture and Order: Approaches to Social Space* (Routledge: London/New York): 98–112.

Rapoport, Amos, 1990. Systems of activities and systems of settings, in Susan Kent (ed.), *Domestic Architecture and the Use of Space,: An Interdisciplinary Cross-cultural Study,* (Cambridge University Press: Cambridge): 9–20.

Richardson, Lawrence Jr., 1988. *Pompeii: An Architectural History* (Johns Hopkins University Press: Baltimore).

Rizzo, G.E., 1936. *Le Pitture della 'Casa dei Griffi',* Monumenta della Pittura Antica III: Roma, fascicolo I (Rome).

Sauron, Gilles, 1980. *Templa serena*: à propos de la 'Villa dei Papiri' d'Herculaneum: contribution à l'étude des comportements aristocratiques romains à la fin de la république, *Mélanges de l'Ecole Française de Rome, serie Antiquité* 92: 277–301.

Scagliarini Corlaita, D., 1974–76. Spazio e decorazione nella pittura pompeiana, *Palladio* 23–25: 3–44.

Wallace-Hadrill, Andrew, 1988. The social structure of the Roman house, *Papers of the British School at Rome* 56: 43–97.

Wallace-Hadrill, Andrew, 1991. Elites and trade in the Roman town, in John Rich and A. Wallace-Hadrill (eds.), *City and Country in the Ancient World* (Routledge: London): 241–272.

Wiseman, T.P., 1987. *Conspicui postes tectaque digna deo*: the public image of aristocratic and imperial houses in the late Republic and early Empire, in Charles Pietri (ed.), *L'Urbs: Espace urbain et histoire (I siècle avant J.-C. – III siècle après J.-C.)*, Collection de l'Ecole Française de Rome 98: 393–413.

Wojcik, Maria Rita, 1986. *La Villa dei Papiri di Ercolano: Contributo alla riconstruzione dell'ideologia della nobilitas tardorepubblicana*, Soprintendenza Archeologica di Pompei Monografie, 1 (L'Erma di Bretschneider: Rome).

7 The Pompeii Forum Project 1994–95[1]

John J. Dobbins

INTRODUCTION

Like the forum in Rome itself, the forum at Pompeii was the focal point of urban life housing institutions of government, cult buildings, and retail markets. This urban core and the questions it presents are the focus of the Pompeii Forum Project. The Project is a collaborative venture that is archaeologically based, heavily dependent upon advanced technology, and broadly conceived so that it transcends its archaeological component and addresses broad issues of urban history and the ways in which an ancient city can serve modern architectural theoreticians and designers. In its most succinctly stated form, the archaeological goal of the Pompeii Forum Project is to understand the evolution of Pompeii's urban center. The multiple dimensions of this goal involve questions of chronology, decoration, building function, patronage, individual building design, overall urban design, relationship to Rome, and the social and economic implications of urban development.

BRIEF HISTORY

Phase One of the Project began in 1988 as a one-person research project conducted by the principal investigator[2] whose appointment in 1993–94 to the Institute for Advanced Technology in the Humanities at the University of Virginia[3] transformed the research, first into a project that employs advanced technology at all levels, and secondly into the present interdisciplinary, collaborative research venture. It was clear that data (numerous, complex, and three-dimensional) could be recorded and analyzed most appropriately by existing CAD technology. At the same time, the entrance of the Project into the realm of advanced technology

---

[1] My colleagues and I are grateful to Pietro Giovanni Guzzo, Soprintendente alle Antichità di Pompei, Baldassare Conticello, former Soprintendente alle Antichità di Pompei, and to the staff at the Soprintendenza Archeologica and the Direzione degli Scavi for facilitating our work in the forum at Pompeii. Appreciation is also extended to the National Endowment for the Humanities, the University of Virginia, the Institute for Advanced Technology in the Humanities, the Center for the Study of Architecture, and private donors. Photographs are by Dobbins. CAD plans and models are by Eiteljorg, Hanna, Cooper, and Dobbins.

[2] Results of those investigations have been presented already (Dobbins 1992; 1994a; 1994b).

[3] The Institute, whose acronym is IATH, maintains a Web site at http://jefferson.village.virginia.edu.

provided an opportunity to expand the research design and interpret the developments at Pompeii in more broadly based urbanistic ways. Thus began Phase Two. The on-site team now includes CAD specialists, classical archaeologists, an architect, an architectural and urban historian, and an urban designer.[4] Colleagues in architecture, civil engineering, and environmental sciences, who are interested in the response of buildings to earthquakes and volcanoes, are collaborators who are not part of the on-site team.

THE 1994 AND 1995 FIELD SEASONS

A two-week preliminary season in June of 1994 tested equipment and data gathering procedures and refined the research design. In 1995 the Project received a three-year grant from the National Endowment for the Humanities for field seasons during June of 1995–1997. On-site surveying is performed using a total station (an electronic theodolite with data recorder) and data are transferred daily to a 3D CAD model. To enhance data gathering efficiency, photogrammetry is employed. Reflective targets are taped to a wall and surveyed using the total station. The same wall with targets still attached is then photographed. Upon our return to the United States the photographs and the survey data are combined in order to add to the model. Advanced technology also plays a central role in the analysis of data as the computer model and data bases are developed and studied at the University of Virginia and the Center for the Study of Architecture.[5]

An important component of the 1995 season was large format archival black-and-white photography, especially of the buildings on the east side of the forum, by archaeological photographer Aaron Levin. As our goal is to present much of our data and preliminary observations as the project evolves, we have created on the World Wide Web a home page for the project at http://jefferson.village.virginia.edu/pompeii/. Offerings available at the Web site include a selection of photographs by Aaron Levin and preliminary observations by C. W. Westfall regarding the larger urban issues that the project raises, a discussion that results from on-site investigations by Westfall and Mark M. Schimmenti in 1995.

Two interrelated observations of the 1995 season are highlighted here. The first concerns the forum colonnade whose absence in front of the Sanctuary of the Genius of Augustus is a feature of most plans. A good case can be made for filling this lacuna with a colonnade. The second concerns the Imperial Cult Building whose geometric design continues to be examined. Preliminary comments on some larger issues of social and economic history conclude this report.

---

[4]   The on-site team consists of Larry F. Ball, James G. Cooper, Harrison Eiteljorg, Karim M. Hanna, Mark M. Schimmenti, Carroll William Westfall and John J. Dobbins (Principal Investigator). The 1995 team also included Sally Butler and Aaron Levin.

[5]   Project member Harrison Eiteljorg II, Director of the Center for the Study of Architecture, describes the equipment and field procedures used at Pompeii in the *CSA Newsletter* 7.2 (August 1994), 7.3 (November 1994), 8.1 (May 1995), 8.2 (August 1995), 8.3 (November 1995), 9.1 (May 1996), 9.2 (August 1996). World Wide Web site http://csaws.brynmawr.edu:443/web1/newslet.html.

OBSERVATIONS ON THE FORUM COLONNADES[6]

An examination in 1995 of the forum colonnades and associated stylobates leads to the conclusion that the stylobate in front of the Eumachia Building and the Sanctuary of Augustus is probably a nineteenth-century restoration. Mau drew the same conclusion in 1892 without elaborating on evidence or implications (Mau 1892, 114).[7] This paper provides an opportunity to present the evidence and reopen the question of whether or not an ancient colonnade once stood in front of the Sanctuary of the Genius of Augustus. Present observations also help in reconstructing the colonnade in front of the Imperial Cult Building and understanding the relationship between the cult building's façade colonnade and the adjacent forum colonnades.

Fig. 7.1 Porticus of Popidius at the south-east corner of the Forum, from the south.

Long stretches of what appear to be the forum's authentically ancient stylobates establish a point of reference for several anomalous features identified here as nineteenth century restoration. Ostensibly ancient stylobates still *in situ* are found south of the Via dell'Abbondanza along the east side of the forum, along the entire southern edge of the forum, along most of the west side, and finally, in front of the Macellum. These *in situ* stylobates consist of precisely cut, smoothly dressed blocks of white limestone that are carefully laid to produce level upper surfaces and straight front edges. The stylobate associated with the Porticus of Popidius at the southeastern corner of the forum is a good example. Visible in Fig. 7.1 are the stylobate and colonnade, a broad apron of white limestone set one step

---

[6]   As important observations were made by Sally Butler and James Cooper, this section is jointly authored by Butler, Cooper and Dobbins.

[7]   Mau's commentary is unfortunately limited to one sentence. In speaking of the chalcidicum in front of the Eumachia Building he says 'Il margine attuale sull'intero lato e senz'alcun dubbio moderno' – the present edge of the entire western side is without doubt modern.

Fig. 7.2   *Detail of the Forum colonnade in front of the Macellum.*

below the colonnade, and the white limestone pavement of the forum one step below the apron. The pavement of the forum is therefore set two steps below the portico that defines the forum's open space. The same conditions exist along the southern and western sides of the forum. The section of the west colonnade where this pattern is interrupted also appears to be a restoration.

Everywhere, except in front of the Sanctuary of the Genius of Augustus and the Eumachia Building, columns rest on lava footings; they are not set directly on the limestone stylobate. While this condition can be detected throughout, the clearest evidence comes from the north-western corner of the forum where missing columns reveal the underlying keyhole-shaped lava footings. The limestone blocks of the stylobate are cut to surround the lava footing. As the stylobate blocks extend to the rear of the columns and their footings, the illusion is created that the columns are set on the stylobate itself.

The treatment in front of the Macellum is somewhat different, but still follows the familiar pattern of bedding the columns on lava footings (Fig. 7.2). Here the footings are approximately square in plan. Limestone stylobate blocks fit precisely between the footings and project a few centimeters beyond them. The ends of the stylobate blocks are notched or stepped to accommodate the plinths of the Corinthian columns which overhang the footings by a few centimeters on the north and south. This arrangement is quite clear at the right of Fig. 7.2 where the column and plinth are missing. Part of the arrangement is a facing block that masks the front (western) face of the footing and aligns with the stylobate block. The column at the left of Fig. 7.2 illustrates the finished condition: the footing is completely masked and the

Fig. 7.3 Stylobate and colonnade in front of the Eumachia Building, from the south-west.

appearance is created that the marble Corinthian order is bedded directly on a stylobate of white limestone. Here, too, the stylobate extends to the rear of the plinths.

In summary, the hallmarks of most forum stylobates are precision in the cutting and laying of blocks, a two-step descent to the forum that includes a broad apron as an intermediary level, columns set on lava footings, and columns not extending beyond the rear line of the stylobate. As there is no reason to doubt the authenticity of these stylobates, they are considered normative for authentically ancient stylobates in the forum.

By contrast, the stylobate in front of the Eumachia Building and the Sanctuary of the Genius of Augustus is anomalous in several ways. Many of its blocks are smaller than those used in the stylobates just described and many are set headerlike among larger blocks (Fig. 7.3). The blocks themselves are laid in an irregular fashion that lacks precision and produces an upper surface that is less regular than the forum's other stylobates. The vertical sides that face the forum are not finely dressed. The broad apron is lacking as are forum pavement slabs themselves. And finally, the alignment of the blocks fails to produce a straight line along the stylobate's western face. The outward curve in front of the Eumachia Building and the Sanctuary of the Genius of Augustus (Fig. 7.4) contrasts markedly with the straight edge of the stylobate in Fig. 7.1.

It is also clear that two blocks cut to surround the footings of a Doric column in the manner discussed above have been incorrectly incorporated into the section in front of the Eumachia portal (Fig. 7.5). As their curved cuttings are improperly aligned to receive a column and as the columns in front of the Eumachia Building are set on plinths, it is clear that these two

Fig. 7.4 *Stylobate and colonnade in front of the Eumachia Building and Sanctuary of the Genius of Augustus, from south.*

blocks are not in a primary use-related context. It is likely that they derived from a disturbed and now restored section of the western colonnade. In addition, the small pieces of broken marble veneer visible in Fig. 7.5 are additional features pointing to modern reconstruction. Furthermore, the relationship of the columns to the stylobate is anomalous. The columns are bedded directly on the limestone stylobate rather that on tufa footings, and they overhang the stylobate on the eastern side. Taken together, these observations suggest that the stylobate in front of the Eumachia Building and the Sanctuary of the Genius of Augustus is a completely modern arrangement. Nineteenth century photographs provide a *terminus ante quem* for the reconstruction of the stylobate and indicate that the reconstruction, if modern, took place shortly after the excavation of the east side of the forum (Conticello et al. 1990, nos. 8, 9, 33, 45; the earliest is no. 9, ca. 1862). Ancient salvaging in this region must have been particularly vigorous and probably accounts for the removal of pavement, apron, stylobate, and numerous elements of the columnar order. A partially salvaged section of the forum's western stylobate probably provided the two circularly cut blocks that the restorers apparently incorporated into the rebuilt Eumachia stylobate.

Using the evidence presented so far it is possible to offer some reconstructions of the forum's eastern colonnade. The apron can be restored as an intermediary level along the east side of the forum. This is easily achieved in a CAD model by connecting the preserved patch of apron at the Imperial Cult Building with the apron at the southeastern corner of the forum (Fig. 7.6, a schematic model that contains measured points, dimensions derived from existing plans, and arbitrary extrusions to give volume to the buildings). The apron is restored as a unifying element interposed between the forum porticoes and the forum pavement and extending from the front of the Temple of Jupiter around the whole forum.

Fig. 7.5 *Stylobate in front of the Eumachia Building, detail, from the west.*

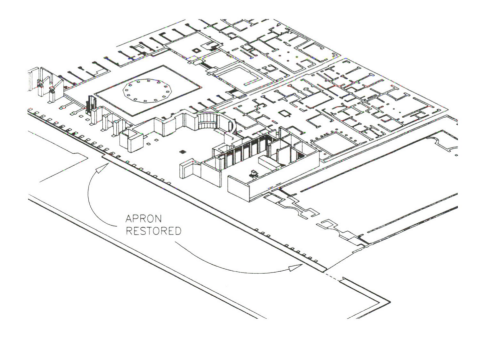

APRON
RESTORED

Fig. 7.6 *Schematic CAD model illustrating the restored apron along the east side of the Forum.*

The argument that there was never a colonnade in front of the Sanctuary of the Genius of Augustus presumably stems from the absence of any trace of columns on the stylobate. That is, there are no lava footings of the type seen elsewhere in the forum and there are no indications on the stylobate itself, such as setting marks or dowel holes as seen on the lava stylobate inside the Eumachia Building (Dobbins 1994b, 660 for the Eumachia Building). Moreover, no columns that might have belonged to a colonnade in this location were recovered in the excavations. However, once it is recognized that this stretch of stylobate is not ancient, it ceases to play a role in the debate and no longer constitutes evidence for the absence of a colonnade in this area.

Apart from a *prima facie* likelihood that a colonnade surrounded the entire forum, there are intimations in the colonnade of the Imperial Cult Building that point to a colonnade where there is now a lacuna. As reported by Mau 100 years ago, seven of eight original tufa footings for a colonnade are still *in situ* in front of the Imperial Cult Building (Mau 1896, 291, and plan on 285). These are the seven southernmost footings. The northernmost footing had been robbed out and is restored on Mau's plan as a (barely) dotted square. Mau emphasizes the proximity of the footing to the southernmost footing of the Macellum's forum colonnade. He did not develop the argument any further.

The colonnade in front of the Imperial Cult Building can be reconstructed as an octastyle portico that relates directly to the cult building. The order was taller than the order of the adjacent porticoes and therefore raises the question of the manner in which the transitions were effected.

Fig. 7.7 presents the Imperial Cult Building, the seven large footings in front of it, the southernmost footing associated with the Macellum's forum colonnade, the edge of the re-

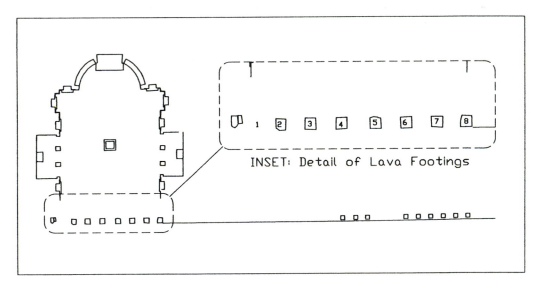

Fig. 7.7 *CAD plan of the Imperial Cult Building and standing columns in front of the Eumachia Building.*

Fig. 7.8 Colonnade in front of the Macellum, from the south .

stored stylobate that extends to the south, and the nine columns that have been erected in front of the Eumachia Building. Although the lava footings are generally squared in plan, the inset makes it clear that they are not perfect squares. Within the inset, the footings are numbered from north to south; footing 1 is lacking.

The alignment of the Macellum colonnade with the oddly shaped footing next to the lacuna for footing 1 makes it clear that the footing belongs to the Macellum colonnade (Fig. 7.8). The footing is larger than the 0.75 m. square Macellum footings and is anomalous in shape (and damaged as well). Its surface presents two separately dressed surfaces. The northern half bedded the southernmost column of the Macellum's forum colonnade. The southern half accommodated the northern end of the colonnade in front of the Imperial Cult Building. Also clear from the plan and from photographs is that the colonnade for the Imperial Cult Building projects forward of the colonnade of the Macellum.

Fig. 7.9 presents additional steps in the reconstruction. Footing 1 is easily restored by mirroring footing 8 around the central east-west axis of the Imperial Cult Building. The northern termination of the Imperial Cult Building's colonnade against the Macellum colonnade argues for a balancing treatment at the southern end. The oddly-shaped (and damaged) Macellum footing is mirrored in a similar fashion to locate the northernmost footing for the colonnade in front of the Sanctuary of the Genius of Augustus.

Fig. 7.10 restores a colonnade in front of the Eumachia Building and the Sanctuary of the Genius of Augustus. The column spacing of the present columns in front of the Eumachia Building is uneven. From south to north, the first five interaxial distances are (in meters) 2.269, 2.323, 2.315, 2.270, 2.293. The interaxial distance used in Fig. 7.10 is 2.313. This results in the placement of a column on the prepared bedding of the footing that is restored by the mirroring process just described. The overlap between the northernmost plinth and its footing is

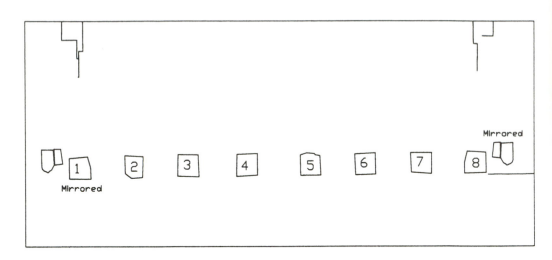

Fig. 7.9 *CAD plan reconstructing the column footings associated with the Imperial Cult Building.*

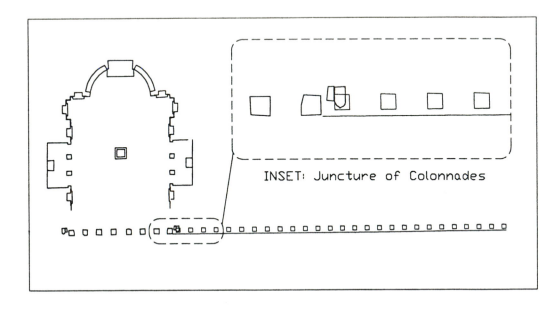

Fig. 7.10 *CAD plan of the Imperial Cult Building with the Forum colonnade to the south restored.*

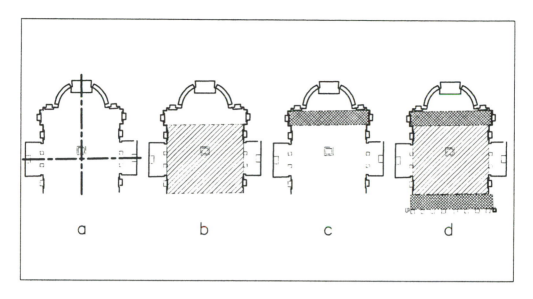

Fig. 7.11 Imperial Cult Building. Plans. (a. major axes; b. zone centered on intersection of axes and lateral exedrae with flanking niches; c. zone between arched bays; d. arched bay zone and colonnade)

awkward because the mirroring process employed the damaged footing seen in the foreground of Fig. 7.8. A further step in the reconstruction (not shown) restores the footing to its original dimensions.

THE IMPERIAL CULT BUILDING

Investigation of the Imperial Cult Building's design continues. The building itself is noteworthy for several reasons: the complexity of plan, the bold open front, the highly articulated interior wall surfaces, the marble revetment throughout (now lacking), and the creative insertion of the building into the previously existing urban fabric.

A visitor to the building is aware of the central-plan quality of the interior space, of the interplay of axes, vista, and the now-missing sculpture. Nonetheless, the plan itself appears not to be a central plan. The intersection of the two main axes does not fall in the center of the building and the center of the building is not significant in any architectural sense (Fig. 7.11a). At the same time, however, the building is prescient in that it anticipates the articulated wall surfaces of Domitian's Aula Regia and the central plan quality of the Pantheon.

Moreover, each of the large, lateral exedrae was screened by two columns and each was flanked by statue niches creating on the north and south side of the building a symmetrical arrangement of a screened exedra framed by statue niches (Fig. 7.12), a motif that anticipates the familiar arrangement of the Pantheon's interior. This design created a spatial zone within the building that centers on the intersection of the two main axes (emphasized by hatching

Fig. 7.12 *Imperial Cult Building. Interior, south side, from the north*

in Fig. 7.11b). The odd, or extra, arched bay at the eastern end of the north and south sides (at the left in Fig. 7.12) appears to be an anomaly that interrupts the symmetrical arrangement of elements just described; cross hatching in Fig. 7.11c emphasizes the zone defined by the two arched bays.

Our continuing investigation of the building's design has led to a new interpretation that better explains the arched bays. Project member James Cooper has made important observations that reveal the essentially symmetrical nature of the plan. The width of the arched bays is the same as the distance between the building's front walls and the forum colonnade thereby suggesting that the designer of the building intended the forum colonnade to be an integral part of a symmetrical design (Fig. 7.11d). If the symmetry of design visible in plan also existed in elevation, then it is likely that arches spanned the openings between the corner columns of the façade and the end walls of the buildings. An as-yet unfinished CAD model restores the colonnade and associated arches of the Imperial Cult Building (Fig. 7.13).

Two additional conditions support the symmetrical design thesis and demonstrate that the forum colonnade was integrated into the design as an octastyle façade of grand proportions. First, large footings for columns much taller than others in the forum colonnade remain in front of the Imperial Cult Building indicating that this stretch of colonnade emphasizes the building that lies behind it; and second, the projection of the footings in advance of the line of the forum colonnade further distinguished the group of eight columns and confirms that special attention was paid to the presentation of the Imperial Cult Building. From the open space of the forum the projecting octastyle façade announced the presence of an important building while people walking within the forum colonnade were perforce drawn into the building whose design had co-opted the forum colonnade itself.

WATER AND CIRCUSES?

Two of the most important questions that drive the Pompeii Forum Project conclude this report: (1) What were the main concerns of the Pompeians after the earthquake of 62?, and (2) to what extent did these concerns include the forum? By determining what the Pompeians built or rebuilt after the earthquake we should be able to determine what was important to them. To the extent that the rebuilding involved the forum, we can identify civic design concerns prevalent, at least in Pompeii and perhaps more widely in Roman Italy, during the third quarter of the first century AD. Lacking information on the debates that must have taken place among the *decuriones*, lacking the records of decisions made, and lacking building inscriptions of new and restored structures we must turn to the built evidence itself to determine the nature and extent of the recovery.

The standard view is familiar (citations in Dobbins 1994b, n. 8). John-Ward-Perkins reports that after the earthquake 'only two public monuments (the Amphitheater and the Temple of Isis) had been completely restored and there was little or no new public building' (Ward-Perkins and Claridge 1978, 50). Paul Zanker considers that the center of daily commerce had shifted from the forum to the more frequented streets, above all the Via Stabiana, the Via

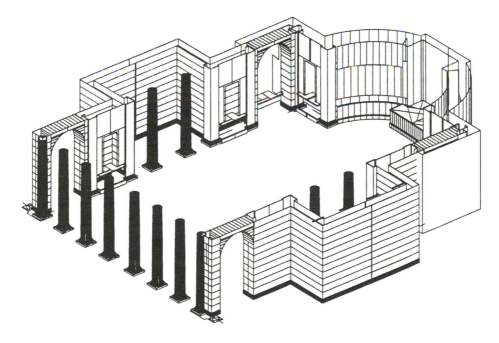

Fig. 7.13 *CAD model of the Imperial Cult Building, its colonnade, and associated arches*

dell'Abbondanza, and the Via degli Augustali and that the largo in front of the Stabian Baths had become the center of town life (Zanker 1987, 41; 1993, 139; 1995, 135).[8] Jean-Pierre Adam, whose claim that the Pompeians had focused on 'l'eau et les loisirs' inspires the heading for this section, sees a post-62 preoccupation with baths and spectacles (Adam 1986, 86).

The standard view of post-62 Pompeii sees no role for the forum in the life of the city. The radical nature of this view should be emphasized since, for any Roman city, the forum was the center. An abandonment of the forum would have had a crippling effect on civic institutions and on the social, religious, and economic aspects of life that focused on the forum. Were the institutions that were housed in the forum also in ruin? We know that certain civic institutions survived because elections continued to be held. Did the social and political rituals associated with the forum (for example, the arrival of élites with clients) cease to exist? Could the streets of Pompeii and even the largo at the Stabian Baths really have served as the focus of civic life when they were more suited to directing traffic toward the forum?

The Pompeii Forum Project has turned to the buildings themselves. They tell a very different story and reveal that the Pompeian forum provides an unexpected opportunity for reassessing the urban development of the city's core. Evidence gathered and presented during phase one of the Project (Dobbins 1994b) clarifies the Augustan-period developments and, perhaps more surprisingly, points to a comprehensive post-earthquake plan for the forum, a design whose hallmarks are the unification and monumentalization of the urban center. Even if every detail had not been completed by 79, the evidence allows us to see a renewed emphasis on the forum and the institutions it housed. The modern model of rejecting the center in favor of peripheral spaces does not apply. Post-62 urbanism gave enhanced physical embodiment to the institutions that belonged on the forum. More fully than in any previous period the forum became a showcase of civic pride, aspiration, and achievement. While this assessment of the post-62 forum is new, it is not as radical as 'the standard view.' The new interpretation is compatible with the nature of a Roman city and recognizes a continuity with previous developments in Pompeian urbanism that had already aggrandized the forum and linked it to neighboring streets (for example, the arches, colonnade, and temple associated with the Via del Foro).

This new understanding raises its own difficult questions. What was the design process by which the forum achieved its new form? Who financed it? Did the old élite families play a major role? How are we to understand in social and economic terms the increased 'industrialization' (i.e., within existing houses) and the simultaneous enhancement of the forum? Was there a causal relationship between the closing of the east side of the forum and the development of industrial establishments that occur in the blocks to the east of the forum? In other words, was the east side of the forum closed to isolate it from the region immediately to the east or did industrialization in those blocks occur after they were isolated from the forum? These are some of the larger questions that will occupy the Pompeii Forum Project in coming seasons.

---

[8]   The plans accompanying Zanker's text indicate that only the chalcidicum of the Eumachia Building had returned to use.

References

Adam, J.-P., 1986. Observations techniques sur les suites du séisme de 62 à Pompéi, in C.A. Livadie (ed.), *Tremblements de terre, éruptions volcaniques des hommes dans la Campanie antique* (Bibliothêque de l'Institut français de Naples, ser. II, 7, Naples.)

Conticello, B., et al., 1990. *Fotografia a Pompei nell'800 dalle collezioni del Museo Alinari* (Alinari: Florence).

Dobbins, J.J., 1992. The Altar in the Sanctuary of the Genius of Augustus in the Forum at Pompeii, *Römische Mitteilungen* 99: 251–263.

Dobbins, J.J., 1994a. The Pompeii Forum Project, IATH Research Reports, Second Series, 1994: World Wide Web, URL: http://jefferson.village.virginia.edu/pompeii/page-1.html

Dobbins, J.J., 1994b. Problems of Chronology, Decoration, and Urban Design in the Forum at Pompeii, *American Journal of Archaeology* 98: 629–694.

Mau, A., 1896. Der städtische Larentempel in Pompeji, *Römische Mitteilungen* 11: 285–301.

Mau, A., 1892. Osservazioni sull'edificio di Eumachia in Pompei, *Römische Mitteilungen* 7: 113–143.

Ward-Perkins, J. and Claridge, A., 1978. *Pompeii A.D. 79* (Alfred A. Knopf: New York).

Zanker, P., 1987. *Pompeji: Stadtbilder als Spiegel von Gesellschaft und Herrschaftsform* (Phillip von Zabern: Mainz).

Zanker, P., 1993. *Pompei: Società, immagini urbane e forme delle'abitare* (Giulio Einaudi: Turin).

Zanker, P., 1995. *Pompeji: Stadtbild und Wohngeschmack* (Philipp von Zabern: Mainz).

8 New Directions in Economic and Environmental Research at Pompeii

Jane Richardson, Gill Thompson and Angelo Genovese

INTRODUCTION

New environmental research at Pompeii is offering a fresh angle on the analysis and interpretation of the ecology and economy of the city. This environmental team and its collaborators are keen to study three interrelating topics: the urban economy, the environment of the city and the environment of the surrounding landscape. The evidence employed includes animal bones, macroscopic plant remains, pollen, insects and soil micromorphology. The emphasis is on the systematic investigation of all excavated contexts, from the earlier phases of this city as well as the first-century AD layers directly sealed by the volcanic deposits. In addition to recently excavated animal bones, those that were excavated from other contexts in the city prior to standardized recording are also under analysis. The former provide information on diet, refuse disposal and dumping patterns, and levels of cleanliness and squalor, while the latter, which are mainly complete skeletons, indicate the 'living' population present at the time of the eruption.

During early periods of excavation at Pompeii, considerable quantities of bioarchaeological remains were excavated and have subsequently been stored in the city and at the National Museum at Naples. The charred debris of plant foods recovered mainly from ceramic storage vessels in shops and houses, for example, have provided an extensive list of commodities used in the city (Licopoli 1890; Wittmack 1904; Meyer 1980). These include cereals (oats, emmer wheat and six-row barley, as well as Italian and common millets), nuts (hazel, chestnut, almonds and walnut), fruits (figs, dates, cherries, pears and grapes), pulses (broadbeans, chickpeas, vetches and lentils), olives, pine nuts and carob. This material evidence provides a correlate for the literary and art historical sources on Roman cuisine, but a full interpretation is limited by the lack of detailed stratigraphical associations for the samples.

Further environmental research has concentrated on the *in situ* first century AD deposits, in particular the gardens, vineyards and other open spaces sealed by the falling ash and lapilli of the eruption (Jashemski 1973; 1993; Meyer 1980; Ciarallo 1992; 1993; De Simone 1993). Sampling deposits for environmental data has generally been small-scale and from discrete, well-separated parts of the city. Their analysis has produced valuable snapshots of parts of

Pompeii, and provides the basis for developing a more coherent picture of the environmental and economic structure of the city.

New research is now linked to the work of the Anglo-American Pompeii Project (cf. Bon et al. this volume) but its range extends beyond that program. Our aim is to consider city-wide evidence, to integrate urban and rural research and to compare results from the cityscape preserved by the AD 79 eruption with the more piecemeal bioarchaeological data recovered from deposits which accumulated during the earlier centuries of Pompeii's history. Most importantly, the Anglo-American Pompeii Project will integrate interpretations of the environmental data as part of a wide range of research questions. In the new program of excavations, contextual information will inform environmental interpretations, and vice versa. These are, of course, well-established and standard approaches to environmental archaeology elsewhere, but new at Pompeii.

The importance of intensive sampling for bioarchaeological investigations has already been realized on large scale urban excavations (Hall and Kenward 1990, 289). In investigating the Pompeian economy, it has been possible to examine biological materials from all deposits excavated by the Anglo-American Pompeii Project in Regio VI, Insula 1. Soil samples have been screened, and further sub-samples floated to retrieve animal and fish bones, mollusks and botanical remains. Analysis of these may reveal dietary evidence including food preparation methods, the fuels used in cooking and also in industry and may help to identify the use of certain rooms and other areas. In addition, the levels of refuse dumped in this part of the city can be used as indicators for the presence and success of organized refuse disposal.

This paper will deal with the progress already made and the aims for studying the economy and environment of Pompeii and the surrounding Campanian region. It will briefly compare previous work on first-century AD deposits with the current project in VI,1. Particular attention is paid to the faunal evidence. The dearth of faunal remains from the early phases of deposits or from the animals which died during the eruption is addressed here. Indeed the detailed study of four equids and four canids carried out by Jane Richardson and Angelo Genovese during 1995 attempted to rectify this. The preliminary results presented here provide a glimpse of a few domestic animals and begin to redress the balance between animal bone studies and the plethora of work already carried out on botanical evidence from Pompeii.

THE POMPEIAN ECONOMY

Previous environmental work at Pompeii has focused on the garden plots and open spaces of the city while the excavation of buildings has usually concentrated upon the identification of architectural structures and the retrieval of material artifacts. In contrast, our work is moving away from a partial environmental sampling strategy, to a more systematic investigation of every excavated deposit. All excavated soil from VI,1 was sieved through a 5 millimeter mesh to ensure near-perfect retrieval of faunal remains. A 20 litre sample from each securely sealed stratigraphic unit excavated was also floated using a modified Ankara-style of flotation sys-

Fig. 8.1 *Flotation tank in use during the 1995 excavations by the Anglo-American Pompeii Project.*

tem (French 1971). This combined a flotation tank, two settling tanks and a pump for recycling water (Fig. 8.1).

During the 1995 excavations in the House of the Vestals (VI,1, 5–8, 24–26) a wide variety of context types were investigated, including a pit with ritual associations cut prior to the construction of the atrium building, drains and drainage channels, a small peristyle garden area and rooms with floors packed with broken painted wall plaster (Bon et al. 1995; this volume). Further down the Via Consolare in the workshop commonly called the 'soap factory' (VI,1,14) some small-scale industrial activity and a flush toilet have been identified. With this wide ranging data source of animal and fish bones, charred and mineralized seeds and wood charcoal, we can begin to investigate aspects of provisioning Pompeii.

The animal bones excavated from VI,1 in 1995 have already been identified. A total of 1838 bone fragments were recovered from this season of excavation and 253 of these were identifiable to species. Pig dominated the identifiable assemblage at 30 percent, sheep and goat together equaled 13 percent and cow accounted for only 2 percent of the sample. Dog was represented by a single bone. 12 bird bones were found and most were identified as galliformes, most probably chicken. The only comparable evidence is from Jashemski's excavations of essentially AD 79 deposits (Jashemski 1974, 403; 1979a, 95–96; 1993, 242). All the bones recovered from Jashemski's garden excavations are reported, but numbers are so low from these excavations as well as from VI,1 that interpretation becomes difficult. The common domesticates are all present and pig is often represented by the greatest number of bones although cow and sheep are also significant. These results may indicate a uniformity of dietary habits over time and space, but bone frequencies are very low. There also seem to be other activities affecting the samples, in particular the possible collection of rubbish and the processes involved in ritual activities (Jashemski 1979a, 254; Richardson 1995).

The excavated bone from VI,1 was poorly preserved and found in a highly fragmented state. This is reflected in the low numbers of bones that were identifiable to species, only 14 percent of the sample. This dearth of faunal evidence, however, is not surprising as the deposits in question come from within buildings. We would expect the majority of kitchen waste to have been discarded at the very least outside the buildings if not outside the city walls. The proportion of taxa may also be influenced by such discard patterns as it is easier to discard or displace the bones of the smaller pigs and sheep within a house than the much larger remains of cows. It is possible then that kitchen refuse was disposed of elsewhere. The scarcity of animal bones may even reflect a refuse collection service. Tacitus (*Annals* 11.32) and Valerius Maximus (1.7) indicate that an organized rubbish collection and street cleaning service were in operation in Rome with carts being used to take away all kinds of refuse. It is quite probable that the city of Pompeii had such a system in use.

Some larger remains, olive stones and grape pips, were noted while sorting in the field the heavy fraction from flotation. The full identification and analysis of the botanical remains from VI,1 is currently under way at the Department of Archaeological Sciences, University of Bradford. The laboratory identification of further food debris will increase our information on this range of edibles. Certain weed assemblages may aid in the reconstruction of microenvironments in the insula, while arable weed seeds brought into the city as contaminants of food products may provide information about rural ecology and land management further afield. In addition to seeds and fruits, the recovery of wood charcoal will allow the investigation of fuel supplies for cooking and industry. One particular charcoal spread excavated from the light industrial, possibly metal-working features in the front of the workshop at VI,1,14 may provide one example of the fuels used in industrial activities (cf. Fig. 5.7).

Sampling every excavated archaeological context for environmental evidence is likely to be valuable for interpreting the functions of certain areas. For instance, the faunal remains from the pit in the tablinum of the House of the Vestals included parts of the carcasses of at least three piglets (two teeth, an astragalus and eight limb bones). Most of these were found in

association with six small ceramic cups which have been interpreted as having a votive purpose (cf. Bonghi Jovino 1994, 175–176; Bon et al. 1995). These remains, together with the
observation that piglets are the most commonly depicted sacrificial animals at Pompeii
(Jashemski 1979a, 120), have led to an interpretation of ritual activity related to the construction of the atrium house which seals this pit. Such an interpretation is possible due to the
detailed attention paid to formation processes and the stratigraphic record. De-contextualized
faunal deposits excavated before systematic recording became the norm can offer no clues to
ritualized deposition. While this analysis is an example of environmental data aiding the interpretation of a feature, it also provides a salutary lesson for the interpretation of faunal
evidence. A number of studies elsewhere have identified the use of animals in ritual activities:
some deposits once identified with assurance as food-processing waste must now be considered as potential indicators of both economic and symbolic events (cf. Grant 1989, 81; Hill
1995, 1).

ENVIRONMENTAL ASPECTS OF THE CITY OF POMPEII

Gardens have already received much attention at Pompeii, largely due to the work of Professor Wilhelmina Jashemski and her colleagues from the University of Maryland. They have
catalogued and excavated a number of gardens and other open areas which provide detailed
information about the use of space within the city and the inter-relation between interior and
exterior architecture (Jashemski 1973; 1974; 1979a; 1981; 1993). While these plots would have
contributed to the economy of Pompeii, and indeed Jashemski has identified commercial
activities such as vineyards and the flower garden of Hercules (II,8,6) where scented oils were
prepared (1979a, 279; 1979b), the gardens also formed an integral part of the urban environment and must have served an aesthetic role, providing areas of tranquillity and beauty. Indeed the ability to identify and differentiate between the economically productive plots and
the elegant and artistic gardens is only possible through systematic environmental sampling
and integrated analysis of soil micromorphology, micromolluscs, pollen, phytoliths and macroscopic plant remains.

   The aim is to build on the results of past excavations and to continue to identify and analyze
garden areas and open spaces. One example currently under analysis is the garden area identified in the small peristyle of the House of the Vestals (cf. Fig. 5.12). The difference, however, is that this new research includes the analysis of open spaces first uncovered in the early
excavations of the city. Since these areas have been exposed for two centuries, the root holes
of the plants once growing there are not preserved in the same ways as in the freshly excavated areas investigated by Jashemski. Our research will therefore need to exploit a further
source of evidence, the characteristics of the soil itself. Soil chemistry, such as high phosphate
levels may indicate past manuring, while micromorphology may indicate the *in situ* development of garden soil, or its import from elsewhere (Murphy and Scaife 1991, 84). Although
garden soils are not ideal for pollen preservation (Murphy and Scaife 1991, 90), palynological
evidence will still be sought from the newly identified garden plots (A. Ciarallo, pers. comm.).

Indeed, both Dimbleby and Ciarallo have already had some success in the extraction and identification of pollen from gardens, albeit from first-century contexts rapidly sealed by metres
of volcanic lapilli (Jashemski 1974, 402; Dimbleby 1985, 46; Ciarallo 1992; 1993).

Other dimensions of the urban environment concern increasing population density and
social complexity, changing land use and urban in-filling. Archaeological evidence from VI,1
has already identified an increasingly complex use of space, growing inequalities in property
size and increased social disparities (Bon et al. this volume). Environmental correlates of such
processes are pollution and refuse, and further environmental data may help us to consider
the quality of life and health in Pompeii (cf. Arthur 1993). Already we have some environmental indications of refuse levels in the form of the animal remains. As already mentioned,
the quantity of faunal debris from excavations in Pompeii is remarkable low which may indicate that refuse was routinely deposited away from living areas. There remain however a number
of potential alternative microenvironmental indicators that have successfully demonstrated
squalor in archaeological contexts elsewhere. Beetles, with their chitinous bodies, can survive
remarkably well in archaeological deposits and the synanthropic beetles, those that are directly
associated with humans and their rubbish, could be particularly useful here (cf. Hall et al. 1980,
132). Beetles can be temperature, moisture and habitat specific and certain species can be indicative of dung, rotting flesh or general foulness (Kenward 1978, 40). Less habitat specific
than beetles are small mammals and amphibians. Wood mice and voles can indicate the presence of light scrub (O'Connor 1994, 141–142) and a predominance of frogs may imply fairly
damp conditions. An abundance of rats and house mice are usually linked to the presence of
humans and a build up in their waste materials (cf. Brothwell and Jones 1978, 52). In the future
such environmental data may provide a more precise reconstruction of the amount and type
of refuse deposited and the areas it was most likely to be dumped in. Importantly, environmental data from the earliest phases at Pompeii may help us to point to a time when the
concentration of refuse within the city gave rise to a specifically urban flora and fauna. Signs
of site abandonment may also be detected through the diversity of micromolluscan assemblages. Here an interdisciplinary approach can add an extra dimension to new chronological
and structural paradigms for interpreting the birth and development of the city (cf. Carafa
this volume).

THE URBAN HINTERLAND

It is difficult to begin a study of the urban environment and economy of Pompeii without
giving thought to the city's surroundings. For a town the size and complexity of Pompeii, the
hinterland probably supplied the bulk of the food, fuels and other natural resources for the
townspeople, although access to marine trade means that some commodities may have been
imported from a greater distance. The city would have needed supplies of cereals, fruit and
vegetables, animals for meat, leather and wool, grapes for wine production and olives for oil.
The possibility that these resources were produced in the near vicinity raises questions about

the integration of crop production and animal husbandry. Perhaps stock raising was mainly practiced on higher ground, cereal agriculture restricted to the plain and viticulture concentrated on the hill slopes (consider Columella III,ii,2 and III,viii,4 and Varro *R.R.* I,vi,5).

Such questions make it necessary to investigate agricultural production and trade in Pompeii's hinterland. Pompeii sat in the Campanian plain with its fertile and well-drained volcanic soil. It is reported that the land was rich enough to allow four harvests each year (Jashemski 1981, 31), but could it also provide adequate pasture for livestock? Was there the potential to integrate animal grazing and crop growth using a rotation system? How far were the villas supplying the city with valuable crops such as grapes and wool for textile manufacture, at the same time as trading in cereals and vegetables? Bioarchaeological data from both urban and rural sites could be used to address these issues. To date environmental archaeology has not been a high priority when investigating rural sites in the region. Nevertheless, exceptional finds came from the first-century AD villa of Oplontis (Ricciardi and Grazia Aprile 1988, 318). Here large quantities of charred seeds and fruits from more than one hundred species of grasses and other herbs have been interpreted as fodder for tethered animals. This provides the clearest picture yet of the flora of the hay meadows in the vicinity of Pompeii and the remarkable preservation illustrates the potential for further environmental studies at sites in the Vesuvian region.

THE 'HORSES' AND DOGS OF POMPEII

In the same way that the Anglo-American Pompeii Project is looking to reinterpret the architectural structures, as well as the first-century and earlier evidence, so the faunal team has identified two avenues for archaeozoological research. First there is the systematic retrieval and analysis of faunal assemblages from new excavations, and second the study of bones from earlier excavations (for which contextual evidence is usually unavailable). In particular a few complete skeletons have been stored and these have the potential to shed light on the types of animals kept in the city at the time of the eruption. The number of animals retrieved and stored is very small, but nevertheless, they can provide some quite precise information about species, age, size and pathologies. Research on four equid and four canid skeletons kept in the Sarno Baths is part of an ongoing analysis of the stored bone assemblages. Among the equids, the aim is to distinguish between horses, donkeys or mules (bred from male donkeys and female horses) and hinnies (bred from female donkeys and male horses). This may be possible through morphological differences, in particular dental patterns and a morphometric analysis (Tables 1 and 2). For the dog remains, the goal is to identify 'type' and to compare the skeletal remains with the wall paintings, mosaics and statues of Pompeii. Ultimately we hope to provide a clearer picture of the animals in the city and to provide comparative data for the analyses of hinterland deposits and stratified assemblages from Pompeii.

Metric analysis on the equids (A-D) has focused mainly on the post cranial skeleton as most of the skulls were fragmented. A wide range of measurements was taken following the standards of von den Driesch (1976) and only fused bones were measured. The results are recorded in Tables 1 and 2. Using the metacarpal and metatarsal measurements (Table 1) it is possible to compare these Pompeii equids with modern data for ponies, heavy horses, donkeys, mules and hinnies (Eisenmann and Beckouche 1986, 156–163). The measurements used to compare the two data sets are the breadth of the proximal and distal ends of the metapodials. These criteria were selected because the measurements were easy to make, and these parts of the bones were very well preserved.

The Pompeii equids exceed all the standard measurements for the modern ponies and hinnies and all are smaller than those for the heavy horses. All the bones lie within the range for mules while some of the measurements from all four equids also fit within the upper end of the range for donkeys. Metrical analysis seems to indicate that the four equids are probably mules, though some may be large donkeys. The height at withers for the four Pompeian equids ranges from 132 to 153 cm (using formulae from Boessneck and von den Driesch 1984, 329). It is also necessary to consider the evidence of dental eruption and epiphyseal fusion (Silver 1969). These criteria indicate that equids A and B were only around 24 to 30 months old while equid C was a fully grown adult and equid D around 42 months of age.

The morphological distinctions of dental patterns were also studied. Armitage (1979, 344) has suggested that the shape of the internal sinus (metaconid-metastylid valley) may be used to separate horse, mule and donkey, while Churcher and Richardson (1978, 387) use the pli cabilline to separate horses and donkeys. The presence/absence of the pli cabilline indicates that the Pompeii equids are not donkeys. Describing subtle changes in shape of the internal sinus, however, is more subjective and was not attempted here. A number of characteristics were noted on the post-cranial skeleton. The morphological criteria established by Barone (1976) for separating horses and donkeys were used where possible and apparently confirm the results of the morphometric and dental data. While the limb bones of equid C seem to compare with the horse, equids A, B and D have a number of intermediate morphological features which suggest they may be mules. Consequently, the evidence from the metrical, dental and morphological studies together suggest that the Pompeii equids are mules. These equids are not the heavy horses of war or the large, prestigious animals of the élite. It seems likely they were work animals, carrying travelers and tradespeople, pulling carts and transporting loads, possibly similar to the animals recently found stabled behind the bakery at the House of the Chaste Lovers (IX,12,6–7) which had been tethered and died in the eruption (F. Tessuta, pers. comm.).

Similarly, analysis of canine skeletons can suggest how dogs were being used in Pompeii. A number of Greek and Latin descriptions detail the physique, achievements and character of dogs (such as Martial 1.CIX), as well as the well-known guard dog mosaics, the cast of the chained dog and a number of statues from Pompeii. They suggest a distinction between hunting dogs and household pets. The pictorial and literary evidence indicates that hunting dogs were long in the muzzle, ear and tail, with lean flanks and broad chests (compare the dogs from the boar and hunting dogs statue from the House of the Citharist, I,4,25). By contrast with the hunting animals, images of pet dogs often show overweight, short-eared and short-tailed animals which are slight in stature (such as the pet depicted in a wall painting in the House of Epigrams, V,1,18). Of course only some of these aspects are visible in the zooarchaeological record. Though it is possible to make use of pictorial representations there is no way of knowing how accurately they represent shape or size. While there is an assumption that the smallest dogs were pets and the largest were kept for hunting, we should be aware that size is only the merest guide to function. Dogs bred as hunters are occasionally recorded as the most cosseted of pets (Toynbee 1973, 121).

Fortunately there are also comparative data from archaeological collections. Four canid skeletons were available for metrical analysis during 1995 (Table 3). All four dogs provided postcranial metrical data, while only two of the skulls were suitable for a visual examination. Both these skulls are best described as mesaticephalic, that is more like the blunt-nosed images of watch dogs, than the thinner and longer-faced hunting animals. Postcranial data indicate a range of shoulder heights from 34 to 61 cm. These values are calculated using the equations of Harcourt (1974, 154) and an average is determined from the sum of all the measurable long bones. Similarly, the Pompeii dog skeleton analyzed by Giordano and Pelagalli (1957, 172) has a height of 58 to 60 cm. The skull of that dog, however, is described as dolicomorphic, with the long, narrow head typical of hunting hounds. According to Harcourt (1974, 164), dogs in Roman Britain were characterized by variability in height, build and skull shape. The Pompeian results fit with Harcourt's height range for Romano-British dogs but are greater than those for the British Iron Age, Bronze Age or Neolithic samples (Harcourt 1974). We see therefore, even in a small sample of only five individuals from Pompeii, a significant variability in canid sizes and a reaffirmation that the Roman inhabitants of the city bred varieties of dogs for companionship and for specific tasks.

CONCLUSION

The city of Pompeii can still provide varied ecological and economic evidence for an integrated archaeological investigation of life in the city before and at the time of the eruption. The advantages available to current research can be realized through systematic sampling and through interdisciplinary collaboration. On-going research is documenting the animal skeletons from the AD 79 deposits which were sealed by the eruption, and current environmental investigation of the city's earlier deposits is being used to identify the development of the urban setting and to reconstruct the living conditions of the inhabitants. The potential of the Campanian region to allow a comparison of the 'usual' archaeological deposits of passing societies with the 'living' community that was preserved by the eruption of Vesuvius is also being realized. Current work on the environmental deposits is giving rise to a clearer, more complete picture of the economy, environmental conditions and interconnections between Pompeii and its rural hinterland over time.

Table 1. *Measurements (in mm.) from the metapodials of the equids from the Sarno Baths store.*

	EQUID A		EQUID B		EQUID C		EQUID D	
	LEFT	RIGHT	LEFT	RIGHT	LEFT	RIGHT	LEFT	RIGHT
METACARPAL								
GL	235	235	-	236.5	236.5	-	-	-
Bp	52.2	52.6	51	49.8	-	-	50.8	50.6
Bd	53.3	52	51.6	52.7	52.3	51	49.8	49.8
Dp	35.3	-	36.2	36.7	34.5	-	32.9	33
SD	33.8	33.9	32	32.2	35.4	34	33.4	32.4
METATARSAL								
GL	-	215.5	275.5	275	274	274.5	-	335
Bp	50.4	50.8	50.3	50.6	48.1	48.2	57	54.4
Bd	51.5	51.8	51.8	52.6	47.4	47.9	53.1	52
SD	31	32.2	30.7	31.2	30	30	-	-

Table 2. *Measurements (in mm.) from the post cranial elements of the equids from the Sarno Baths store.*

	EQUID A		EQUID B		EQUID C		EQUID D	
	LEFT	RIGHT	LEFT	RIGHT	LEFT	RIGHT	LEFT	RIGHT
SCAPULA								
SLC	58.8	59.3	59.4	60.3	58.4	57.8	61.45	60.8
GLP	88.3	88.1	95.1	93.8	85.75	90.5	-	94.5
LG	55.9	56.1	58.8	58.1	-	55.2	-	55.2
BG	-	52.5	-	48.6	-	47.6	-	49.5
HUMERUS								
GL	-	-	-	-	277.5	-	-	-
Bp	-	95.1	-	-	93.5	-	-	-
BT	75.2	75.6	75.8	76	71.6	-	-	76.1
GLl	-	-	-	-	275	-	-	-
RADIUS								
GL	-	-	-	-	331	-	338	338
Bp	84.7	85.2	86.5	84.9	-	-	85	83.7
BFp	78.1	78.35	76.8	78.1	73.2	-	75.5	76.1
Bd	-	-	-	-	74	-	77.2	77.7
BFd	-	-	-	-	63.8	-	65.6	65.6
SD	38.4	39.4	-	37.1	36.2	-	39	38.9
ULNA								
BPC	46.9	47.5	47.1	46.4	45.3	47	-	-
OS CARPALE III								
GB	44	44.1	44.6	43.6	-	-	41.2	40.5

PHALANX 1

GL	-	89.35	-	90.1	89.6	-	-	-
Bp	57	56.4	57.8	57.4	57.1	58	55	-
Bd	47.2	47.5	-	44.7	48.7	-	47.8	-
BFd	44.5	44	-	43.7	45.3	-	45.2	-

PHALANX 2

GL	-	48.2	-	52.7	-	-	-	-
Bp	-	56	52.7	53.7	52.7	-	-	-
Bd	-	52.5	50.6	47.5	50.4	-	-	-

PHALANX 3

GL	-	-	-	63.5	-	-	-	-
GB	-	75.7	-	73.5	-	-	-	-

PELVIS

LAR	68.8	69	-	66.6	-	-	-	-

FEMUR

Bd	-	-	-	-	85.8	86.5	94.4	95.5
DC	-	-	-	-	54.2	53.65	-	-
SD	-	-	-	-	-	34.4	-	-

PATELLA

GL	71.8	71.2	69.35	69.6	66.25	68.5	-	69.7
GB	69.2	69.4	67.4	67.5	65.4	69.4	-	69.1

TIBIA

GL	-	-	-	-	-	-	345.5	-
Bp	-	-	-	-	91.5	-	95	99.9
Bd	73.4	73	74.4	74.3	69.7	71.1	71.5	75.7
Dd	-	46.8	48.6	50	45.2	47.8	46.05	-
SD	49.5	40.1	38.1	37.2	37.2	38.1	38	42

TALUS

GH	59.6	-	62.2	-	-	59.3	57.35	57.75
GB	64.7	63.1	66.4	-	-	-	58.9	59.8
LmT	61.8	61.75	60.8	61.2	63.6	59.7	59.1	59.3
BFd	52	53.5	52.1	-	-	50.2	51.4	51

CALCANEUM

GL	112.7	112	-	-	-	114.6	106.5	106.7
GB	50.5	51.1	55.1	-	-	56	49.9	49.5

TARSI CENTRAL

GB	49.7	51	49.1	-	49.4	47.5	54.4	49.6

TARSALE III

GB	47.9	48.2	48.9	-	47.2	45.8	-	50.9

PHALANX 1

GL	-	92.7	94.5	93.2	-	89.6	-	86.6
Bp	55.4	55.7	57.3	55.8	-	57.9	57	56.8
Bd	48.8	49.1	46.4	45.3	-	49.6	44.2	46.7
BFd	-	46	44.6	44.2	-	43.8	-	44.7

PHALANX 2

GL	-	50.5	50.4	52.3	-	-	-	-	
Bp	55.2	55.7	53.15	53.3	-	-	55.4	53.1	
Bd	49	49.4	50.7	47.6	-	-	50.8	-	

PHALANX 3

GL	-	65.4	-	-	-	-	-	-	
GB	-	79.6	-	-	-	-	-	-	

Table 3. Measurements (in mm.) from the limb bones of four canids excavated from Pompeii.

	DOG 1		DOG 2		DOG 3		DOG 4	
	LEFT	RIGHT	LEFT	RIGHT	LEFT	RIGHT	LEFT	RIGHT
SCAPULA								
SLC	29.3	-	28.1	27.9	16.3	-	-	-
GLP	33.9	-	34.3	33.9	20.4	-	-	-
BG	-	-	20	20.1	12	11.8	-	-
HUMERUS								
GL	182	183	187	188.5	105	103.2	-	-
Dp	46.2	45.9	46	46.4	28.6	-	-	-
Bd	37.7	37.6	39.5	39.4	23.2	23.1	-	-
SD	14.4	-	13.8	13.8	-	9.1	-	-
RADIUS								
GL	185	184.5	-	183.5	100.6	-	-	-
Bp	20.75	21.1	21.5	21.9	12.6	-	-	-
Bd	28.5	28.25	27.7	27.6	16.6	-	-	-
SD	15.4	15.3	-	13.8	-	-	-	-
ULNA								
BPC	20.8	20.4	21.7	23	12.5	-	15.5	15.2
FEMUR								
GL	203	-	-	-	-	112	-	-
Bp	44.2	-	-	-	27.8	27.9	-	-
Bd	36.8	-	-	-	-	22.8	-	-
SD	13.3	-	-	-	9.25	9.2	-	-
TIBIA								
GL	209	-	-	-	-	-	174	-
Bp	39.9	-	-	-	-	-	31.6	-
Bd	25.95	-	-	-	-	-	20.6	-
SD	13.4	-	-	-	-	-	9.9	-
SHOULDER HEIGHT (average)	60.9	-	61.3	-	33.5	-	51.7	-

ACKNOWLEDGMENTS

We wish to thank the Directors of the Anglo-American Pompeii Project for the opportunity to study the biological remains from VI,1 and Prof. P.G. Guzzo, Dott.ssa A. Ciarallo, Dott. A. D'Ambrosio and Dott.ssa T. Cocca for their support for this research. Financial support for fieldwork has been provided by the Anglo-American Pompeii Project and the Department of Archaeological Sciences at the University of Bradford. We also wish to acknowledge funding from the Department of Archaeology and Prehistory, University of Sheffield, the British Academy and the Archaeological Institute of America Graduate Travel Award which made it possible for Jane Richardson to present a previous version of this paper at the 1995 AIA Annual Conference.

References

Armitage, P., 1979. Jawbone of a mule from the Roman levels, Billingsgate Buildings (TR 74), City of London, *London Archaeologist* 3: 340–345.

Arthur, P., 1993. Le città vesuviane: problemi e prospettive nello studio dell'ecologia umana nell'antichità, in L. Franchi dell'Orto (ed.), *Ercolano 1738–1988, 250 anni di ricerca archeologia*, Soprintendenza Archeologica di Pompei Monografie, 6 (L'Erma di Bretschneider: Roma): 193–199.

Barone, R., 1976. *Anatomie Comparée des Mammifères Domestiques* (Vigot Frères: Paris).

Boessneck, V.J. and von den Driesch, A., 1984. Die zoologische Dokumentation der Reste von vier Pferden und einem Hund aus einem mykenischen Schachtgrab in Kokla bei Argos (Pelponnes), *Spixiana* 7: 327–333.

Bon, S.E., Jones, R., Kurchin, B. and Robinson, D., 1995 *Anglo-American Research at Pompeii 1995. Preliminary Report* (Bradford Archaeological Sciences Research 1: Bradford).

Bonghi Jovino, M., 1984. *Ricerche a Pompei. L'Insula 5 della Regio VI dalle origini al 79 d.c.* Università degli Studi di Milano, Instituto di Archeologia. Biblioteca Archaeologica 5 (L'Erma di Bretschnedier: Rome).

Brothwell, D. and Jones, R., 1978. The relevance of small mammal studies to archaeology, in D.R. Brothwell, K.D. Thomas and J. Clutton-Brock (eds.), *Research Problems in Zooarchaeology* (Institute of Archaeology: London): 47–57.

Churcher, C.S. and Richardson, M.L., 1978. Equidae, in V.J. Maglio and H.B.S. Cooke (eds.), *Evolution of African Mammals* (Harvard University Press: Cambridge): 379–422.

Ciarallo, A., 1992. *Orti e Giardini di Pompei* (Fiorentino: Napoli).

Ciarallo, A., 1993. La botanica e le aree archeologiche vesuviane, in L. Franchi dell'Orto (ed.), *Ercolano 1738–1988, 250 anni di ricerca archeologia*, Soprintendenza Archeologica di Pompei Monografie, 6 (L'Erma di Bretschneider: Roma): 643–646.

De Simone, A., 1993. Recenti esperienze di scavi paleobotanici a Pompei: prime considerazioni, in L. Franchi dell'Orto (ed.), *Ercolano 1738–1988, 250 anni di ricerca archeologia*, Soprintendenza Archeologica di Pompei Monografie, 6 (L'Erma di Bretschneider: Roma): 647–653.

Dimbleby, G.W., 1985. *The Palynology of Archaeological Sites* (Academic Press: London).

Eisenmann, V. and Beckouche, S., 1986. Identification and discrimination of metapodials from Pleistocene and modern *Equus*, wild and domestic, in R.H. Meadow and H.-P. Uerpmann (eds.), *Equids in the Ancient World* (Dr Ludwig Reichert Verlag: Wiesbaden): 117–163.

French, D.H. 1971. An experiment in water sieving, *Anatolian Studies* 21: 59–64.

Giordano, C. and Pelagalli, G., 1957. Cani e canili nella antica Pompei, *Atti dell'Academia Pontaniana* Nuova serie 7: 165–201.

Grant, A., 1989. Animals and ritual in early Britain: the visible and the invisible, in P. Meniel (ed.), *Animal et Pratiques Religieuses: les Manifestations Materielles* (Anthropozoologica Troisième Numéro Special: Paris): 79–86.

Hall, A.R. and Kenward, H.K., 1990. *Environmental Evidence from the Colonia: General Accident and Rougier Street,* Archaeology of York 14/16 (Council for British Archaeology: London).

Hall, A.R., Kenward, H.K. and Williams, D., 1980. *Environmental Evidence from Roman Deposits in Skeldergate,* Archaeology of York 14/3 (Council for British Archaeology: London).

Harcourt, R.A., 1974. The dog in prehistoric and early historic Britain, *Journal of Archaeological Science* 1: 151–175.

Hill, J.D., 1995. *Ritual and Rubbish in the Iron Age of Wessex: a study on the formation of a specific archaeological record* (British Archaeological Reports, British Series 242. Tempvs Reparatvm: Oxford).

Jashemski, W.F., 1973. The discovery of a large vineyard at Pompeii: University of Maryland excavations, 1970, *American Journal of Archaeology* 77: 27–41.

Jashemski, W.F., 1974. The discovery of a market-garden orchard at Pompeii: the garden of the 'House of the Ship Europa', *American Journal of Archaeology* 78: 391–404.

Jashemski, W.F., 1979a. *The Gardens of Pompeii, Herculaneum and the Villas Destroyed by Vesuvius* (Caratzas Brothers: New York).

Jashemski, W.F., 1979b. 'The garden of Hercules at Pompeii' (II,viii.6): the discovery of a commercial flower garden, *American Journal of Archaeology* 83:403–411.

Jashemski, W.F., 1981. The Campanian peristyle garden, in E.B. MacDougall and W.F. Jashemski (eds.), *Ancient Roman Gardens* (Dumbarton Oaks Trustees for Harvard University: Washington D.C.): 31–48.

Jashemski, W.F., 1993. *The Gardens of Pompeii, Herculaneum and the Villas Destroyed by Vesuvius II: the Appendices* (Caratzas Brothers: New Rochelle/ New York).

Kenward, H.K., 1978. *The Analysis of Archaeological Insect Assemblages: A New Approach,* Archaeology of York 19/1 (Council for British Archaeology: London).

Licopoli, G., 1890. Sopre alcune sementi provenienti degli scavi di Pompei, in *Rendiconto dell'Accademia delle Scienze fisiche e matematiche* (sezione della Società Reale di Napoli. 2 (4) anno 39): 85.

Meyer, F.G., 1980. Carbonized food plants of Pompeii, Herculaneum, and the villa at Torre Annunziata, *Economic Botany* 34(4): 401–437.

Murphy, P. and Scaife, R.G., 1991. The environmental archaeology of gardens, in A.E. Brown (ed.), *Garden Archaeology* (Council for British Archaeology Research Report 78: London): 83–99.

O'Connor, T., 1994. 8th-11th century economy and environment in York, in J. Rackham (ed.), *Environment and Economy in Anglo-Saxon England* (Council for British Archaeology Research Report 89: London): 136–147.

Ricciardi, M. and Aprile, G.G., 1978. Preliminary data on the floristic components of some carbonized plant remains found in the archaeological area of Oplontis near Naples, *Ann. Fac. Sci. Agrar. Univ. Napoli in Portici.* Ser. IV, 12: 201–212.

Richardson, J., 1995. Faunal remains, in Bon et al. 1995: 27–29.

Silver, I.A., 1969. The ageing of domestic animals, in D. Brothwell and E. Higgs (eds.), *Science in Archaeology* (2nd. ed., Thames and Hudson: London): 283–302.

Toynbee, J.M.C., 1973. *Animals in Roman Life and Art* (Thames and Hudson: London).

von den Driesch, A., 1976. *A Guide to the Measurement of Animal Bones from Archaeological Sites* (Peabody Museum Bulletin 1: Boston).

Wittmack, M.C.L., 1904. Die in Pompeji gefundenen planzlichen Reste, *Bot. Jahr. Syst.* 33 (73): 38–66.

9 Pompeii AD 79: A Population in Flux?

Estelle Lazer

INTRODUCTION

It has generally been assumed that Pompeii in AD 79, with its mixed background and its function as a river port, housed a heterogeneous population (e.g. Nicolucci 1882, 3–5,-21–23; Mau 1907, 16; Maiuri 1962, 17). This notion was primarily derived from ancient literary and epigraphic sources. Strabo (V,IV,8) wrote that Pompeii and Herculaneum were occupied over time by various groups of people: Oscans, Etruscans, Pelasgians, Samnites and Romans. Oscan inscriptions etched on plaster, ostensibly dating to the last seventeen years of occupation, have been cited as evidence of the presence of Italic people. The identification of Greek names in a list of accounts and Greek inscriptions on walls and amphorae have been seen as a reflection of a Greek element in the population. Similarly, names like Martha and Mary on wall inscriptions and Semitic inscriptions on amphorae have been interpreted as proof of a Jewish community in Pompeii (Mau 1907, 16–18; Ward-Perkins and Claridge 1980, 15, 33; Corti 1951, 208; Giordano and Kahn 1979, 44). It should be noted that certain scholars have been circumspect about the interpretation of some of this evidence; for example, Mau (1907, 18) suggested that names inscribed on amphorae could reflect either the dealers of commodities or the owners of the estates where they were found.

Archaeological evidence has also been used to determine the composition of the population of Pompeii. The subject matter of wall paintings interpreted as depictions of Old Testament stories, such as the Judgement of Solomon (Naples Museum 73879 from house VIII,6, 6), have been cited as evidence for a Jewish presence in Pompeii. More spurious is the identification of some sculptures as representations of Semitic types on the questionable basis of stereotypical features associated with Jews, like the shape of the nose (Giordano and Kahn 1979, 56–58, 60–70). It has also been suggested that the discovery of a temple dedicated to Isis is proof for the presence of Egyptians at Pompeii (Mau 1907, 17; Tran Tam Tinh 1964; Witt 1971). Alternatively, it could be argued that this, like all the evidence presented above, merely implies that there was contact between different cultures.

An emphasis on written evidence is traditional in Mediterranean archaeology. It relates to the history of the discipline, where the remains of material culture were seen as an adjunct to the historical records. Until relatively recent times, archaeological discoveries were never used to test the historical sources, only to illustrate them (cf. Daniel 1981, 13). In this paper, the established notions about the composition of the Pompeian population will be tested against the skeletal evidence.

FACTORS THAT MAY HAVE INFLUENCED
THE POMPEIAN POPULATION AND THE SAMPLE OF VICTIMS

It is necessary to establish the parameters of the Pompeian sample before results of the skeletal study can be interpreted. Discussion about the AD 79 Pompeian population has generally been based on the assumption that Pompeii was a thriving town that was destroyed quickly and without warning (e.g. Jongman 1988, 55,56). Recent Pompeian scholarship acknowledges that the notion of the site as a frozen moment in time is somewhat simplistic (e.g. Allison 1992, 42). It has been suggested that the destruction of Pompeii was not confined to the AD 79 event but that it had been a protracted process that commenced with the earthquake of AD 62 (e.g. Wallace-Hadrill 1991, 203).

IMPACT OF THE AD 62 EARTHQUAKE. DID IT RESULT IN CHANGES TO THE POPULATION?

The ancient literature records an earthquake in AD 62 which caused major damage to Pompeii and the Campanian region (Seneca *Nat. Quaest.* VI,I,2; Tacitus *Ann.* XV,22). Signs of damage and partial or completed repairs have traditionally been attributed to the AD 62 earthquake. These include: damage and possible interruption to the water supply; villas and houses that had been damaged so badly that they were virtually uninhabitable; partial or complete destruction of public buildings, such as the Capitolium and the Temple of Venus in the region of the Forum; and reconstruction of the Temples of Vespasian and Isis. Many of the larger houses were roughly repaired and subsequently subdivided into what appear to have been separate apartments. Some were also converted for commercial or industrial uses, such as the modification of a house into a fuller's shop, the so-called Fullonica Stephani (I,6, 7). Houses that were restored were supposedly recognizable by a new system of wall decoration, the so-called fourth style. Some houses, such as the House of the Vettii (VI,15, 1–2), were totally rebuilt (Andreau 1979, 40–44; Maiuri 1943; Corti 1951, 44–45, 48; Brion 1973, 21–24; Descoeudres 1994a, 34–37; Richardson 1978, 84, 86; 1988, xxi-xxii; Allison 1994, 8–9).

SEISMIC ACTIVITY IN THE LAST SEVENTEEN YEARS OF OCCUPATION OF POMPEII

There has been considerable debate as to whether all the pre-eruption damage and repair that is evident in the Pompeian archaeological record was the result of the AD 62 earthquake or whether some of it was due to a series of earthquakes in the seventeen years leading up to the eruption (e.g. Allison 1994, 86–97; 1995, 162–169; Descoeudres 1993, 173; 1994a, 35).

The ancient sources are unambiguous about the fact that the AD 62 earthquake was neither the first nor the last in the region (Suetonius *Nero*, 20; Tacitus *Ann.* XV,34:1; Pliny the Younger

VI, 20). That this earthquake is the best recorded is due to its magnitude. Despite this evidence which leaves little doubt that earthquakes were relatively common in Campania, the concept of change as a result of multiple or continuous seismic events in the latter years of Pompeii's occupation has only been a comparatively recent consideration. It is notable that the volcanological literature accepts that there were intermittent earthquakes throughout the period between AD 62 and 79 (e.g. Bullard 1984, 190; Francis 1993, 65, 67). This is not surprising as earthquake activity often precedes volcanic eruptions (Francis 1993, 65, 67).

Both Allison (1994; 1995) and Descoeudres (1993) argue for partial abandonment of the site in the years between the AD 62 earthquake and the eruption. Descoeudres (1993, 173) explained the lack of expected finds as evidence for an undocumented earthquake between the two events. Allison (1994, 10) criticized the notion of a second major earthquake on the grounds of insufficient evidence. She argued that many of the signs of repair, change of function and apparent abandonment that she observed in her study of the house contents of thirty Pompeian residences could be best explained by continued seismic activity in the last seventeen years of occupation (Allison 1994, 86–97; 1995, 162–169). It is probable that the AD 62 earthquake and subsequent seismic activity was a contributing factor in the apparent signs of changes in occupation patterns in the archaeological record. It is, however, simplistic to assume that these would have been the only reasons for change.

Another possibility that does not appear to have received much attention from scholars working on Pompeii is that at least some of the observed occupation changes attributed to the last seventeen years of settlement were the result of factors unrelated to earthquake activity. The complexity of urban settlement patterns has been demonstrated by archaeological investigations of sites with long occupation sequences, such as the English city of Winchester (Biddle 1974, 35–43). A long term project in Winchester revealed that changes over time, such as the abandonment of certain areas and changes in function of specific urban precincts, were influenced by a variety of factors. These included the change from Roman to Anglo-Saxon cultural dominance, shifts in national and religious importance of the town over time, increasing industrialization and the development of certain trades in specific areas (Biddle 1974, 35–43).

There is no need to invoke disasters to explain all the alterations in occupation and building usage in Pompeii. The dynamic nature of a society that is suggested by apparent changes in the occupation patterns may indicate that the population was undergoing change both in size and composition.

EVIDENCE OF ABANDONMENT AFTER THE AD 62 EARTHQUAKE

The notion of abandonment probably dates back to Seneca (*Nat. Quaest.* VI,II, 10–12) who railed against survivors for emigrating and refusing to return to the region. This, in turn, influenced Winckelmann in the eighteenth century. From the little he had been able to observe on his early abortive visits to Herculaneum, he concluded that there was evidence for the abandonment of Pompeii and Herculaneum by a large number of the inhabitants after the earthquake of AD 62 (Leppmann 1968, 73). The idea that Pompeii may have been entirely abandoned after the earthquake was proposed in the second decade of the nineteenth century, but was rejected after much debate (cf. Lippi and Tondi as cited by Ciprotti 1964, 40). The notion of partial abandonment has sporadically been suggested (Maiuri 1933, 11–16; Corti 1951, 46, 47; Allison 1994, 97) and has been resurrected in the recent literature.

The lack of certain expected finds at Pompeii has traditionally been interpreted as evidence of post-eruption looting (e.g. Richardson 1988, 25–27; Corti 1951, 82–83). For example, numerous statue bases were found in the forum, though no trace of the statues that should have surmounted them remained. In addition, most of the marble flagstones and marble veneers that once covered buildings in the forum were missing. The possibility that this negative evidence could reflect pre-eruption abandonment has been offered as an alternative explanation. Descoeudres (1993, 173) suggested that the site was stripped of many items of value in the years between the earthquake and the eruption by inhabitants choosing to leave Pompeii, possibly as a result of further earthquake activity. He concluded that Pompeii was already a ruined city with a diminished population prior to the eruption of AD 79 (1993, 173). Allison (1994, 97) has also argued that there was a diminution of the population size in the last seventeen years of occupation.

While it is quite probable that there was a decrease in population size in the last seventeen years of Pompeii's existence, it is unlikely that the entire AD 79 population was killed by the eruption, given the literary evidence for survivors and the stratigraphic evidence that infers the possibility of escape in the first eighteen hours of the eruption (see below). In addition, evidence of the instigation of construction programs that have been dated to the last seventeen years of occupation, such as the building of a new bath complex, the so-called Central Baths (IX,4, 5/18), suggests that the population could not have been too depleted.

COMPOSITION OF THE POPULATION OF POMPEII IN THE LAST PERIOD OF OCCUPATION

Perhaps the most difficult factor to assess in relation to changes between AD 62 and AD 79 is whether the composition of the population was altered as a result of certain sections of the community abandoning the site. Since there is no certainty about the original makeup of the population, it is not possible to do more than postulate about the types of changes that could have been expected.

It has been assumed that the people who chose to abandon the town were, on the whole, the members of the upper strata; people who were financially independent and whose economic base was not totally based on working the land in the Campanian region. A case has been mounted for some wealthy owners to have left their properties in the hands of household staff during rebuilding (Corti 1951, 48, 204; Maiuri 1933, 11–16; Allison 1994, 97; Descoeudres 1994, 36).

Evidence has also been presented to support the suggestion that the old aristocracy was replaced by *nouveaux riches* individuals, such as the Vettii brothers who were credited with the reconstruction and refurbishment of the so-called House of the Vettii (VI,15, 1–2). Similarly, it is thought that the Villa of the Mysteries changed hands to a Greek freedman called Zosimus after the AD 62 earthquake, either because of abandonment or the death of the previous owner. It should be noted that the basis for determining the status of the presumed owners of property is often subjective and open to question, e.g. it has been claimed that the Vettii brothers were wine merchants because of representations of Mercury and his attributes in the House of the Vettii (Della Corte 1965, 67–71; Corti 1951, 52; Richardson 1988, 324; Trevelyan 1976, 17).

It has been argued that though there may have been an initial drop in the population, growth would have resumed along with reconstruction (Corti 1951, 54). If this were the case then it is possible that new arrivals may have come from outside the region. Descoeudres (1994, 36), though he argued for site abandonment, considered that there would have been a significant increase in demand for people with building and wall painting skills in the final years of occupation.

Although the archaeological evidence for this period is difficult to interpret, it does appear likely that there was some level of change in the Pompeian population in terms of size and, perhaps, also composition between AD 62 and 79. The available data suggest that the response of the population to the earthquake and possible subsequent seismic activity was complex and varied. Ultimately, there is insufficient evidence to draw firm conclusions about the degree of change that occurred. The likelihood that the Pompeian community was in a state of flux at the time of the eruption challenges the notion that the AD 79 level of Pompeii represents a bustling community frozen in time.

THE AD 79 POPULATION AND THE AVAILABLE SKELETAL SAMPLE

Size of the population in AD 79

Knowledge of the proportion of the community that was killed by the eruption would greatly enhance the value of a population study of the Pompeian skeletal remains. To determine this, it is necessary to have some idea of the size of the population at the time. It would also be beneficial to know the number of skeletons that have been uncovered in the last two hundred and fifty-odd years.

There are no definitive figures for the size of the population of Pompeii on the eve of its destruction in AD 79. Estimates of the number of inhabitants vary widely between authors. The arguments for the various figures have been summarized and discussed by Jashemski (1979, 343, n. 56), Jongman (1988, 55, 108–112) and Wallace-Hadrill (1991, 199–202). The size of the population of Pompeii has been estimated to range between 6,400 and 30,000 individuals. Population size has been variously based on estimates of the seating capacity of the amphitheater (Fiorelli 1873, 14; Russell 1985, 1), an extrapolation of the number of excavated rooms in relation to the area of the site still to be excavated using the assumption that the number of people who occupied the site was proportional to the number of rooms in a dwelling (Fiorelli 1873, App.3, 12–13), house and room numbers (Mau 1907, 16), and population density estimates derived from medieval population information (Russell 1985, 3;

Eschebach 1978, 6). The validity of all the methods used for the reconstruction of the size of the AD 79 Pompeian population can be questioned. Despite the recognition of this problem, there has been a tendency for scholars to support a population estimate of between 8,000 to 12,000 individuals (Jashemski 1979, 24, 343 n.56; Jongman 1988, 108–112; Wallace-Hadrill 1991, 203, 225).

At best, population estimates can only provide a very rough guide to the size of Pompeii's population. Such figures should be used with extreme caution as they tend to be based on simplistic and sometimes spurious assumptions.

Number of individuals thought to have perished

There is no reliable figure for the number of individuals who perished as a result of the AD 79 eruption. The calculation of the number of Pompeian victims of this event was based on extrapolation from the estimated number of bodies found in the sample of the site that had been excavated up to that time to a figure for the whole area of the city (Gell 1832, xix; Lytton 1897, 304; Fiorelli 1873, 172). Various results were obtained but that determined by Fiorelli has been most widely accepted. He calculated that about 2000 individuals did not manage to escape. This figure has never been revised and has been accepted virtually without question in a number of publications on Pompeii (e.g. Corti 1951, 81; Grant 1976, 34; Bisel 1990, 31).

There is no evidence to suggest that any estimate for the number of victims based on the extrapolation of the number found in a portion of the site would be reliable because this assumes an even distribution of bodies across Pompeii.

Number of skeletons that have been discovered

There was minimal documentation during the first century of excavation and estimates of the number of skeletons that were found during this period were not very reliable. The initiation of systematic recording by Fiorelli in the latter part of the nineteenth century could not compensate for the loss of information from the preceding generations of excavators. It is not possible to establish the number of skeletons that were excavated over the last two hundred and fifty years from the written records. The skeletons that have been unearthed cannot be counted to provide a total because of the post-excavation treatment of skeletal material, including reburial, poor storage and the removal of some of the material to be stored in collections that are not easily accessible (De Caro pers. comm.).

The information that has been presented regarding the size and composition of the Pompeian population prior to the eruption demonstrates the complexity of this issue and underlines the difficulty of interpreting a sample of bones that merely represent the victims of the eruption. To gain some appreciation of what sort of sample these victims may represent, it is necessary to examine issues that relate to the possibility of survival from this eruption, such as the form it took and its duration.

Were people able to escape from the eruption?

There seems little doubt that a number of Pompeians were able to escape from the eruption. The issue is whether the sample of victims is representative.

It is essential to have an understanding of the nature of the volcanic event to establish whether certain sections of the community would have been more likely to perish in this disaster. Current theory favors a two phase eruption using the 1980 eruption of Mt. St. Helens in Washington, USA, as a model (Sigurdsson et al. 1982, 47–50; 1985, 339–363; Francis 1993, 198–202, 241–244). It is important to note that all volcanic eruptions are different and that this model should be treated with caution. The effects of the eruption varied throughout the region. From the stratigraphic evidence and historical sources (Pliny the Younger VI,16), it appears that the Pompeians initially experienced a fall of ash and pumice which would have lasted for about eighteen hours. This phase was not considered to have been particularly lethal. Escape was possible, though it probably would have been hampered by darkness and a constant hail of small pumice stones (Pliny the Younger VI,16). The second phase consisted of a series of hot gas avalanches or *nuées ardentes*. There would have been no possibility of escape from these as they travel at speeds of between 100 and 300 kph, have temperatures between 100 and 400 degrees Celsius, contain little free oxygen, have a high toxic gas content and are extremely turbulent (Sigurdsson et al. 1982, 49; Scott 1989, 11–14). From a study of the autopsy reports of the Mt. St. Helens eruption it has been suggested that death would probably have been from asphyxiation or thermal shock and would have occurred within two minutes (Eisele et al. 1981, 933; Baxter 1990, 533–534; Sigurdsson et al. 1985, 365). These views are consistent with recent finds of bodies in Pompeii, such as the victims that were discovered in the House of Stabianus (I,22, 1–2) in the early 1990s, within the layer of fine ash identified as that of the *nuée ardente* above the layer of ash and lapilli.

From the volcanological and archaeological evidence, there is no reason to believe that either a significant number of people were unable to escape or that certain groups were more predisposed to become victims of the AD 79 eruption. Studies of modern disasters suggest that all levels of a community tend to be equally affected by this kind of event (Grayson and Sheets 1979, 626–627; Russell 1985, 7–8).

Date of the eruption

Knowledge of the season in which the eruption occurred could provide some insight into the composition of the population of Pompeii at the time of the eruption.

Strabo (5.4.8) stated that the whole of the Bay of Naples appeared like a continuous town as a result of the number of villas that lined the coastline. Many of these villas were owned by Romans. For example, the Younger Pliny had six villas, Cicero, three, and it is thought on the basis of inscriptions, that the Villa of Oplontis near Pompeii belonged to Nero's wife, Poppaea. Chance finds that included inscriptions have also been employed as evidence to suggest that the family of the latter, the Poppaei, were the owners of the so-called House of the Golden Cupids (VI,10,7) and House of the Menander (I,10,4) in Pompeii (Trevelyan 1976, 25; De

Franciscis 1975, 14–15; Grant 1976, 74; Ward-Perkins and Claridge 1980, 9; Richardson 1988, xv). It has generally been assumed that the villas that were owned by wealthy Roman citizens were mostly used as summer resorts. This assertion is probably based on the knowledge that a number of these coastal properties were, at various times, owned by citizens who were obviously based in Rome, like the dictator Sulla who had a villa near Cumae and the Emperor Augustus who had a retreat in Capri (Ward-Perkins and Claridge 1980, 9). If it were possible to establish the exact time of the year when Mt. Vesuvius erupted, it would be possible to infer whether or not it was likely to be associated with a significant Roman presence in Campania.

Despite the fact that most authors confidently assert that the eruption occurred on August 24 (e.g. Ward-Perkins and Claridge 1980, 8; Perl 1982, 21; Sigurdsson et al. 1982, 39; Descoeudres 1994, 37), there is no conclusive evidence for this date. Ciprotti (1964, 41–42) reviewed the arguments for the dating of the eruption. The various versions of the letters of Pliny the Younger that have survived suggest dates of either November 3, 23 or August 24. Dio Cassius (LXVI, 24) mentioned autumn as the season of the eruption but one must bear in mind that he wrote a considerable time after the event. In addition, there is no consensus with respect to the length of this season in the ancient world. Opinion varies and suggestions have been made that autumn ranged from mid-August to mid-December or from mid-September to mid-November. Contradictory archaeological finds of seasonal fruit and other plant remains, evidence of wine making activities, carpets and braziers have been used to support claims for both summer and late autumn.

More recently, Pappalardo (1990, 209–210) cited traces of a fur beret associated with a skeleton, along with impressions of heavy clothing in the casts of the Pompeian bodies, as evidence of cooler weather than that generally encountered in August. It is possible, however, that the inhabitants donned heavier clothing as protection against falling debris of the ash fall. Pliny the Younger's first letter to Tacitus (VI,16) mentioned that people tied pillows to their heads for this purpose. Similarly, the bodies in the garden of the House of the Cryptoporticus (I,6, 2) were discovered with roof tiles covering their heads (Ciprotti 1964, 48). In addition, the first phase of the eruption was associated with a lengthy period of darkness which might have produced colder weather than would normally be expected in summer. Ultimately, contradictory evidence is available for both the summer and autumn eruption dates and no truly convincing argument has been mounted.

THE SKELETAL SAMPLE

A large number of skeletons excavated in Pompeii were stored in ancient buildings on the site. The majority of the human skeletons have been stored in the Sarno Baths (VII,2,17) since the nineteenth century, or earlier (Nicolucci 1882, 2). These were stored haphazardly and had become disarticulated over time. It was not feasible to rearticulate skeletons except in the case of gross pathology. In the late 1970s, a small collection of human skeletal material was removed from the Sarno Baths for study and storage in the Forum Baths (VII,5, 2/8/24; D'Amore et al. 1982, 928).

Since very few complete skeletons were available for study, it was decided to concentrate on statistical studies on samples of specific bones. For example, sex determination was based on pelves, femora, humeri and skulls.

It was important to establish whether the sample was biased in any way, such as by sex, age or infirmity, as this would suggest that the sample would not be a reliable indicator of the AD 79 population. A normally distributed sample would suggest that the sample might be random and therefore would provide a good reflection of the AD 79 population in Pompeii.

Sex and age-at-death

The skeletal evidence from adults suggested that there was no significant sex or age bias in the sample of victims (Lazer 1995, 110–199). Very young juveniles were underrepresented in the collection. This is not unusual in archaeological contexts as the bones of neonates and young juveniles are either not preserved or are not recognized by excavators as human and are therefore not collected (Vallois 1960, 186).

Pathology

There did not appear to be a bias towards bones with pathological changes in the sample (Lazer 1995, 200–267). The disarticulation of the sample proved to be a constraint to the study of pathology since many diagnoses require the examination of the entire skeleton. As a result of this, and the lack of access to x-ray equipment, it was only possible to study gross pathology that could be interpreted from individual bones. The main archaeological issue was whether pathological changes to the bones had an impact on the potential for escape from the eruption.

Healed Fractures

The observed frequency of healed fractures in the Pompeian sample is about 0.6%, which is comparable to, or slightly lower than, that reported from other archaeological sites (Roberts and Manchester 1995, 74–79). While it does not appear that the sample was skewed towards people with healed injuries, it is possible that specific individuals did not escape as a result of gross pathology.

Hyperostosis Frontalis Interna

An age-related pathology, hyperostosis frontalis interna (HFI) proved to be a most useful population descriptor. HFI is a syndrome with a suite of signs and symptoms which include obesity, hirsutism, non-insulin dependent diabetes and headaches (Ortner and Putschar 1981, 294; Cocheton et al. 1974, 2946; Pawlikowski and Komorowski 1983, 474; Fernández-Nogueras and Fernández-Nogueras 1993). The syndrome is usually associated with post-menopausal women. It presents on the skull as bilaterally symmetrical deposits of bone overgrowth on the inner table of the frontal bone.

Forty three of 360 skulls that were examined displayed hyperostotic change consistent with an interpretation of HFI (Lazer 1995, 244–266). This represents 11.9% of the sample. The frequency is comparable with the upper end of the normal range for a modern western population. As HFI is often sub-clinical, it is likely that it is underreported in modern populations. It is therefore more likely that the incidence of HFI observed in the Pompeian sample of victims is a reflection of its population occurrence rather than a skewing of the sample. This suggests that the total Pompeian sample is representative of a normally distributed population with no bias toward this pathology.

SKELETAL EVIDENCE FOR POPULATION VARIABILITY

Metric evidence

The fact that many of the skulls were incomplete hampered the collection of cranial metric data. A series of twelve measurements were made on 117 adult skulls (Lazer 1995, 269–277). To establish whether there was consistency between samples, the results of the analysis were compared with similar analyses based on the raw craniometric data collected by Nicolucci (1882) in the nineteenth century.

To gain some understanding of the Pompeian population affinities, the twelve cranial measurements were compared with data from a variety of European and African populations (Howells 1973; 1989), the Pompeian skeletal sample studied by Nicolucci (1882) and the data collected from the Herculanean sample by Bisel (1991). Because the Pompeian data set was not complete and the data sets of Nicolucci and Bisel did not contain all the measurements used by Howells (1973; 1989), it was decided that the use of unpaired t-tests of the means for comparable measurements would be more appropriate than principal components analysis.

Metric evidence from the skull sample provided insufficient evidence to establish whether the Pompeian sample reflects a homogeneous or heterogeneous population. Comparison with other samples from European and African contexts tended to confirm the European affinities of the sample. As expected, the data from the current Pompeian sample were closest to Nicolucci's earlier sample and Bisel's Herculaneum sample, though there were exceptions for some measurements. A large portion of the observed differences were not interpopulational but intrapopulational reflecting male and female variation.

Non-metric studies

Both cranial and post cranial non-metric data were collected to establish whether the Pompeian population was heterogeneous, as has been claimed in the general literature. Non-metric traits are anomalous skeletal variants, which are generally non-pathological. They are also known as epigenetic traits and occur with varying frequency in all populations. A study of the pattern of cranial and post-cranial anomalies may provide information about population variability.

Because skeletal inheritance is multifactorial, the genetic and environmental components of non-metric traits cannot easily be distinguished. Human pedigree and mouse studies have established that there is a genetic component in a number of traits (Berry and Berry 1967, 362–363; Ossenberg 1970, 357; Pardoe 1984, 14–20; Saunders 1989, 103–105). It should be noted that a genetic basis is not essential for a non-metric trait to be a useful population descriptor. The development of traits as a result of shared environmental factors can also provide useful population indicators (Saunders 1989, 106; Brothwell pers. comm.).

Twenty eight cranial non-metric traits were scored on 126 skulls in the Forum Bath collection. These included metopic suture, metopic fissure, supranasal suture, frontal grooves, trochlear spine, infraorbital suture, condylar facet, coronal ossicle, ossicle at bregma, sagittal ossicle, ossicle at lambda, lambdoid ossicles, ossicle at asterion, occipito-mastoid ossicles, inca bone, sutura mendosa, pars incoidea, anterior ethmoid foramen, posterior ethmoid foramen, parietal foramina, occipital foramen, condylar canal, hypoglossal canal, infraorbital foramen, highest nuchal line, precondylar tubercle, palatine torus and auditory torus (Lazer 1995, 277–313).

Intra and interobserver variation in scoring traits has been well documented (Rösing 1984; De Stefano et al. 1984; Saunders 1989, 102). Standard definitions for scoring traits were provided by Hauser and De Stefano (1989).

Only one non-metric variable was scored for teeth. This involved the investigation of canines for the presence or absence of two roots.

Ten non-metric traits were scored on the post cranial material. These were Allen's fossa, Poirier's facet, plaque, hypertrochanteric fossa, exostosis in the trochanteric fossa and third trochanter in the femur; medial and lateral squatting facets in the tibia; and septal aperture and supracondyloid process in the humerus.

Interpretation was hampered by the dearth of appropriate comparative material. This is because cremation was the primary method of disposal of the dead in the Roman world in the first century AD. Herculaneum is virtually the only other site with comparable material. Unfortunately, the non-metric traits have not been published and it was not possible to gain access to this material. It would be desirable to determine the degree of similarity between these sites, but this appears unlikely in the foreseeable future. In lieu of contemporary material, the Pompeian cranial non-metric traits have been compared with the most appropriate available data. These include samples that are temporally and geographically different to the Pompeian sample. It should be borne in mind that there is no reason to assume regional immutability over time, especially for traits with an environmental component.

The most appropriate comparative material that was available for the crania in this study was from the excavations at the medieval monastery at San Vincenzo al Volturno in central southern Italy. Two groups of skeletons were unearthed at this site, the first were from the late Roman period and the second from the early medieval period. These two groups of skeletons have been interpreted as eighty-four workers from a large villa estate of the fifth century AD and sixty-nine lay workers from the monastery. The latter set of burials comprised individuals from family groups of tenants who worked the monastic land. The monastery was in use from the eighth to the end of the ninth century AD (Higgins 1989, 175–176).

The other cranial material that could be used for comparison with the Pompeian sample was less satisfactory and consisted of an assortment of European populations which dated from the prehistoric to the modern period. In addition, when data was available, a sample of ancient Egyptian skulls, prehistoric Africans from Mali and historic Nubian sample were compared with the Pompeian material as an acknowledgment of the possibility of Pompeian contact with Africa. The data for these samples was presented in Brothwell (1981, 92) and Hauser and De Stefano (1989).

There was very little published data for the population incidence of double rooted canines and post-cranial non-metric traits. As a result comparisons were made with all the available material.

A major consideration in relation to comparison of traits with other published material is the lack of standardization in the presentation of trait incidence. Scholars have not always described the techniques they used to record incidence. There are further problems when making comparisons between data sets for different populations. These include differences in sample sizes and whether they reflect random samples or are representative of the populations from which they were drawn. Apart from the acknowledgment that they exist, it is very difficult to account for these problems (Hauser and De Stefano 1989, 17).

Statistical analysis to identify association between sides, traits and sex

Because these non-metric data do not tend to be normally distributed it was not appropriate to use parametric correlation tests. Instead, non-parametric tests were applied to establish whether there were any intertrait, side or sex associations for particular traits. Spearman's rank correlation coefficients were calculated to identify side or intertrait association. The Mann-Whitney U test was used to discern relationships between sex and specific traits. Spearman's rank correlation is based on ranks rather than raw scores and can be used to detect non-linear correlations (Stevens 1987, 100). The Mann-Whitney U test was designed to test for difference between the means of two independent samples. This test can be used to compare samples of unequal sizes (Stevens 1987, 127). Sex determination was based on the sex index generated from the observations of features considered diagnostic of sex from the skull.

RESULTS

The results for the majority of these traits were inconclusive. This is largely attributable to the lack of appropriate comparative material. The non-metric traits that yielded the most interesting results in relation to the issue of heterogeneity in the Pompeian sample were palatine torus, double rooted canines and lateral squatting facets on the tibia.

Palatine Torus

This is a hyperostotic trait. This means that it is associated with excessive ossification into structures that are usually made up of cartilage or dura (Ossenberg 1970, 362–263). Palatine tori can be observed on the palate as a median, or more frequently, paramedian bony mound varying in height, width and length. They tend to be bilateral but can be unilateral. There can be a considerable range of expression of this trait from very slight and more pronounced at either the anterior or posterior end of the bone to excessive and covering the entire length of the palate. No convincing argument has been presented to ascribe a function to this trait. There does appear to be a genetic potential for the development of a palatine torus as it is has been observed in monozygotic twins though it has been suggested that its presence can be influenced by other factors, such as pathology (Hauser and De Stefano 1989, 174, 176, 177; El Najjar and McWilliams 1978, 143–144).

Some degree of expression for palatine torus was present on all but 2 cases of 52 skulls in the Forum Bath collection where the palate had been preserved. A similar frequency was observed in the Sarno Bath collection though the survival rate of the palate was much lower in this collection. Contrary to the suggestions in the literature (Hauser and De Stefano 1989, 174, 176; El Najjar and McWilliams 1978, 143–144), this trait was not found to be age or gender related in the Pompeian sample. The Pompeian cranial index for palatine torus is 96.2%. No other population presented in the available literature has a comparable incidence of this trait. A modern Roman sample had a reported incidence of 7.4% and an undated Sardinian population had a frequency of 7.3%. An Iron Age Romano-British sample had a frequency of 9.71% (Hauser and De Stefano 1989, 178–179). The sample from San Vincenzo had a cranial index of 23.7% (Higgins 1991, Table 4). The highest rate of occurrence amongst the comparative European material is 49.8% for a modern Polish sample. The prevalence for a first millennium African sample from Mali is 7.2%, 3% for a modern Nubian sample and 1.33% for an ancient Egyptian sample (Brothwell 1981, 92; Hauser and De Stefano 1989, 178–179). It is notable that high frequencies have been reported for this trait in populations that are very genetically distant from the Pompeian sample. For example, Pardoe (1984, 115–117; Fig. 33) reported an incidence of palatine torus of up to 74.5% for Aboriginal samples from the border area between New South Wales and Victoria in Australia.

The frequency of palatine torus in the Pompeian sample is extraordinary in comparison with all the available data and requires some investigation. It could be argued that the high frequency is an artifact of the relatively small sample size (n–52), which, in turn is the reflection of the survival rate of this portion of the skull. There is, however, no reason to assume that preservation is not random. Even if it were strongly skewed toward individuals with this trait, the frequency would still be higher than for most of the comparative material. In addition, as mentioned above, observations of palatine torus for the available Sarno Bath palate sample, which were not included in this study were consistent with the frequency of those in the Forum Bath collection.

The next issue to consider is scoring. Berry and Berry (1967, 376) claimed there was a discrepancy between observers in scoring this trait as the results obtained varied considerably from other published data. This led them to postulate the existence of two separate entities that could be scored as palatine torus. This problem ostensibly should have been solved by the publication of Hauser and De Stefano's standard atlas (1989) which includes photographic references to minimize ambiguity for each trait. Another source of possible overidentification of this trait in comparison to the results of other scholars is the inclusion of trace scores. It is possible that some observers could score trace expression as absent. This explanation would only account for 12 cases or 23.1% of the Pompeian sample, which still leaves an unequivocal 73.1% presence.

It does appear that the high frequency of this trait is not an artifact and that the palatine torus could possibly be a useful population indicator for the Pompeian sample. As already mentioned, the aetiology for this trait is not well understood. It appears that both environmental and genetic components contribute to the expression of palatine torus, though it has been claimed that it is an abnormality determined by one or more genes (Brothwell 1981, 95). It has been suggested that its presence is a genetically determined response to irritation (Hauser and De Stefano 1989, 176). Whatever the mechanism for the formation of the palatine torus, it has the potential to be a population descriptor for the ancient Pompeians. It could be argued that the almost total presence of the trait in the sample might suggest a type of homogeneity that was not necessarily based on similarity of genotype but perhaps a shared environment during the period of osseous development.

It would be most instructive if other ancient and contemporary skulls of the Vesuvian region could be examined for palatine torus to establish if this is a regional feature or specific to ancient Pompeii.

Double Rooted Canines

The roots of canines in the mandible or lower jaw, are occasionally divided into labial (facing the lips) and lingual (towards the tongue) parts. The degree of division can vary and be either partial or complete. It is most uncommon to find a furcated root on an upper (maxillary) canine (Woelfel 1990, 78). This characteristic can be a useful population marker. When possible, loose canines were routinely removed from their sockets to facilitate measurement. During the course of this work a number of double rooted canines were observed. Observations were also made of the sockets of canines that had been lost post-mortem. This is only useful for the identification of the trait when the roots are well divided. Only unequivocal cases were scored. There was only mandibular occurrence of this trait. Six of the 21 mandibles from which it was possible to make observations had teeth with roots that were divided. It is perhaps misleading to use percentages for such small sample sizes but the prevalence of double rooted canines was about 28.6%.

There is minimal comparative data for this trait in the literature. Turner (pers. comm.) has found double rooted canines to occur more frequently in European populations. It is extremely rare in Australian Aboriginal, Oceanic, Asiatic and African populations. He observed this trait in varying frequencies in small samples of a diverse sample of populations. Because of the small sample size and the lack of comparative data it is not reasonable to draw too many conclusions from the presence of double rooted canines in the Pompeian sample. All that can be stated is that the frequency appears to be higher for the Pompeians than for any other recorded population, though this may be an artifact of the small samples for all the populations that have been studied. It would be useful to investigate this further, possibly through x-ray analysis of the mandibles where canines could not be removed for inspection as well as the cast collection.

Lateral Squatting Facets

This trait is scored present when the inferior articular surface extends into the lateral fossa of the transverse depression on the lower anterior surface of the tibia. This latter forms the attachment for the articular capsule of the ankle joint. It has been argued that tibial squatting facets result from biomechanical stress. It has been postulated that lateral squatting facets are caused by a particular type of squatting posture. These facets have not generally been recorded in association with European adults, though they can be observed on European fetuses (Kennedy 1989, 149–150). This suggests that biomechanical stress can hardly be the only cause of such facets, and a genetic origin must also be considered.

A sample of 127 left and 124 right tibiae were examined for the presence of medial and lateral squatting facets. There was a much higher prevalence of lateral than medial squatting facets. This trait occurred more frequently on the right side, with an 87% prevalence as compared to a frequency of 78.7% on the left side. It is notable that the majority of cases for both sides exhibited strong expression of the trait. No comparable population data were available. A modern American sample of white males yielded a left side frequency of 26% and a right side frequency of 23%. The side incidences for a sample of American white females are 24% for the left and 33% for the right (Donlon 1989, 87, 90).

Lateral squatting facets are so common in the Pompeian sample that one could hazard a guess that the inhabitants shared certain habitual behavioral traits. Shared behavior that results in similar skeletal changes in a population can indicate a type of homogeneity. Comparison with other contemporary skeletal samples from the region and other sites from the Roman Empire would be necessary to determine whether this was specific to Pompeii, Campania in general, or was common for Roman communities.

Discussion and Conclusion

The relatively high frequency of certain non-metric traits in relation to other populations, like palatine tori and double rooted canines, may indicate homogeneity. Further research, involving both non-metric trait analysis of the Pompeian collections and comparative studies of contemporary material from the region is required for corroboration.

It could be argued that the apparent tendency towards homogeneity in the skeletal sample is the result of sample bias produced by selective collection in the nineteenth century. Nicolucci (1882), for example, intentionally selected what he considered more unusual skulls for examination. It appears that at least some of these skulls are now in collections in Naples and are no longer accessible (D'Amore et al. 1979, 301). It is impossible to assess the impact of this practice on the sample. The skulls that have been excavated and stored over the last hundred years have not been subjected to this treatment and so should be random.

As it has always been assumed that the Pompeian population was heterogeneous, an explanation is required for the apparent homogeneity of the Pompeian skeletal collection. Evidence provided by approximately equal sex ratios, representative age ranges and the frequency of HFI suggests that this is a statistically representative sample. It is possible that the composition of the population may have been altered in the period between the AD 62 earthquake and the eruption of AD 79 by the abandonment of the site, either as a direct result of the earthquake or because of continuing seismic activity. The population could also have changed for other reasons as would be expected in a dynamic community with a long history of occupation.

Consideration should also be given to the fact that the Pompeian skeletal sample is a reflection of the victims of the eruption. While it may constitute a statistically representative sample, it may not include certain portions of the original population. It is possible, for example, that the indigenous core of the population either chose or were forced to remain in Pompeii during the eruption in order to protect estates or because they had no alternative refuge, whilst people with fewer ties to the town, such as Roman seasonal visitors, chose to escape.

It is also possible that the apparent homogeneity of the sample could be explained by a combination of these factors. Alternatively, the Pompeian population may never have been as mixed as the historical sources suggest. The sample could simply be a reflection of the Pompeians as they always were.

Whilst the skeletal analysis did not yield conclusive results, it did provide information which challenges traditional views about the composition of the Pompeian population. Though other explanations are possible, the unexpected homogeneity of the sample is consistent with the suggestion that the AD 79 population was in a state of flux in the last seventeen years of occupation.

ACKNOWLEDGMENTS

I would like to thank the staff of the Soprintendenza Archeologica di Pompei for making my work possible. Firstly, I am grateful to the successive Superintendents, Dott. Baldassare Conticello and Prof. Pietro Giovanni Guzzo, for granting me permission to work on the collections of human skeletons from Pompeii. I would also like to thank Dott. Antonio D'Ambrosio, Dott. Antonio Varone, Dott.ssa A. Ciarallo, as well as Vincenzo Matrone, Luigi Matrone, Ciro Sicignano and Franco Staiano from the Direzione. I thank Simon Hayman, Department of Architectural and Design Science, University of Sydney for his statistical expertise. I would also like to thank Ruth Lazer and Dr. Carol Lazer for their comments and criticisms of the manuscript.

References

Allison, P.M., 1992. Artefact assemblages: not the 'Pompeii Premise', in E. Herring, R. Whitehouse and J. Wilkins (eds.), *Papers of the Fourth Conference of Italian Archaeology*. Volume 3. New Developments in Italian Archaeology, Part 1 (Accordia Research Centre: London): 49–56.

Allison, P.M., 1994. *The Distribution of Pompeian House Contents and its Significance*. Volumes I and II. (PhD Thesis, School of Archaeology, Classics and Ancient History, University of Sydney, 1992. UMI: Ann Arbor).

Allison, P.M., 1995. On-going seismic activity and its effects on the living conditions in the last decades, in T. Fröhlich and L. Jacobelli eds., *La Regione Vesuviana dal 62 al 79 d.C.: Problemi Archeologici e Sismologici*. Colloquium, Boscoreale,-26–27 November, 1993 (Verlag Biering und Brinkmann: Munich): 183–190.

Andreau, J., 1979. Il terromoto del 62, in F. Zevi (ed.), *Pompei 79: raccolta di studi per il decimonono centenario dell'eruzione vesuviana* (Gaetano Macchiarolo Editore: Naples): 40–44.

Baxter, P.J., 1990. Medical effects of volcanic eruptions, *Bulletin of Volcanology* 52: 532–544.

Berry, A.C. and Berry, R., 1967. Epigenetic variation in the human cranium, *Journal of Anatomy* 101: 361–379.

Biddle, M., 1974. The archaeology of Winchester, *Scientific American* 230 (5): 32–43.

Bisel, S.C., 1991. The human skeletons of Herculaneum, *International Journal of Anthropology* 6,1: 1–20

Bisel, S.C. (with Bisel, J. and Tanaka, S.), 1990. *The Secrets of Vesuvius* (Madison Press: Toronto).

Brion, M., 1973. *Pompeii and Herculaneum: The Glory and the Grief* (Cardinal: London).

Brothwell, D.R., 1981. *Digging up Bones: The excavation, treatment and study of human skeletal remains*. 3rd ed. (British Museum (Natural History)/ Oxford University Press: London).

Bullard, F.M.,1984. *Volcanoes of the Earth*. 2nd. ed. (University of Texas Press: Austin).

Ciprotti, P., 1964. Der letze Tag von Pompeji, *Altertum* 10: 40–54.

Cocheton, J.J., Finaltain, L., and Poulet, J., 1974. Le syndrome de Morgagni-Stewart-Morel: Mythe ou realité? *Semaine des Hôsitaux* 50: 2945–2950.

Corti, E.C.C., 1951. *The Destruction and Resurrection of Pompeii and Herculaneum*. Translated by R.G.Smith (Routledge and Kegan Paul: London).

D'Amore, C., Mallegni, F. and Schiano Di Zenise, M., 1979. Antropologia pompeiana del 79 d.C.: sesso ed età di morte, *Archivio per l'Antropologia e la Etnologia* CIX: 297–308.

D'Amore, C., Mallegni, F. and Schiano Di Zenise, M.,1982. Primi risultalti degli studi sull'antropologia pompeiana del 79 d.C., in *La Regione Sotterrata dal Vesuvio: Studi e Prospettive, Atti del Convegno Internazionale* 11–15 Novembre 1979 (Università degli Studi: Napoli): 927–943.

Daniel, G.,1981. *A Short Histroy of Archaeology* (Thames and Hudson: London).

De Franciscis, A., 1975. *The Pompeian Wall Paintings in the Roman Villa of Oplontis* (Verlag Aurel Bongers Recklinghausen: Germany).

De Stefano, G.F., Hauser, G., Guidotti, A., Rossi, S., Gualdo Russo, E. and Brasili Gualandi, P., 1984. Reflections on Interobserver Differences in Scoring Non-metric Cranial Traits (with Practical Examples) *Journal of Human Evolution* 13: 349–355.

Della Corte, M.,1965. *Casa ed Abitanti di Pompei*. 3rd. ed. (Fausto Fiorentino: Napoli).

Descoeudres, J-P., 1993. Did some Pompeians return to their city after the eruption of Mt. Vesuvius in AD 79? Observations in the House of the Coloured Capitals, in L. Franchi Dell'Orto (ed.), *Ercolano 1738–1988: 250 anni di ricerca archeologica*. (L'Erma di Bretschneider: Rome): 165–178.

Descoeudres, J-P., 1994a. A Brief History of Pompeii, in D. Harrison (ed.), *Pompeii Revisited: The Life and Death of a Roman Town* (Meditarch: Sydney): 1–39.

Descoeudres, J-P., 1994b. Discovery and Excavation, in D. Harrison (ed.), *Pompeii Revisited: The Life and Death of a Roman Town* (Meditarch: Sydney): 41–53.

Donlon, D.,1990. *The value of postcranial nonmetric variation in studies of global populations in modern Homo Sapiens*. (PhD thesis, University of New England: Armidale).

Eisele, J.W., O'Halloran, R.L., Reay, D.T., Lindholm, G.R., Lewman, L.V., and Brady, W.J., 1981. Deaths during the May 18, 1980, eruption of Mt. St. Helens, *The New England Journal of Medicine* 305 (16): 931–936.

El-Najjar, M. Y. and McWilliams, K.R., 1978. *Forensic Anthroplogy: The Structure, Morphology and Variation of Human Bone and Dentition* (Charles C. Thomas: Springfield).

Eschebach, H., 1978. *Pompeji: Erlebte antike welt* (VEB E.A. Seeman Buch und Kunstverlag: Leipzig).

Fernández-Nogueras, F.J., and Fernández-Nogueras, V., 1993. The Stewart-Morel Syndrome in the differential diagnosis of patients with frontal headache, *Anales Ortorrinolaringológicos Ibero-Americanos* 20 (4): 383–391.

Fiorelli, G., 1873. *Gli Scavi di Pompei dal 1861 al 1872* (Tipografica nel Liceo V. Emmanuele: Napoli).

Francis, P., 1993. *Volcanoes: A Planetary Perspective* (Clarendon Press: Oxford).

Gell, W., 1832. *Pompeiana: the Topography, Edifices and Ornaments of Pompeii. The results of Excavations since 1819* (Chaplin: London).

Giordano, C. and Kahn, I., 1979. *The Jews in Pompeii, Herculaneum, Stabiae and in the cities of Campania Felix* (Procaccini Editore: Napoli).

Grant, M., 1976. *Cities of Vesuvius: Pompeii and Herculaneum* (Penguin: Middlesex).

Grayson, D.K. and Sheets, P.D., 1979. Volcanic disasters and the archaeological record, in P.D.Sheets and D.K. Grayson (eds.), *Volcanic Activity and Human Ecology* (Academic Press: New York): 623–632.

Hauser, G. and De Stefano, G.F., 1989. *Epigenetic Variants of the Human Skull* (Schweizerbart: Stuttgart).

Higgins, V., 1989. A model for assessing health patterns from skeletal remains, in C.A. Roberts, F. Lee and J. Bintliff (eds.), *Burial Archaeology: Current Research, Methods and Developments.* (British Archaeological Reports 211: Oxford).

Higgins, V., 1991. in R. Hodges (ed.), *San Vincenzo al Volturno 1: Excavation and Survey 1980–86* (British School at Rome: London).

Howells, W.W., 1973. Cranial variation in Man: A study by multivariate analysis of patterns of difference among recent populations, *Papers of the Peabody Museum of Archaeology and Ethnology* 67 (Harvard University: Cambridge, Massachusetts).

Howells, W.W.,1989. Skull shapes and the map: craniometric analyses in the dispersion of modern Homo, *Papers of the Peabody Museum of Archaeology and Ethnology* 79 (Harvard University: Cambridge, Massachusetts).

Jashemski, W.F., 1979. *The Gardens of Pompeii, Herculaneum and the Villas Destroyed by Vesuvius* (Caratzas Brothers: New York).

Jongman, W., 1988. *The Economy and Society of Pompeii.* Dutch Monographs on Ancient History and Archaeology, Vol. IV. Edited by P.W. De Neeve and H.W. Pleket (J.C. Gieber: Amsterdam).

Kennedy, K.A.R., 1989. Skeletal markers of occupational stress, in M.Y. Iscan and K.A.R. Kennedy (eds.), *Reconstruction of Life from the Skeleton* (Alan R. Liss: New York).

Lazer, E., 1995. *Human Skeletal Remains in Pompeii.* Volumes I and II. (PhD Thesis, Department of Anatomy and Histology, University of Sydney: Sydney).

Leppmann, W., 1968. *Pompeii in Fact and Fiction* (Elek: London).

Lytton, E.B. 1897. *The Last Days of Pompeii* (Putnam: New York).

Maiuri, A., 1933. *La Casa del Menandro e il suo tesoro di argenteria* (La Libreria dello Stato: Rome).

Maiuri, A., 1943. *Pompei.* 2nd. ed. (Istituto Geografico De Agostini: Novara).

Maiuri, A., 1962. *The New Excavations, the Villa dei Misteri, the Antiquarium* (Istituto Polografico dello Stato: Rome).

Mau, A., 1907. *Pompeii. Its Life and Art.* Translated by F.W. Kelsey (Macmillan: London).

Nicolucci, G., 1882. Crania Pompeiana. Descrizione de'Crani Umani Rinvenuti fra le Ruine dell'Antica Pompei, *Atti della R. Accademia della Scienze Fisiche e Matematiche* IX, No. 10.

Ortner, D.J., and Putschar, W.G.J., 1981. Identification of pathological conditions in human skeletal remains, *Smithsonian Contributions to Anthropology* 28 (Smithsonian Institution Press: Washington).

Ossenberg, N.S., 1970. The influence of artificial cranial deformation on discontinuous morphological traits, *American Journal of Physical Anthropology* 33:357–372.

Pappalardo, U., 1990. L'eruzione pliniana del Vesuvio nel 79 d.C., *Ercolano* 25 (10): 197–215.

Pardoe, C., 1984. *Prehistoric Human Morphological Variation in Australia.* (PhD Thesis, Australian National University: Canberra).

Pawlikowski, M. and Komorowski, J., 1983. Hyperostosis Frontalis Interna and the Morgagni-Stewart-Morel Syndrome, *Lancet*, Feb 26, 1 (8322): 474.

Perl, G., 1982. Pompeji-Geschichte und Untergang, in M. Kunze (ed.), *Pompeji: 79–1979: Beiträge Zum Vesuvausbruch und seiner Nachwirkung.* Beiträge der Winckelmann Gesellschaft, Band 11 (Stendal): 9–24.

Richardson, L., 1978. Life as it appeared when Vesuvius engulfed Pompeii, *Smithsonian* 9 (1): 84–93.

Richardson, L., 1988. *Pompeii: An Architectural History* (John Hopkins University Press: Baltimore).

Roberts, C. and Manchester, K., 1995. *The Archaeology of Disease*. 2nd. ed. (Cornell University Press: Ithaca).

Rösing, F.W., 1984. Discreta of the human skeleton: a critical review, *Journal of Human Evolution* 13: 319–323.

Russell, J.C., 1985. *The Control of Late Ancient and Medieval Population* (American Philosophical Society: Philadelphia).

Saunders, S.R., 1989. Nonmetric Skeletal Variation, in M.Y. Iscan and K.A.R. Kennedy (eds.), *Reconstruction of Life from the Skeleton* (Alan R. Liss: New York): 95–108.

Scott, W.E., 1989. Volcanic and related hazards, in R.I. Tilling (ed.), *Volcanic Hazards* (American Geophysical Union: Washington D.C.): 9–23.

Sigurdsson, H., Cashdollar, S., and Sparks, S.R.J., 1982. The eruption of Vesuvius in A.D. 79: reconstruction from historical and volcanological evidence, *American Journal of Archaeology* 86: 39–51.

Sigurdsson, H., Carey, S., Cornell, W., and Pescatore, T., 1985. The eruption of Vesuvius in A.D. 79, *National Geographic Research* 1 (3): 332–387

Stevens, G., 1987. *Statistics Course Notes*. (Faculty of Architecture, University of Sydney: Sydney).

Tran Tam Tinh, V., 1964. *Essai sur le culte d'Isis à Pompei* (Boccard: Paris).

Trevelyan, R., 1976. *The Shadow of Vesuvius: Pompeii AD 79* (Michael Joseph: London).

Vallois, H.V., 1960. Vital statistics in prehistoric population as determined from archaeological data, in R.F. Heizer and S.F. Cook (eds.), *The Application of Quantitative Methods in Archaeology* (Quadrangle Books: Chicago): 205–222.

Wallace-Hadrill, A., 1991. Houses and households: sampling Pompeii and Herculaneum, in B. Rawson (ed.), *Marriage, Divorce and Children in Ancient Rome* (Oxford University Press: Oxford): 191–227.

Ward-Perkins, J.B., and Claridge, A., 1980. *Pompeii AD 79: Treasures from the National Archaeological Museum, Naples and the Pompeii Antiquarium, Italy*. 2nd. ed. (Australian Gallery Directors' Council: Sydney).

Witt, R.E., 1971. *Isis in the Graeco-Roman World* (Thames and Hudson: London).

Woelfel, J.B., 1990. *Dental Anatomy: Its Relevance to Dentistry*. 4th. ed. (Lea and Febiger: Philadelphia).

Ancient Sources

Dio Cassius, *Dio's Roman History*. Translated by E.Carey, 1914–1927. (Loeb Classical Library. Harvard University Press: Cambridge, Massachusetts).

Pliny the Younger, *Letters and Panegyrics*. Translated by B. Radice, 1969 (Harvard University Press: Cambridge, Massachusetts).

Seneca, *Naturales Quaestiones*. Translated by Corcoran, 1972. (Loeb Classical Library. Harvard University Press: Cambridge, Massachusetts).

Strabo, *The Geography*. Translated by H.R. Jones, 1988. (Loeb Classical Library. Harvard University Press: Cambridge, Massachusetts).

Suetonius, *The Twelve Caesars*. Translated by Robert Graves, 1957 (Penguin: Middlesex).

Tacitus, *Annals of Imperial Rome*. Translated by B. Radice and R. Baldick, 1971 (Penguin: Middlesex).

10 Private Toilets at Pompeii: Appearance and Operation[1]

Gemma Jansen

Now that the emphasis of classical archaeology is shifting from art historical research to the study of daily life, it seems only natural to investigate one of the most 'everyday' of daily events: the use of the toilet. The excavation of Pompeii makes it a highly suitable site to study this aspect of daily life. We not only find many toilets there, but the environment in which they were used is preserved as well, which enables us to study their position in the house and in the urban infrastructure.

Until now, almost no specific and systematic investigation has been carried out into the public and private toilets of Pompeii. Toilets are regularly mentioned by Fiorelli (1873, 24f.; 1875), Thédenat (1910, 96–97), Blümner (1911, 49–50), Strell (1913, 99–103) and Squassi (1954, 25–26). Some of them are described in more detail in monographs on specific houses at Pompeii.[2] More analytical descriptions can be found in Mygind (1921, 310–319), Scobie (1986), Grassnick (1992, 21–28), Jansen (1993), Neudecker (1994,-17–21) and Koloski-Ostrow (1996).

The study of the private toilets of Pompeii must be divided into two stages, since so little previous work has been done. First, I completed an inventory of the excavated toilets to get a clear picture of the way they looked and operated as well as of their position inside the house. This inventory also allowed me to discover the relationship between this specific private provision and urban provisions for water supply and waste water disposal in general. This part of the research has been completed and the present article presents its first results. It is only in the second stage that more specific research questions can be formulated about the actual use of the toilet and its socio-cultural implications. In this article stage one will be our focus. However, some restrictions have to be made. I will describe only that place in the house that was especially designed and built to allow people to relieve themselves. That is why piss-pots,

---

[1] The present paper forms part of the doctoral research carried out by the author into sanitary facilities and methods of water supply and discharge in Roman cities. The situation in Pompeii features prominently in this research project, which is financed by the Netherlands organization for scientific research (NWO) and will be completed in 1996. I would like to thank the Soprintendente of Pompeii for his willingness to give the permission to study all the houses of Pompeii. Furthermore I would like to thank all those people who collaborated in this research both in Pompeii and at home. I feel especially grateful to Drs. M.C.A.E. van Binnebeke and A.O. Koloski-Ostrow (Ass. Prof. at Brandeis University) for their comments on this paper.
[2] For instance: Curtis (1979, 10, 19), Strocka (1984, 21, 46, Abb. 72–73), Descoeudres and Sear (1987, 13, 17), Ehrhardt (1988, 36, Abb. 145–146, 148), Michel (1990, 26–28, 30), Strocka (1984, 21; 1991, 62–63, 95–96), Peters (1993, 6, 87–88, Fig. 2, Fig. 99–102).

public toilets, urinals or amphorae that were put in the street to collect urine will not be discussed here, and neither will other places – such as graves or statues – where the Romans
used to defecate or urinate. In addition, only the situation during the last years of Pompeii will
be dealt with; the way the city was found when it was excavated. This is because the walls of
the toilets, which were often not an integral part of the rest of the structure of the house,
proved difficult to date.

This article consists of five sections. Section I presents the criteria used to define a toilet
and goes into some of the problems connected with the research. Section II provides a detailed description and explanation of the appearance and operation of the toilets. Section III
deals with the location of the toilet inside the house. Section IV shows how the private toilets
fit into the urban infrastructure and relate to the supply and disposal of water and how these
provisions in their turn affected private toilets. Finally, section V formulates starting points
for the second stage of the research.

I. CRITERIA AND PROBLEMS

Although a large number of toilets are preserved at Pompeii, few of them are still completely
intact. The most complete ones found are those in the House of the Silver Wedding (V, 2, 1)
and the House of Apollo (VI, 7, 23). From these and other Pompeian toilets in good condition we can identify the elements which must be present in order to classify a room as a toilet.
It is easy, for instance, to take a closet or a small lime-kiln for a toilet. The definition used in
this research is: a toilet is a small room or part of a room with the visible remains of a seat
and/or a tiled, sloping floor. Rooms without these features have not been put on the inventory list of toilets. Rooms that are called toilets in the literature but now no longer meet the
requirements of the definition have been excluded from the list.

I was not able to investigate all the toilets at Pompeii. For one thing, a number of them
were inaccessible. In 1992 and 1993, when the inventory was being made, the northern part
of the city was for the most part overgrown.[3] Other toilets could not be studied because at
the time in question they are still used as toilets by tourists and others.[4] A few small rooms
that may have been toilets could not be investigated because they were filled with bricks, roof
tiles and pieces of marble.

Another reason is that many toilets that were excavated years ago have in the meantime
been destroyed. Most of the toilets from Region VIII described by Fiorelli (1873; 1875) can
no longer be found. Many toilet walls (which were less strong than the rest of the walls to
begin with) have fallen down after having been excavated because they were not protected
from the rain and the wind. Some toilets disappeared on account of modern rebuilding.[5]

---

[3] Nearly all of Region VI and a number of insulae in Region VIII were overgrown.

[4] The shoulder-height walls of the ancient toilets offer, apparently, enough privacy and shelter for the modern visitors to
Pompeii to relieve themselves. For instance the toilet in the House of the Sailor (VII, 15, 1.2.15) and in IX, 2, 12.

[5] The toilet in the House of the Vettii (VI, 15 1.27), for instance, was destroyed to make way for the tourist exit; the toilet

Nevertheless, it was possible to investigate 195 toilets. Statements in this article, however, must not be regarded as statistical statements about the toilets of Pompeii as a whole; they only apply to the toilets that were investigated within the framework of this research.[6]

II. TOILETS AT POMPEII

The different features of the toilets at Pompeii will be described on the basis of what the Pompeians apparently demanded of their toilets. It appears from our investigation that people built their toilets in such a way that: 1) they were able to sit down;[7] 2) they were able to clean themselves with the Roman version of toilet paper, the sponge-stick;[8] 3) they could not be seen by people outside the toilet; 4) there was enough light to see by; 5) urine and feces could easily be disposed of, possibly through flushing with water.

1) They wanted to sit down.

The seat was constructed simply: it consisted of a board with a hole in it which either rested on two brick supports or on a kind of cut-away ledge in the wall (see Figs. 10.1 and 10.2). Often, the board was placed on a brick support on one side and on a ledge in the wall on the other. Most toilets were provided with an extra board to put the feet on while one was sitting down. This board was fixed in place in the same way as the seat. Sometimes the seat was built into a niche in the wall (Figs. 10.3 and 10.4), in which case one sat right above the drainpipe, which was built into the wall. One could not sit upright on these toilets; one had to bend a little forward.

2) They wanted to use the sponge-stick.

For the user of the toilet to be able to use a sponge-stick, two requirements had to be met. Firstly, to use the stick, the front of the toilet seat either had to be open or had to have a hole. The toilet seats at Pompeii were made of wood and have disappeared now, so we cannot know

---

in IX, 7, 13 disappeared under the stairs leading to the exhibition room of Casina dell'Aquila; and the toilet in VII, 3, 24.25 is now part of a technical laboratory. Eschebach (1991, 282–284) claims that when the restaurant (VII, 5) was built five private toilets (VII, 5, 13; VII, 5, 14; VII, 5, 15; VII, 5, 17; VII, 5, 20) and one public toilet (VII, 5, 1a) were lost.

[6] Some toilets had better chances of survival (multi-user toilets) or of being recognized (niche toilets) than others.

[7] Saying that people wanted to sit down while the definition of a toilet already stipulates that there must be a seat may not seem to make sense at first sight. What is intended here is to distinguish this type of toilet from the toilets found in Southern European and Arab countries where people have to squat instead of sitting down. In Pompeii, no evidence has been found for squat toilets.

[8] The sponge stick is the generally accepted cleaning device used in Roman antiquity. It is mentioned in at least two texts. Mart. Ep. 12.48.8: '... damnatae *spongea* virgae ...'; Seneca Ep. 70.20: 'ibi lignum id, quod ad undanda avscena adherente *spongia* positum est'. In addition to sponges, there were two other options. Curtis (1979, 19 note 33) suggests that in I, 12, 8 the fig tree that grew next to the toilet not only provided shelter, but also toilet paper in the form of the large fig leaves. Pieces of cloth may also have been used. An investigation of the contents of the cesspits of Pompeii might yield information on how the Romans cleaned themselves after having used the toilet.

Fig. 10.1 *Flush toilet with raised tile floor in the kitchen of the House of Apollo (VI,7, 23).*

Fig. 10.2 *Reconstruction of the use of a flush toilet.*

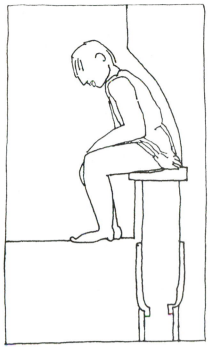

Fig. 10.4 *Reconstruction of the use of a niche toilet.*

Fig. 10.3 *Niche toilet on upper floor of V,1, 30.*

which of the two solutions was chosen.[9] Secondly, it was necessary to clean the sticks with water, either before or after use. Three toilets contained small brick water basins constructed for that purpose (Fig. 10.5).[10] In other toilets the sponge-sticks may have been cleaned in a bucket or moveable basin. In the toilet of the House of the Silver Wedding (V, 2, 1) a small, moveable bronze basin was found (*Notizie degli Scavi di Antichità* 1896, 430). It is not clear where the sponge-stick was left after use: perhaps it was hung on the wall or left in the basin.

3) They did not want to be seen from the outside.

A number of the private toilets were meant for more than one person. This discovery has made researchers think that the Romans felt no need for privacy and had no feelings of shame

---

[9] The toilet in house VII, 11, 4.5 is the only one where the stucco still holds an imprint of the board that closed the front of the seat.

[10] Caupona of Euxinus (I, 11, 10–12); I, 12, 9.14; I, 12, 10.11.

Fig. 10.5 *Entrance to the toilet in the garden of the Caupona of Euxinus (I,11, 10–12), with sponge basin.*

or awkwardness on the subject of these particular bodily functions. That assumption is only partly true. It was indeed quite common to use the toilet together with other people. Most of the 'multi-seaters' were 'two-seaters' (Fig. 10.6); private toilets for three, four or five people together were rare.[11] Toilets with two or more seats were most common in big workshops or in large houses where there was an extensive staff. In small houses and apartments, where there was little space, only single toilets are found. The size of the toilets, then, depended on the number of people that had to use them and on the space that was available.

Although they felt no shame about sharing the toilet, the Pompeians still did not want to be looked at from the outside when they were relieving themselves. A private toilet was either a separate room or, if it was situated in another room, it was hidden behind a shoulder-high brick wall or wooden screen (Seiler 1992, 69, 94). It was virtually impossible to look inside through the windows, which were small and narrow. Only the windows above head height were bigger. One was not completely hidden from view, however, because in most cases there was no door. Of all the thresholds found at entrances to toilets, only two suggest the presence of a door.[12]

---

[11] We calculated about fifty centimetres per person. A toilet seat narrower than one metre was considered a single toilet; a seat wider than one metre was considered a 'two-seater'. Thirty-three of the toilets investigated were two-seaters. One toilet, in the House of the Dioscuri (VI, 9, 6.9) seated three people; two toilets in the House of the Caetroni (VI 9,7.8) and in the House of Marcus Lucretius (IX, 3, 5.24) seated four; and in the House of the Centenary (IX, 8, 6.3.a) a toilet was excavated that seated five.

[12] The toilet at the Caupona of Euxinus (I, 11, 10–12) and the kitchen toilet in the House of the Citharist (I, 4, 5.25–28). The fact that the thresholds are there does not necessarily mean that there once was a door; the thresholds may have been taken from another room and may have been reused here without a door.

4) They wanted to be able to see.

When a toilet was a separate room it was small, with a low ceiling, and rather dark. Some toilets had small windows which let in a little light. Other toilets had no windows and this strengthens the assumption that there was no door, or that, if there was a door, it was left open. A number of toilets were lit by means of oil lamps, as is shown by little niches in the walls.[13] Toilets that were situated in other rooms mostly had no window of their own, but had to make do with the light that was available in that room. The walls of these rather dark toilets were painted white. The dadoes, however, were painted in dark patterns to hide stains (Jansen 1993).

Fig. 10.6 *'Two-seater' toilet in the kitchen of the House of the Ephebe (I,7, 10–12.19) (photo by A. Willemsen).*

5) They wanted to get rid of urine and feces, possibly through flushing with water

In the case of niche toilets there was a drain pipe in the wall underneath the seat. The drains are clearly visible – especially in toilets on upper floors. They consisted of several terra cotta pipes fitted together. Since the seat was right above the drain, this type of toilet needed hardly any flushing. Other toilets had seats that were not right above the drain and there water was needed to wash away urine and fecal matter. They had a raised tile floor which was always higher than the surrounding floors and sloped towards a drain to facilitate the disposal of the waste water.[14] The edges of the floor were sealed off with a curved layer of opus signinum to prevent leakages. A thin layer of this water-resistant opus signinum was also spread on the walls, up to at least knee-height. To where the specific drains led the urine and feces is one of the questions to which this research has as yet not found an answer.

---

[13] Niches for oil lamps were found in the House of the Arches (I, 17, 4) and in V, 4, 6–8. Mygind (1921, 314) mentions another one in the House of the Diadumeni (IX, 1, 20.30). Thédenat (1910, 93, 97) mentions a niche for a lamp in the toilet of IX, 2, 12 and a console in the toilet of the House of Trebius Valens (III, 2, 1a) that may have held a lamp.

[14] House of Paquius Proculus (I, 7, 1.20) and house I, 20, 4.

Fig. 10.7 Toilet in the courtyard of the Fullonica of Stephanus (I,6, 7).

III. THE POSITION OF THE TOILET INSIDE THE HOUSE

Nearly all the toilets were found in the working areas of the houses. Most of them were situated in the kitchen (33 in number) or near it (18 in number). That is not surprising because in that part of the house water was available and the toilet could also be used to drain waste water away. Toilets may also have been used for the disposal of garbage. Other places where toilets were often found are courtyards and gardens (22 in number) (Figs. 10.7 and 10.8). This holds particularly for Regions I and II, where large gardens were excavated. Many toilets were built near the side entrance to the house. Toilets were found in large houses and also on upper floors (9 in number)[15] and in shops (25 in number). On account of shared drains, the position of the toilet sometimes depended on that of the next-door neighbors' toilet[16] or on that of the neighbors downstairs.[17]

Only six houses were found to have had more than one toilet.[18] The fact that in most cases

---

[15] Toilets on upper floors: I, 1, 6–9; I, 2, 2–4; V, 1, 30; House of M. Holconius Rufus (VIII, 4, 2–6.49.50); VIII, 6, 6; IX, 2, 7.8; IX, 3,4; House of Julius Polybius (IX, 13, 1–3).

[16] The toilets in house II, 9, 1 and II, 9, 2, for instance.

[17] Toilet on upper floor linked to toilet on ground floor: I, 1, 6–9; I, 2, 2–4; V, 1, 30; VIII, 6, 6; IX, 3, 4.

[18] In the House of the Menander (I, 10, 4.14–17) no less than four toilets were excavated. Two toilets were found in the Caupona of Euxinus (I, 11, 10–12), in Praedia of Julia Felix (II, 4, 2–12) (we consider the toilet near the baths a public toilet), in the House of the Labyrinth (VI, 11, 8–10), the House of the Golden Cupids (VI, 16, (6).7.38) and in the House of Obellius Firmus (IX, 14, 2.4.b). The House of Paquius Proculus (I, 7, 1.20) has three toilets, but they were probably not all in use at the same time. In the House of Queen Margherita (V, 2, 1.a.a¹) two toilets were excavated, but one of them had been bricked up.

Fig. 10.8 Toilet in the courtyard of the garum workshop (I,12, 8)

they are not far apart seems to indicate that they were meant for different groups of people living or working in those houses. The House of the Labyrinth (VI, 11, 8–10) had one toilet in the kitchen and another in the slave quarters nearby. In the Caupona of Euxinus (I, 11, 10–12) two toilets were found next to each other; one could be reached from inside the house and the other was accessible from the garden. The second toilet probably served the clients of the caupona.

IV. THE TOILET AND THE URBAN INFRASTRUCTURE

Nearly every toilet was supplied with water which was then drained away again, together with urine and feces. In this respect the toilet functions as a kind of turning point between two water systems. In this section we will look at the relationship between toilets and water supply on the one hand, and the disposal of waste water on the other.

The supply of water

The inhabitants of Pompeii had several ways of obtaining water. There were, for instance, deep wells scattered throughout the city. Drinking water could be obtained by collecting rain-water on the roof of the house and storing it in an underground cistern. Such a cistern was located in one of the courtyards of the house.

At a given moment the city built a water pipe system to which a large number of private houses came to be connected. This system led water to the courtyards, where the inhabitants were already used to having water available from cisterns. In the courtyards the pipes fed a number of fountains and then filled the cisterns. Surplus water was directed to the streets via drains. It was only seldom that the water was led directly to the places where it was used: the kitchens, baths, or toilets.

Pompeii not only had large houses with courtyards, but apartments on upper floors and shops facing the street as well. Such units did not have courtyards and consequently their inhabitants could not collect their own rainwater. No water pipe system was found in any of these housing units either. The inhabitants had no water supply system of their own at their disposal and therefore they had to go and fetch water from one of the street fountains that were connected to the mains system.

Toilets and the supply of water

As was already mentioned above, water was needed both to rinse the sponges and to flush away urine and feces. Rinsing the sponges did not take much water, but flushing the toilet required considerable quantities. We found that housing units where little water was available usually had niche toilets, which required little flushing. All upstairs toilets are niche toilets. Nearly all the kitchen toilets in large houses, however, are flush toilets: here enough water was available. In some kitchens the brick storage basins for water have been preserved.[19] They were filled from the cistern with buckets or directly connected to an internal pipe system. The water from these basins was used in the kitchen and to flush the toilets. It seems likely that waste water from the kitchen was also used to flush the toilets. The water basins that were found in the toilets themselves were too small to have supplied water for flushing the toilets; they were only meant for rinsing the sponges.

Pompeii appears not to have had private toilets that – like many public toilets – were flushed directly with mains water.[20] The bronze tap in the House of the Silver Wedding (V, 2, 1) which was connected to the mains system, fed water into a bronze sponge basin. The same probably also applies to the toilet at the House of the Faun (VI, 12, 1–3.5.7.8), where the hole for the water pipe can still be seen next to the toilet. Some researchers (cf. de Haan 1996, 61) claim that the waste water of the private baths was used to flush the toilets.[21] It does not seem likely that this was the primary aim for the flush toilets, however. It seems more probable that it was considered convenient to get rid of the bathwater through an already existing drain.

---

[19] Examples of a water basin in a kitchen with or near a toilet: House of Caecilius Iucundus (V, 1, 23.25–27.10); VI, 3, 3.12.12.22; House of the Bear (VII, 2, 44–46); Villa of Fabius Rufus (VII, 16, 17.20–22); House of M. Holconius Rufus (VIII, 4, 2–6.49.50); House of Obellius Firmus (IX, 14, 2.4.b). Examples of a water basin near kitchen and toilet: House of the Ephebe (I, 7, 10–12.19) and IX, 5, 6.17.

[20] I want to distance myself from statements I made earlier about continual flush toilets at Herculaneum (Jansen 1991, 156). The presence of lead pipes in some of the toilets in that city led me to believe that there must have been continual flush toilets there, but the research in Pompeii, and particularly an investigation of the tap in the toilet of the House of the Silver Wedding (V, 2, 1) now seems to indicate that those pipes were not used for flushing toilets, but for filling the sponge basins.

[21] As in the House of the Centenary (IX, 8, 6.3.a) or the House of the Faun (VI, 12, 1–3.5.7.8).

To summarize, housing units that had no water supply systems of their own had niche toilets which did not need flushing. In other housing units the toilet was flushed with a bucket filled with water from a basin in or near the kitchen. The water basin contained either rainwater or water from the main.

The discharge of waste water

Pompeii had a number of simple but efficient facilities for disposing of waste water, rainwater, overflow from fountains, urine and feces. The city was built on a slope and therefore it was easy to lead the rainwater away through the streets. That is why the streets were paved and the sidewalks raised (Koga 1992). The overflow from the fountains and the waste water were disposed of in the same way. The porous subsoil of Pompeii (Mygind 1917, 297; 1921, 252; Arthur 1986, 29) made it possible to install cesspits to collect urine and feces. The existence of all these methods of disposing of waste water in fact made sewers superfluous, but several places in the city had a sewer anyway. Apparently it was thought preferable to dispose of the waste water from the baths via an underground system and not via the streets. A sewer was also installed to prevent the Forum from flooding. After the different sewers had been laid, openings were made to connect them to streets where rainwater caused trouble.[22]

Toilets and discharge systems

Which of the discharge methods was actually used can only be seen in a small number of cases because most of the toilets have only been excavated to ground level and therefore it cannot be established to where their drains led. At this moment only two toilets can be seen to be connected to a cesspit[23] and one to a cess-cellar.[24] From the two cesspits in question and a number of others described by excavators and researchers[25] it appears that a cesspit was either round or square and dug out from the porous subsoil of the city. The upper part was

---

[22] P. Dicker, Technical University Delft, has made a computer model that can simulate different types of rainfall in the streets of Pompeii. This enables us to see what happened when streets were connected to the sewer and when they were not. The computer simulation also shows the ways in which the Pompeians manipulated the water.

[23] Mygind (1921, 316) writes that Spano investigated the cesspit of the House of the Silver Wedding (V, 2, 1) and coated its walls with cement. According to him the cesspit of the House of Marcus Lucretius (IX, 3, 5.24) was coated with cement as well and collects 'jezt als Zisterne Wasser zu Bewässerung pompejanischen Gärten'.

[24] In the House of the Colored Capitals (VII, 4, 31–33.50.51) part of the cellar was bricked up and turned into a cesspit (cf. Descoeudres and Sear, 1987, 12, Fig. 1, 17).

[25] Cozzi (1900, 587–590) describes four cesspits: VI, 9, 1.14 (now overgrown); VII, 4, 23–25 (now closed); VII, 7, 10.13 (now filled up); VII, 12, 11 (now filled up). Arthur (1993, 194) reports having excavated two cesspits; one of them in the southeastern corner of the grounds of the Temple of Apollo. He claims that here there was a temporary toilet for the workers who rebuilt the temple. He also excavated a cesspit in the forum, in front of the public toilet. Eschebach (1979, 52, Taf. 25d) found a cesspit under the Stabian baths. Wynia (Peters 1993, 6) describes the remains of the cesspit from the House of Marcus Lucretius Fronto (V, 4, a.11). Strocka (1984, 18) describes the pear-shaped cesspit in the pavement in front of the House of the Prince of Naples (VI, 15, 7.8). Mygind (1921, 317) mentions a number of other cesspits, but gives no details about their possible connection to a toilet, their sizes, depth, etc.: House of the Citharist (I 4, 5.25.28); House of the Dioscuri (VI 9, 6–9); House of Caius Vibius (VII 2, 18.19.42) and House of the Hunt (VII, 4, 48.43). There is no cesspit visible in any of the four houses anymore.

built of bricks. Cesspits could be up to eleven metres deep but, unlike wells, they were never dug deeper than the first hard lava bank. Because of their size and the highly porous subsoil – which meant that waste water and urine were immediately absorbed – the cesspits probably did not need to be emptied very often. Cozzi (1900, 590) states that he found a dark stinking layer at the bottom of one of the pits (VII 4, 23–25). Arthur (1993, 194–95) is the only one ever to have studied the contents of a cesspit. What he found was mainly fragments of pottery and bone material.

Fig. 10.9 Opening of the cesspit in the garden at the back of the toilet in the House of the Silver Wedding (V,2, 1).

To avoid having to carry the contents of the cesspit through the kitchen or any other part of the house when it was being emptied, its mouth was often situated in an adjoining garden (Fig. 10.9) or in the sidewalk of the street nearby.[26] Thédenat (1910, 97) claimed that three cesspits still had stone covers with metal rings.[27] According to Arthur (1993, 194) the contents of the pits was carried to fields outside the city as well as to gardens within the city. This is supported by the fragments of bone and pottery that Jashemski (1979) found in gardens.

At this moment there is only one toilet, that of VIII, 4, 8, which is visibly connected to a sewer (the sewer in question is that of the Stabian baths). Cozzi (1900, 599), who studied this sewer, claims that a large number of pipes discharged into the sewer under Insula VIII, 4. Unfortunately he does not reveal from which houses these pipes originated. We cannot study the connections of toilets to this sewer because the sewer has become silted up.

---

[26] In the garden: House of the Silver Wedding (V, 2, 1); House of Marcus Lucretius Fronto (V, 4, a.11) (cf. Peters 1993, 6). In the sidewalk of an adjoining street: I, 10, 12; V, 6, 4; House of the Prince of Naples (VI, 15, 7.8); VII, 9, 60.63; VII, 10, 5.8.13; VII, 13, 24; VII, 15, 9.10; IX, 6, 1. In the kitchen itself: House of M. Lucretius (IX, 3, 5.24).

[27] VII, 12, 11; V, 2, 48(?); House of the Golden Cupids (VI, 16, 7.38). Seiler (1992, 52), who studied this last house, does not regard the opening in the room next to the toilet as the mouth of a cesspit, however, but as the mouth of a cistern.

It can still be seen, however, that the houses standing above the sewer had their toilets in the exact location where Cozzi situated the sewer.[28]

Other writers mention toilets that were connected to other sewers.[29] All houses, large and small, as well as other housing units, whether with or without their own water supply facilities, could be connected to a sewer: the only determining factor probably was whether there was a sewer in the vicinity. As far as can be established the shape of the toilets was not affected by whether or not they were connected to a sewer.

V. CONCLUDING OBSERVATIONS

This article has gone into the appearance and operation of toilets at Pompeii. The Pompeians constructed their toilets in such a way that they could sit down and had water available for rinsing their sponges and, where necessary, for flushing. They also took care that there was sufficient light to see by, that they themselves could not be seen from outside the toilet, and that urine and feces were led away towards a drain. The type of toilet (niche or flush) was determined by the amount of water available in the house. The way in which the water was discharged afterwards, whether via a cesspit or a sewer, probably did not affect the shape of the toilet. The most remarkable finding of all was that toilets were found in all the different types of housing. All the inhabitants of Pompeii apparently considered it necessary and natural to have a toilet in their houses.

After this first general inventory, from which we have investigated what toilets looked like and how they functioned technically, a second, more detailed and complete inventory will be made and new research questions asked. This might yield information about the actual use of the toilets and about attitudes and feelings concerning hygiene and privacy.

Moreover, excavating cesspits would make it possible to collect data about the construction and operation of such pits themselves and about the way in which toilets were used. Emptying cesspits would, for instance, show whether or not the toilets were also used for garbage disposal. In addition, it might also be found that all kinds of objects connected with the use of the toilet (sponges, oil lamps) had ended up in the cesspit. Finally, the contents of the pits could give us information about the dietary patterns of the users and about possible diseases that might be related to an unhygenic use of the toilet. Such a research would complement our understanding of life in Pompeii in many respects.

---

[28] We are talking here about a toilet on the upper floor of the House of M. Holconius Rufus (VIII, 4, 2–6.49.50), the kitchen toilet of this house, and the toilets in VIII, 4, 9, VIII, 4, 34 and VIII, 4, 37.

[29] Piranesi (1804, plate II and XXX) shows that the toilet of VI, 17, 1–4 was connected to a sewer. Mau, in *Römische Mitteilungen*, describes three other toilets that were also connected to a sewer: House of Joseph II (VIII, 2, 38.39) (1887, 121), IX, 7, 12–13 (1889, 105) and IX, 7, 15–20 (1890, 238). Strell (1913, 99–103) mentions two other toilets that were connected to a sewer: the toilet in the House of Pansa (VI, 6, 1.8.12.13) and in the House of Sallust (VI, 2, 3–5.30.31).

References

Arthur, P., 1986. Problems of the urbanization of Pompeii: excavations 1980–81, *Antiquaries Journal* 66: 29–44.

Arthur, P., 1993. La città vesuviana: problemi e prospettivi nello studio dell'ecologia umana nell'antichità, in L. Franchi dell'Orto (ed.), *Ercolano 1738–1988, 250 anni di ricerca archeologia*, (Soprintendenza Archeologica di Pompei Monografie, 6. L'Erma di Bretschnieder: Roma): 193–199.

Blümner, H., 1911. *Die römischen Privataltertümer* (Beck: München).

Curtis, R. I., 1979. The garum shop of Pompeii I.12.8, *Cronache Pompeiane* 5: 5–23.

Cozzi, S., 1900. La fognatura di Pompei , *Notizie degli Scavi di Antichità* 1900: 587–599.

Descoeudres, J.P., and Sear, F., 1987. The Australian expedition to Pompeii, *Rivista di Studi Pompeiani* 1: 11–36.

Ehrhardt, W., 1988. *La Casa dell'Orso (VII.2.44–46)* (Häuser in Pompeji 2. Hirmer: München).

Eschebach, H., 1979. *Die Stabianer Thermen in Pompeji* (Denkmäler antiker Architektur 13: Berlin).

Eschebach, L., 1991. Die Forumsthermen in Pompei Reg.VII. ins.5, *Antike Welt* 22 4: 257–287.

Fiorelli, G., 1873. *Gli Scavi di Pompei dal 1861 al 1872* (Napoli).

Fiorelli, G., 1875. *Descrizione di Pompei* (Napoli).

Grassnick, M., 1992. *Bäder und hygienische Einrichtungen als Zeugnisse früher Kulturen* (München/Wien).

de Haan, N., 1996. Die Wasserversorgung der Privatbäder in Pompeji, in de Haan and Jansen 1996: 59–65.

de Haan, N., and Jansen, G., (eds.) 1996. *Cura Aquarum in Campania*. Proceedings of the Ninth International Congress on the History of Watermanagement and Hydraulic Engineering in the Mediterranean Region.

Jansen, G., 1991. Water systems and sanitation in the houses of Herculaneum, *Mededelingen van het Nederlands Instituut te Rome* 50:145–166.

Jansen, G., 1993. Paintings in Roman toilets, in E. M. Moormann (ed.), *Functional and Spatial Analysis of Wall Painting*, Proceedings of the Fifth International Congress of Ancient Wall Painting. Publications of the Dutch Institute in Rome 3 (Stichting BABESCH: Leiden): 29–31.

Jashemski, W., 1979. *The Gardens of Pompeii* (Caratzas Brothers: New Rochelle, New York).

Koga, M., 1992. The surface drainage system of Pompeii, *Opuscula Pompeiana* 2: 57–72.

Koloski-Ostrow, A.O., 1996. Finding social meaning in the public latrines of Pompeii, in de Haan and Jansen 1996: 79–86.

Michel, D., 1990. *Casa dei Cei (I.6.15)* (Häuser in Pompeji 3. Hirmer: München).

Mygind, H., 1917. Die Wasserversorgung Pompejis, *Janus* 21: 294–351.

Mygind, H., 1921. Hygienische Verhältnisse im alten Pompeji, *Janus* 25: 251–281.

Neudecker, R., 1994. *Die Pracht der Latrine, Zum Wandel öffentlicher Bedürfnisanstalten in der kaiserzeitlichen Stadt* (Pfeil: München).

Peters, W.J.Th., 1993. *La Casa di Marcus Lucretius Fronto a Pompei e le sue Pitture* (Scrinium 5. Thesis: Amsterdam).

Piranesi, F et J.B., 1804. *Antiquités de la Grande-Grèce, Antiquités de Pompeïa*, I-II (Paris).

Scobie, A., 1986. Slums, sanitation and mortality in the Roman world, *Klio* 68: 399–433.

Seiler, F., 1992. *Casa degli Amorini dorati (VI 16, 7.38)* (Häuser in Pompeji 5. Hirmer: München).

Squassi, F., 1954. *L'arte idro sanitaria degli antichi* (Tipografia Filelfo: Tolentino).

Strell, M., 1913. *Die Abwasserfrage in ihrer geschichtlichen Entwicklung von den ältesten Zeiten bis zur Gegenwart* (Leipzig).

Strocka, V.M., 1984. *Casa del Principe di Napoli (VI 15, 7.8)* (Häuser in Pompeji 1. Wasmuth: Tübingen).

Strocka, V.M., 1991. *Casa del Labirinto (VI 11, 8–10)* (Häuser in Pompeji 4. Hirmer: München).

Thédenat, H., 1910. *Pompéi, Histoire-Vie privée* (Paris).

11 The Social Texture of Pompeii

Damian J. Robinson[1]

THE SOCIALLY HOMOGENOUS CITY?

The architecture of Pompeii and the social life that it sustained and promoted are intimately intertwined. The spatial structure of the city represents the social choices, habits, customs and relationships of the society that constructed it. The material remains of Pompeii have meaning in their structure and it is possible to 'read' the society that inhabited it. This is possible through a contextual investigation of the cultural document of Pompeian social space, as suggested by Fletcher (1995). The question to be addressed in this paper is the spatial distribution of social class across the urban landscape and its cultural interpretation. The current paradigm concerning the social texture of Pompeii was formed through the pioneering work of R.A. Raper (1977) who suggested that the city's land use was characterized by a disordered usage of space without any evidence for social zoning (1977, 207, 218). Recent work, however, has undermined many of the central premises of Raper's interpretative framework and his theoretical methodology. This paper attempts to critically reassess the conclusions of Raper and then offer another interpretation of the social texture of Pompeii.

The work of Raper stands as a turning point in the genealogy of Pompeian urban analysis. It was written, in part, as a reaction against the contemporary trend in Pompeian studies where the features of daily life – the decoration, the furniture, the graffiti – were described rather than analyzed (Raper 1977, 189). For Raper, the city was more than a repository of beautiful finds and structures, it was an artifact for analysis. The historical framework employed by Raper and the process of 'democratization' which he used to reconstruct the land use patterns of the AD 79 city, however, relied heavily upon Maiuri's interpretation of the social situation in Pompeii during the Roman colony (cf. Maiuri 1960, 116). Under this scenario the traditional élites, in the face of the economic development of Pompeii, underwent a substantial decline and either moved out to nearby villas, or residential towns such as Herculaneum.

This traditional interpretation is based upon a stereotypical view of the non-participation of the urban élite in trade or industry and is apparent in Raper's use of the map of the

[1] I would like to acknowledge the support of a University of Bradford Research Scholarship and also of the Archaeological Institute of America for the Graduate Student Travel Award which enabled me to present an earlier draft of this paper to its 1995 Annual Meeting in San Diego.

'architectonic' structure of the city generated by Hans Eschebach (1970). In this reconstruction Eschebach only differentiated between private houses and shops, entertainment buildings, and private houses incorporating workshops. The social classification of houses was not explicit, although implicit in both of these reconstructions of Pompeian society is the ideal that houses of wealth and status were not associated with trade (cf. Maiuri 1960; and especially 1958). This assumption has been recently refuted (Wallace-Hadrill 1994, 140–188). In contrast to the ideas of Maiuri, Mouritsen in his detailed re-examination of Pompeian epigraphy, has concluded that there was no élite desertion of the city and that there was a core of aristocratic families which were represented through several generations during the last hundred years of the city (1988, 118).

Furthermore both Wallace-Hadrill (1994; 1995) and Grahame (1995) have recently shown that in small discretely sampled areas of the city there is evidence for a whole range of social situations and potential evidence for socio-spatial zoning. Such works have illustrated the need to systematically examine *all* of the dwellings in Pompeii and to look for contrasting areas of social inequality across the urban landscape. This must be done to critically investigate the often repeated hypothesis proposed by Raper, that there was no spatial zoning (e.g. Laurence 1994, 118–119) and to interpret the spatial structure of the city in the light of current ideas about its social history.

HOUSES AND SOCIAL STATUS

In order to read the social map of the city, it is first necessary to investigate how dwellings may be invested with status. The material remains of the Pompeian house are socially communicative. Although not talking explicitly about the Pompeian houses, Cicero says that a man of rank needs accommodation to fit his social standing (*De Officiis* 1.138–139). Consequently the house must be a reflection of the wealth and status of its occupant. Several authors have attempted to socially categorize Pompeian houses. Della Corte (1965), for example, gave a somewhat imaginative reconstruction of the status of the occupants of many houses in the city. This account has been thoroughly discredited by Mouritsen (1988). Most recently there have been two attempts to move away from the arbitrary attribution of status. Grahame (1995) analyzed the ground plans of the majority of the dwellings from Regio VI using a developed form of Hillier and Hanson's space syntax theory (1984). Unfortunately Grahame does not explicitly separate the dwellings in his sample into different social groups, apart from at the most basic courtyard/non-courtyard level. Grahame does suggest, however, that there are different social groups represented and that there may have been some spatial logic behind their distribution.

Secondly, Wallace-Hadrill (1994) used a statistical approach to study a 'representative' sample of dwellings from Regiones I and VI in Pompeii and from insulae III, IV, V and VI in Herculaneum. Unfortunately, he fails to consider the spatial distribution of each type of dwelling, trusting instead Raper's assertion that the city had no social zoning (1977, 207, 218). Nevertheless the methodology proposed by-Wallace-Hadrill proved an effective tool for

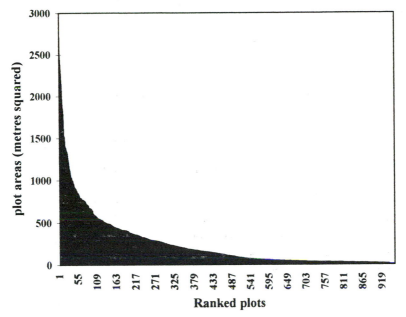

Fig. 11.1 Graph of plot areas when ranked.

ascribing social status to a particular house and a developed form of it was utilized for the analysis of the social texture presented in this paper. The Pompeian house can be socially characterized through a consideration of the interaction of three factors: the size of the property; the quantity and quality of the dwelling's decoration and the presence or absence of certain architecturally distinctive rooms.

Property size

Generally, in the Roman world the size of a house would have been commensurate with the wealth and social status of its owner or occupier. The architect Vitruvius, for example, advises important public figures to have homes with large amounts of reception space in which to carry out the necessary rituals of élite life (*De Architectura* 6.5). The importance of house size is also reflected in the property qualification for admission into the decurionate of Tarentum, where it was necessary to possess a house in the city with a minimum of fifteen thousand roof tiles (*CIL* I 22.290). In order to assess the housing and thus the social profile of Pompeii, the size of all of the completely excavated properties were recovered from a CAD (Computer Aided Design) model of the city[2] and then ranked according to size (Fig. 11.1). The distribution curve of Fig. 11.1 suggests that Pompeii was a very diverse city in social terms as it was characterized by great wealth differences. There was a socio-economic continuum

---

[2] The CAD map of Pompeii was digitised in the Department of Archaeological Sciences with the aid of a teaching grant from the University of Bradford.

between the largest property covering around two and a half thousand square metres (II, 2, 2), to the smallest at less than twenty square metres (e.g. VII, 3, 7). If property sizes are grouped according to Regio, however, differences in the social texture of the city start to become apparent (Table 1). The differences in the values for each regio as percentages of the average score for all known properties illustrate clearly the wide diversity in average property sizes around the city.

Table 1   Average property sizes per regio

Regio	Average area of properties (m²)	% of average of all known properties[3]
I	319	128
II	1004	402
IV	243	97
VI	265	106
VII	156	62
VIII	295	118
IX	199	80
All known properties	250	100

The low average property size of Regio VII is explained by a high proportion of the small dwellings in the central area around the forum. The similarly low average of Regio IX is due to the majority of the excavated insulae lying on two of the major through-routes of the city. These have been characterized by Laurence (1994, 96–103) as areas where small commercial establishments tend to cluster, and which would tend to decrease the average property size. Regiones I and II on the other hand are marked by a large number of dwellings with extensive garden plots, increasing the value of their average property sizes.

Decoration

The ground area occupied by a property, however, is only a crude measure of the wealth expended upon it. As was illustrated above, the large garden properties in Regiones I and II often had small, unpretentious dwelling areas (e.g. II, 1, 10), yet may have covered the same ground area as an imposing élite *domus*. A survey of Regio I highlighted the close relationship between the size of a dwelling and the quality and scale of its decoration (Wallace-Hadrill 1994, 143–174). Unfortunately the area used in the survey is the best preserved and documented part of the city and it was not possible to compare Regio I to other areas of Pompeii to check

---

[3] The value for each regio is calculated by taking the average area of all known properties as a 100%: in Regio I the average size of properties is 319m², equivalent to 128% of 250m², the average area of all known properties.

the validity of this conclusion. The House of Pansa (VI, 6, 1) for example, one of the largest dwellings in the city and the domus of a long established aristocratic family, has no walls with surviving decoration (Bragantini et al. 1983); whereas the more recently excavated and smaller House of the Vettii (VI, 15, 1) has fifteen decorated rooms surviving (Bragantini et al. 1983, 303–322). Consequently although decoration has the potential to differentiate, both economically and socially, between similarly sized properties, it can only be used in very small regions of the city and can not be used to aid in the reconstruction of the social texture of dwellings across Pompeii.

Reception rooms

In a survey of the dwellings in Regio VI, it was suggested that there was a relationship between increasing property size, the number of courtyards the property possessed and the social class of the building (Grahame 1995, 175–178). Such courtyards are the large atrium and peristyle reception spaces which Vitruvius alludes to (*De Architectura* 6.5) and are easily identifiable in the material remains of Pompeii.[4] Consequently when analyzing the social texture of the city the distribution of these architectural features should highlight areas of differing social class (Table 2). Atrium-peristyle dwellings are equally distributed across the urban landscape, with the exception of Regio VII. It must be suggested then that there was an equal distribution of these socially significant dwellings throughout the city. In contrast, houses with either an atrium or a peristyle appear to be more common in Regiones I, II, IV and VI. These are situated in the more peripheral areas of the city. The central core of Regiones VII, VIII and IX has more dwellings without high status architecture.

*Table 2   The distribution of socially significant architecture across the city
(figures are percentages of properties in each regio)*

Regio	I	II	V	VI	VII	VIII	IX	All known properties
No atrium or peristyle	42	39	50	50	75	65	61	58
Atrium or peristyle	43	44	36	36	16	19	24	28
Atrium and peristyle	15	17	14	14	9	16	15	14
Numbers of properties	160	18	59	213	284	99	106	939

[4] The presence/absence and type of room was derived from an examination of the property plans in the *Corpus Topographicum Pompeianum* maps (Van der Poel 1984). Eschebach et al. (1993) is also a useful reference.

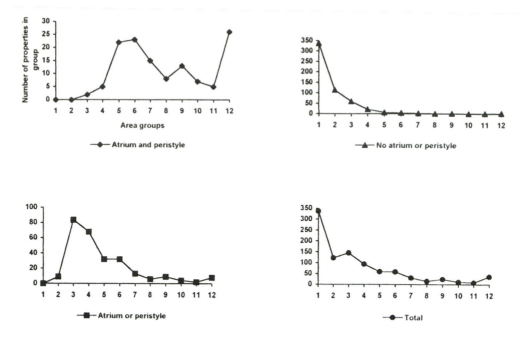

Fig. 11.2 The relationship between the area of the plot and its architectural embellishment.

A typology of Pompeian dwellings

It would appear that individual properties may be socially classified through a combination of their size and the presence or absence of certain architectural features. This combination is graphically represented in Fig. 11.2. The peaks and troughs in the data set suggest that there were essentially four types of dwellings in Pompeii:

Type 1: Such properties are less than one hundred square metres in area and have no status architecture. The type must represent the most socially disadvantaged property owning/ occupying group of citizens in Pompeii.

Type 2: These dwellings are typically small atrium houses and are over one hundred square metres in area. In the smaller properties the atrium tends not to have an *impluvium*. Impluviate atria become more common as the size of the property increases. This type also encompasses larger properties without elaborate architecture such as the garden properties in Regio II.

Type 3: These properties are at least five hundred square metres in area and are likely to have an impluviate atrium. Larger dwellings often having a peristyle with only two or three colonnades.

Type 4: Dwellings in this group are at least eight hundred square metres in area and are dominated by houses which possess both an impluviate atrium and a true four colonnaded peristyle. In the largest houses multiple atria and peristyles become common. Type four properties must represent the dwellings of the social élite of Pompeian society.

The dwelling types may be plotted across the urban landscape to reveal the social texture of Pompeii (Fig. 11.3).

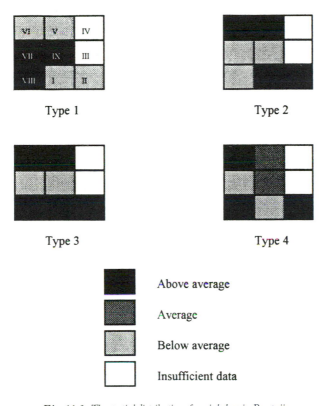

Type 1   Type 2

Type 3   Type 4

Above average

Average

Below average

Insufficient data

Fig. 11.3 *The spatial distribution of social class in Pompeii.*

AN INTERPRETATION OF THE SOCIAL TEXTURE OF POMPEII

From the distribution of type 1 dwellings there appears to have been a densely occupied core in Regiones VII, VIII and IX. This corresponds closely with the major centers of public buildings in and around the forum and the triangular forum. The majority of the dwellings in these areas were also highly integrated into the commercial life of the city. Most of these either had shop units leading off the front of the property or workshops being integrated into the structure of the dwelling. Space was obviously at a premium in the central core of Pompeii and the low average size of the dwellings is also the result of the fragmentation of type 2 and type 3 properties into smaller economic units. The high proportion of type 1 dwellings also continued on the major through-routes of the city. These led to the forum or to the city gateways. The high occurrence of street messages along these routes, as well as the high proportion of commercial establishments suggest that these were areas of high social interaction and helped channel visitors towards the forum and the central economic zone (Laurence 1994, 100; 1995).

A large proportion of the type 4 properties were also located on these through-routes. This has important social implications and suggests that the members of the élite tended to locate their houses in highly visible locations. According to Cicero a grand house gave its owner *dignitas*, indeed he suggests that a house may actively enhance the occupiers' standing in the eyes of the local community (*De Officiis* 1.138–139). The impressive façades of élite houses in Pompeii are a testimony to this social process. Elite houses were located for optimal effect on the main streets. As such they could take advantage of the flow of people along the through-routes. This enabled the house to impress a greater number of the voting public, a task which it would have been unable to perform if it were hidden away in a back street.

Away from the central core of the city, in Regiones I, II and VI there is a more dispersed form of urban activity. Away from the through-routes, commercial activity was limited and by far the majority of dwellings were of a residential nature. Back street activity also tended to involve dwellings from types 2 and 3 as these areas held far fewer opportunities for élite social display. Regio VI however, saw a greater density of urban development than the other peripheral regiones (I and II) where there was not the same pressure on space and which allowed larger garden properties to develop (cf. Jashemski 1979; 1993).

Although the social texture of Pompeii varies from the less wealthy commercialized core of the city into the more spacious and wealthy periphery, underlying this is a roughly even distribution of the type 4 houses of Pompeii's urban élite which blanket the city with the exception of the very central area of Regio VII. The implications of this for Pompeian society are intriguing. In his study of local identity Laurence points out that the city is often perceived as being made up of a mosaic of local communities. These are spatially distinct from other neighborhoods and each would have had their own distinct identity (Laurence 1994, 38). Based upon the distribution of fountains and neighborhood shrines, he proposed that Pompeii could be divided into thirty-eight communities (Laurence 1994, 44–50). If these are compared to the distribution of type 4 dwellings, thirty neighborhoods contain entrances into élite dwellings. Of the remaining eight neighborhoods, three were associated with the forum, two with the main water distribution point of the city, the *castellum aquae*, whilst the remaining two are located in the east of the city in the back streets of Regio I.

Although the exact nature of the association between the élite house and its neighborhood is unknown, a *dipinto* from Regio VI, 6 (*CIL* 4.138) may provide some insight into the probable nature of the relationship. The *dipinto* advertises street front shops, second storey apartments and a townhouse for rent. Presumably these were the properties created around the large élite dwelling, the House of Pansa (VI, 6, 1.8.13.14.22). Here the owner of the insula would have been surrounded in this neighborhood by his tenants. This close interpersonal bond between owner and occupiers represents an asymmetrical power relationship; the direct supervision and control of the tenants. This elementary form of domination (cf. Bourdieu

1977, 184–196) would have been most effective if the dominator was located in close spatial proximity to the dominated, as is suggested by the VI, 6 *dipinto*. The distribution of electoral programata may illustrate how such a power relationship is manifested in terms of political support. Mouritsen (1988, 52–57) notes that electoral notices are often concentrated in the vicinity of the candidates' home, or in the case of joint candidatures (e.g. M. Casellius Marcellus and L. Albucius Celsus) they are clustered around both of their dwellings. The tenants of Gnaeus Allius Nigidius Maius, the owner of VI, 6, could undoubtedly be relied upon to provide the kind of political support that helped him ascend to the highest offices of the city (*CIL* 4.504; Van Buren 1947). Thus we can propose that social and spatial domination of the inhabitants of a local neighborhood was one of the keys to political power in Pompeii.

The widespread distribution of élite houses is closely correlated with the neighborhood structure of the city. Clearly for the Pompeian élite the location of their domus was not just a Ciceronian exercise in self promotion: it was not enough just to locate one's house in a prominent position, it also had to be sufficiently distanced from other houses to avoid being outshone by the grandeur of potential social rivals. Elite houses formed the social nexus of their regions, they had their own *territoria*, a fertile local ground for the cultivation and domination of tenants, clients and perhaps most importantly political support. Indeed it may be suggested that the neighborhoods themselves were little more than 'extensions' of the élite dwelling. The patrician *domus* was a node in the exploitation and domination of neighborhood space and society. If one also considers that the power and influence of a notable patrician would have extended beyond the domination of his immediate neighborhood through a network of relationships across the city, we can begin to understand how the worlds of neighbourhoods, politics and economic and social ties bound Pompeii together around the homes of its élite.

Conclusion

Pompeii was not a city with the dwellings of all social classes randomly scattered across the urban landscape. Instead it was a highly structured society in spatial terms. Pompeii had a vibrant and successful urban economy which radiated out towards the city gates along major routeways and helped direct and channel visitors into the city to the central economic, social and religious space. It was a city with a class of reasonably successful citizens living in more spacious houses away from the bustle of the main streets and core area. The numerically small élite dominated city life from their imposing residences, fronting onto their main street and advertising their social power. Their distribution across the urban landscape surrounded by their dependents and political supporters in a mosaic of neighborhoods was also an exercise in social control. It amply illustrates the domination of this class of citizens over all of Pompeian society.

Abbreviation

CIL   *Corpus Inscriptionum Latinarum*

References

Bourdieu, P., 1977. *Outline of a Theory of Practice* (Cambridge University Press: Cambridge).

Bragantini, I., De Vos, M., Parise Badoni, F., Sampaolo, V., 1983. *Pitture e Pavimenti di Pompei. Regioni V, VI* (Ministero per I Beni Culturali e Ambientali: Roma).

Della Corte, M., 1965. *Case ed Abitanti di Pompei* (Edrice Fiorentino: Napoli).

Eschebach, H., 1970. *Die Städtebauliche Entwicklung des Antiken Pompeji* (Mitteilungen des Deutsches Archäologischen Instituts, Römishe Abteilung 17: Heidelberg).

Eschebach, L., Müller-Trollius, J., and Eschebach, H., 1993. *Gebäudeverzeichnis und Stadtplan der Antiken Stadt Pompeji* (Böhlau: Köln).

Fletcher, R., 1995. *The Limits of Settlement Growth – a Theoretical Outline* (Cambridge University Press: Cambridge).

Grahame, M., 1995. *The Houses of Pompeii: Space and Social Interaction* (Unpublished PhD. thesis, University of Southampton).

Hillier, B., and Hanson, J., 1984. *The Social Logic of Space* (Cambridge University Press: Cambridge).

Jashemski, W.F., 1979. *The Gardens of Pompeii, Herculaneum and the Villas destroyed by Vesuvius* (Caratzas Brothers: New Rochelle, New York).

Jashemski, W.F., 1993. *The Gardens of Pompeii, Herculaneum and the Villas destroyed by Vesuvius. Volume II: the Appendices* (Caratzas Brothers: New Rochelle, New York).

Laurence, R., 1994. *Roman Pompeii: Space and Society* (Routledge: London).

Laurence, R., 1995. The organisation of space in Pompeii, in T.J. Cornell and K. Lomas (eds.), *Urban Society in Roman Italy* (UCL Press: London): 63–78.

Maiuri, A., 1958. *Ercolano – I Nuovi Scavi (1927–1958)* (Instituto Poligraphico dello Stato: Roma).

Maiuri, A., 1960. *Pompeii* (Istituto Geografico de Agostini: Novara).

Mouritsen, H., 1988. *Elections, Magistrates and Municipal Elite: Studies in Pompeian Epigraphy* (Analecta Romana Instituti Danici, 15. L'Erma di Bretschneider: Roma).

Raper, R.A., 1977. The analysis of the urban structure of Pompeii: a sociological examination of land use (semi-micro), in D.L. Clarke (ed.) *Spatial Archaeology* (Academic Press: London): 189–221.

Van Buren, A.W., 1947. Gnaeus Allius Nigidius Maius of Pompeii, *American Journal of Philology* 68: 382–393.

Van der Poel, H.B., 1984. *Corpus Topographicum Pompeianum – Pars III* (University of Texas at Austin: Rome).

Wallace-Hadrill, A., 1994. *Houses and Society in Pompeii and Herculaneum* (Princeton University Press: Princeton).

Wallace-Hadrill, A., 1995. Public honour and private shame: the urban texture of Pompeii, in T.J. Cornell and K. Lomas (eds.), *Urban Society in Roman Italy* (UCL Press: London): 39–62.

12 Sequence and Space at Pompeii: Casual Observations from an Etruscologist

Jane K. Whitehead

To ANYONE who has loved Pompeii, these papers are both refreshing and reassuring: refreshing, in that they do not treat the site as an object or a work of art, fixed in time, but rather as a process, as a nexus of changing developments in both time and space; this is very liberating. It is also reassuring, especially to a field archaeologist such as myself, to know that in spite of the benighted methods and motives of excavation used at Pompeii over the centuries, and in spite of the ravages of war and time upon the exposed area, new research questions can still be formulated and new information gleaned.

Compare this passage from the *New Plan for the Excavations at Pompeii* dated April 22, 1811: 'I have been thinking for some time now that it would be useful to employ two companies of workmen: and one of them should excavate regularly...and be charged with excavating the core of the city, as is being done today...' (The other should dig from a point outside the city toward the city gate and then continuously on to where the other excavation team is digging) '...Otherwise I have projected that, seeing that fortuitously two theaters have already been found and uncovered – one roofed and the other open – one should think also about finding the amphitheater, located on the spot that today is called the Scodella. But I am more attracted to a third project, namely that the second company should work within the circuit of the city walls (a circuit of about three miles), because in this way one may find the other gates, and with the gates, the other major roads that come into the city itself and traverse it.'[1]

Can you imagine what a project like that would cost today? With two armies of paid workmen digging inexorably toward each other with no more of a research plan than to find *either* the city gates *or* amphitheater?' This passage makes field archaeologists of today shudder, but it represents not the worst and not the best of the excavation strategies employed at Pompeii since 1748. It gives an adequate sense of the situation with which the authors of the papers in this collection have had to deal.

Excavations such as that of 1811 have left their scars in other ways, too, however. Sadly, our profession still carries a reputation generated by centuries of projects whose goals were to serve the field of Classical literature – to illustrate or confirm the truth of the ancient texts

---

[1] Fiorelli 1860, 240, quoted in Belli 1978, 583. The abridgment and translation are my own.

– or to retrieve important art, which the art historians are now deconstructing. The stereotype of the Classical archaeologist, in the eyes of our anthropologist colleagues, is of one whose goals are monument-oriented, whose methods are serendipitous, and whose discourse is as far removed from the current debates and theoretical movements afoot in other branches of archaeology as the 1811 excavation methods are from ours.

The papers in this collection labor to dispel that stereotype. The anthropologists have come to Pompeii, a site almost sacrosanct to Classicists, and have found its 'dirty laundry': its standing garbage, its toilets. The architectural historians and Classicists have come with new questions, and they have turned to technology and science to rectify their predecessors' mistakes and misconceptions. A characteristic that all these papers seem to share is a dynamic view of their material: they do not seek to define static conditions or objects or events, but processes, relationships, and environments.

Sara Bon nicely articulates the dilemma of Pompeii: the 'embarrassment of riches.' The seductive quality of the objects preserved from the destruction by Vesuvius has ironically stimulated another destruction, that caused by looting and deterioration after exposure. Ms. Bon begins by defining the forces that shaped Pompeii as an archaeological site with which modern researchers must deal. The destruction level of AD 79 has been the goal of most Pompeian archaeology up to now and it serves as a fixed point between the post-destruction and pre-destruction phases, both of which she views as developmental.

The cities of Vesuvius are uniquely embarrassed by this richness, and are unusual in the fact that they attract diggers to a single chronological point in their existence. Nonetheless, it is a universal tendency for beautiful objects to distract from the archaeological questions. In the Etruscan world we see this most notably at Poggio Civitate di Murlo, which has produced a range of art-textbook-stuffers from elegant ivories to architectural terracottas. If these items are no longer the primary goal of the current excavators, they remain for the rest of the profession the site's chief interest. It is still mostly in the sites that yield few objects of any intrinsic value that the 'transformational' or the anthropological, social-historical issues are stressed. Numerous small excavations in Etruria of all periods come to mind. One larger site is the Archaic mining settlement at Lago dell'Accesa, currently excavated by G. Camporeale; here the Marxist issues of social class interactions can be read in the unspectacular physical remains.

Three of the articles in this volume deal with discrete insulae or structures within the city. Each of these areas offers its researcher a different preservation history and consequently elicits different research issues and methodologies.

Dott. Carafa, through the excavations directed with Prof. A. Carandini, looks toward the multifarious pre-destruction phases; the goal of that project is to determine a history of the founding and development of Pompeii. In this they are seeking not only the origins of the settlement at Pompeii and the pace of its urbanization, but also, more broadly, the nature of the stimuli for urban formation and change. They have designated certain key relationships – between public and private spaces; between Pompeii and the other settlements of the region with respect to their cultural and political similarities; between the various chronological phases with respect to their political and social organization – relationships that may illustrate the city's urbanistic development.

Although I am personally saddened to see the Etruscans lose credit for founding Pompeii, the scenario that Carafa now proposes is a reasonable one. It is logical to suppose that the burst of wealth and population of the Villanovan culture in Etruria, which was primarily stimulated by trade with the Greeks, should have touched the indigenous peoples all along the coast. What was Pompeii's attraction?

Bon, Jones, Kurchin, and Robinson extrapolate significant, broad issues from the House of the Surgeon and its neighbors; they deal with both pre-and post-destruction issues. Their post-destruction problems are complex, since they are dealing with an already excavated site. They are employing new digital imaging systems to record existing phases and conditions in order to determine development and change; this is in itself a valuable contribution. Although only in its beginning stages, this process has already led the group to new insights into the history of houses generally regarded as Pompeii's oldest. Their method for defining the different phases is apparently mere observation: a tricky business, particularly since they accept Chiaramonte Treré's conclusion that buildings cannot be dated by their materials alone. Presumably their work will in part correlate excavation stratigraphy with building sequences.

The pre-destruction issues that Bon, Jones and their colleagues are pursuing through selective excavation relate to the history of the atrium house: its role within the social and economic fabric of the insula and how that role changes over time; the functions of the individual spaces and how they change. They gaze beyond these issues to questions of urbanization. Their preliminary findings in the industrial area are already very illuminating. I look forward to following their research, particularly to see how they make the transfer from the descriptive to the theoretical; that is, how they will ultimately tap the issues of power and hierarchy to which they allude.

John Dobbins appears to be more traditionally architectural-historical in the scope of his research; he is more monument-oriented than the others in his attempt to reconstruct buildings within the environment of the forum. He is also unique in the precise chronological focus of his research (between 62 and 79), and he is thus more event-oriented than the others, who focus more on processes. But he too deals effectively both with the post-destruction transformations – he has detected a 19th century restoration – and with pre-destruction issues, particularly in the way they imply economic conditions at that time. He, like Bon, Jones and colleagues, is defining a technological approach that can be extended to other sites.

I found two very reassuring details in Prof. Dobbins' paper: first, that bad restorations, even on top of inadequate recording of excavation data, can be rectified almost a century later by close observation – that is, if one is working with monumental stone remains. Second, it is affirming when what one assumes by logic and scholarly comparison to be true (namely, that the colonnade continued in front of the Imperial Cult Building) turns out to be true in fact; when our instincts, trained in the traditional methods, turn out to be justified.

Eleanor Leach's article serves as a bridge between those that are keyed to specific structures or built units of the city and those that are based on specific bodies of scientifically or technologically generated evidence. She excavates texts; she calls her work 'an archaeology of nomenclature.' Ironically, she employs sophisticated technology in one of the most traditional kinds of study for textual critics, the word search, and she uses the technique to undermine the ancient literary sources as sole authorities for our understanding of the Pompeian house. Here philology has become the handmaiden of archaeology. Her conclusions overturn entrenched ideas about the functions of certain spaces as well as about the significance of the wall painting styles. Her combination of bodies of evidence brings form and shape to the literary terms and life to the empty excavated rooms. This article does more than any of the others to fill Pompeii with living beings, to deal with intention, experience, family and gender relationships.

How evocative are lines like 'the flora of the haymeadows in the vicinity of Pompeii' or species 'indicative of dung, rotting flesh or general foulness,' so expressive of real existence. The implications of the faunal analysis by Richardson, Thompson and Genovese are very broad and very significant, as they have clearly articulated: they situate Pompeii in its ancient natural environment. They deal with both pre- and post-destruction evidence in order to isolate groups of data for analysis: for example, to separate a refuse deposit from a 'living' (i.e. at the time of destruction) population. The goal of this team is in part to gain an understanding of the changing quantities of standing rubbish over time: what could be farther removed from the traditional monument-oriented research questions? Here, however, I would like to know more about their protocols, their sampling methods and strategies. Scientific results must be reproducible and comparable to be valid; it strikes me here that comparability is especially important where there is so much fragmentation of research.

Comparability is also a significant issue in the research of Estelle Lazer, who is studying the ethnic diversity of Pompeii's population through skeletal remains; her samples appear to be those collections stored since the nineteenth century in the Terme del Sarno and the Terme Femminile del Foro. The puzzling homogeneity of population that emerges from her results raises the further issue, which she addresses, of the representativeness of her sample and of population estimates for Pompeii in general. Here it would be helpful to know more about why she chose to document those particular features or characteristics and with which other studies she is hoping to establish comparability. For example, in her study of teeth (which are often the best preserved skeletal features) she selects only one factor: the presence or absence of double roots in the canines. Comparative studies into the ancient populations of the Italian peninsula currently undertaken by Prof. Alfredo Coppa from the University of Rome (to give only one example) are examining five anomalies of dentition: the shovel shape of the lateral maxillary incisor, the interruption groove in the anterior teeth, the Carabellic tuberculum of the first maxillary molar, the parastyle of the cuspid, and the protostylid of the upper and lower molars (Coppa et al., 1990; 1995). Why is there no overlap?

The paper by Gemma Jansen on private toilets could actually be very funny (and I am not one who enjoys scatological humor) if read aloud in the right tone. What I find surprising, however, are the armies of scholars newly mobilized to study the ancient disposal of fecal matter. Of course toilets are important for both technological and socio-cultural insights. This paper really does illuminate aspects of real life in the ancient world, though in a very harsh light; it enables us to imagine the Emperor Titus gazing out of a window as he uses a toilet sponge.

Damian Robinson, in looking at the diversity of social class across the urban landscape, as he says, is attempting to quantify everything that has simply been comprehended intuitively up to now. Such an approach lacks the poetry of the paleobotanists' 'flora of the haymeadow', and sometimes it points out the stridently obvious: note, for example, his conclusion that the houses of the rich are larger, more expensively decorated, and have more reception space. But expressing everything in terms of hard numbers does expose in rather glaring light certain facts that otherwise are overlooked. This method also exposes silly or misinformed conclusions based on the subjective analysis of a sample of one. This Mr. Robinson does here with a delightful tongue-in-cheek.

Statistical analyses have been employed heretofore mainly on categories of artifacts. For example, Ingela Wiman has grouped Etruscan mirrors and quantified their characteristics by Multiple Correspondence Analysis (Wiman 1989; 1990). Her results yield interesting conclusions that overturn our concepts of 'typology' and render useless the categories based solely on motif or other observed details. Robinson's studies build on the research of Andrew Wallace-Hadrill, as many in this collection do. One hopes that his databases will generate answers to the questions he poses.

A noteworthy aspect of the papers in this collection is that they are the results of international collaboration: another example of the broader vision that this new research brings to archaeology. I look forward to following the results of these various projects.

References
Belli, C., 1978. *Amedeo Maiuri: Mestiere d'Archeologo* (Milan).
Coppa, A., Colarossi, P., Danubio, M.E., Mancinelli, D., and Petrone, P.P., 1990. Aspetti paleodemografici in campioni di popolazione adulta dell'Italia Centrale durante l'Età del Ferro, *Antropologia Contemporanea* 13: 65–93.
Coppa, A., Colafranceschi, M., Vargiu, R., Cucina, A., and Mancinelli, D., 1995. Continuity/discontinuity in Central-Southern Italian populations during the Metal Age: dental metric and non-metric traits evidence,' *American Journal of Physical Anthropology* Supplement 19: 194 (abstract).
Fiorelli, G., 1860. *Pompeianarum Antiquitatum Historia* (Naples).
Wiman, I.M.B., 1989. Indications of inconsistency between physical data and ornamental decoration within two groups of Etruscan mirrors, *OpRom* 17: 213–224.
Wiman, I.M.B., 1990. *Malestria-Malena. Metals and Motifs in Etruscan Mirrors,* SIMA XCI (Göteborg).

13 Some Random Thoughts on a Collection of Papers on Roman Archaeology

Stephen L. Dyson

OUR VIEWS OF ancient Pompeii are driven by two hoped-for perfections. The first is that of a perfect recapture of a segment of ancient Rome, where the past can be understood and recreated with a clarity and completeness not found elsewhere in the messy record of Roman antiquity. The second is that of the perfect archaeological site, where human action was frozen at a sudden moment in past time. It was the dream of the New Archaeologists that a combination of imaginative cultural model building and sophisticated field technique would allow archaeology to become a true interpretive social science (Binford 1972; 1981; Dyson 1981; 1993). A site like Pompeii should allow archaeologists to employ material culture distributions to reconstruct a complex picture of human activity in a way not possible at most archaeological sites (Schiffer 1976; 1985). Lawrence Alma-Tadema and Lewis Binford may make strange bedfellows but they have played that role in shaping Pompeian studies.

From the moments of first discovery in the eighteenth century the special lure of Pompeii was the completeness of its record of the Roman past and the way that preserved record could be used not only to reconstruct but also to visualize what life was actually like in the ancient civilizations so admired by educated Europeans. Both eighteenth century Neo-classicists and early Nineteenth century Romantics revelled in this tangible presence of the much admired and imitated world of Greco-Roman antiquity (Leppmann 1966; Etienne 1992, 14–34). Pompeii soon spawned a major tourist industry which evolved from the erudites to the educated bourgeoisie.

The process of identification with and personalization of the buried city on the Bay of Naples was enhanced by the publication in 1834 of Bulwer Lytton's novel *The Last Days of Pompeii* (Jenkyns 1980, 82–5). That work had enormous circulation in nineteenth century England and America, and for generations it shaped reaction to Pompeii not only as a tourist objective, but also as an object of study. The latest Laterza guide to Pompeii still notes the association between the House of the Tragic Poet and the House of Glaucus 'nel noto romanzo di E. Bulwer-Lytton' (De Vos & De Vos 1982, 223). The world of Glaucus and his associates then became transferred into an infinity of school Latin texts and general guides to Roman civilization.

This literary vision of ancient Rome was complemented by the pictorial vision of the late nineteenth century European Neo-classical painters and especially of the Anglo-Dutch artist Lawrence Alma-Tadema. Alma-Tadema became fascinated with Pompeii during his honeymoon in Italy in 1863, and studied in some detail the discoveries and techniques of that pioneering archaeologist Guiseppe Fiorelli. Alma-Tadema was one of the first painters to realize the potential of the use of a large photographic collection to allow the creation of historical paintings of a new level of archaeological accuracy (Tomlinson 1991, 1–6). While largely scorned and ignored by collectors until recently, Alma-Tadema's paintings were enormously popular and influential in the late nineteenth century. If Bulwer Lytton conveyed in words, Alma-Tadema conveyed in images how cultivated people visualized what Rome and Pompeii had been like (Swanson 1977). It was a world of gentility, taste, and order. People may have gone to the bath, but did not go to the bathroom. Jansen's illuminating paper in this volume would not have been acceptable.

The search for a neat and ordered Pompeii which would represent all of the elements of a quintessential Roman town produced a picture of its historical development that had clarity to it and reflected the influence of the major civilizations of the Italian peninsula and the classical Mediterranean. Since the city bore so much of the weight of our understanding of ancient Rome, the Roman-ness of the later city received special emphasis. Everything from political activity in the forum to the life of the bath and the brothel had to be seen as more generically Rome and less the particular record of a Samnite town on the Bay of Naples.

While relatively little was known of the event-orientated history of Pompeii, enough could be reconstructed to allow some periodization and to pigeonhole major social and economic changes in the city. The impact of the earthquake of AD 62 could not be ignored and in fact served a useful purpose (Andreau 1973). It provided an important archaeological division point in the structural history of Pompeii. It also allowed conservative academics to comment on what happened in a Roman community when one went from the control of the traditional country gentry to that of the vulgar merchant classes.

The Sullan colony provided the historical moment for transforming the Hellenized Samnite center into the Roman town. Interestingly enough, while social historians like Castrén have stressed the social and political impact of the imposition of the colony, much less stress has been placed on what must have been the wrenching physical implications of such massive changes in property holdings and social status (Castrén 1975; Richardson 1988, 154–183). Emphasis for the Samnite period at Pompeii has been placed on the cultured, wealthy, Hellenized community of the second century BC rather than on the more primitive hill folk who had been enemies of Rome.

The origins of the city were usefully vague in both the historical and the archaeological record. The search for the *Altstadt* implied that the archaeologists expected some ordered foundation, which the later street plan seemed to mirror. Etruscan and Greek influences were stressed, which enhanced the sense of ongoing association of Pompeii with the Hellenic civilization of the Bay of Naples. It was seen as a place where the highly Hellenized figure of Glaucus in *The Last Days of Pompeii* could feel very much at home (Jenkyns 1980, 84–5).

The lack of deep excavation and stratigraphic research at Pompeii meant that the archaeological record which could be used for chronological reconstruction took on an abstract order which would tend to simplify more complex historical processes. Major divisions in urban development were provided by the foundation of the Sullan colony (although as has been noted this event has been little read into the archaeological record), the Augustan hegemony, and the AD 62 earthquake. Changes in building techniques like those of the Samnite tufa phase provided some framework for the reconstruction of basic construction history (Richardson 1988, 67–130).

More central to the reconstruction of the history of residential use were stylistic changes in the ubiquitous wall paintings. The four stage division of the decorative schemes found in Pompeian painted walls introduced by the German August Mau in the late nineteenth century and refined by later scholars became the basis of much subsequent interpretation of the history of the houses at Pompeii (Mau 1882). The Pompeian paintings were linked to more precisely dated examples at Rome, and the four styles were given well-defined time periods. Artistic production at the capital and the secondary center off the Bay of Naples became inseparably intertwined, so that any history of Roman painting became to a large degree a history of Pompeian painting. It was comforting for even the well educated amateur to be able to walk into a Pompeian house, distinguish Second from Fourth Style, and reconstruct something of the history of the house.

New research is making it increasingly clear that this well ordered view of Pompeian artistic and archaeological development will have to be seriously modified. What the papers in this present volume make very clear is the complexity, fluidity, and uncertainty of our archaeological knowledge of Pompeii. They demonstrate our relative ignorance of much of the long history of the city, and force an appreciation of the subtle complexity of the events that we now try to reconstruct.

The problem of interpretation begins with the history of the excavations themselves. Anyone who has worked at Pompeii knows how much of the wall painting and other decorations of the houses has been lost through time, wear and neglect since clearing at the site first began in the eighteenth century. Given the propensity of the early researchers to stress only the best elements in ornamentation of houses and their custom of physically removing the best examples of painting from their original location and transporting them to the museum first at Portici and then at Naples, it is fair to say that it is almost impossible to speak definitively about the overall organization of the decorative scheme of many of those houses and public buildings that were excavated in that early period.

What is less frequently stressed is the degree to which what we see and study at Pompeii today is the product of not only deterioration and removal, but also of rebuilding and restoration. This can be seen in our understanding of the basic construction history of particular buildings. The custom of making clear distinctions between ancient originals and restorations in Pompeian wall construction (and at other Italian archaeological sites as well) is a relatively new one. Even experts can confuse constructions of the nineteenth and twentieth centuries with those of antiquity. Detailed wall recording and analysis of the type now being undertaken at Pompeii (see Bon, Jones, Kurchin and Robinson, in this volume) are necessary not only to

provide the basis of reconstruction of ancient building history, but also to advance the process of distinguishing between what was the work of ancient builders at different time periods
and what was the product of nineteenth and twentieth century restorers.

Two lines of current research undermine literally and figuratively the naive processual archaeologists' fantasy that Pompeii represents a complex ancient activity area preserved in
volcanic amber. The first assumption in this model has been that the site of Pompeii was not
only destroyed almost instantaneously by the standards of normal archaeological site abandonment, but also that it remained relatively little disturbed until the start of the excavations
of the eighteenth century. Recent work including papers in the current volume make this
hypothesis very uncertain.

The tops of many of the structures apparently remained visible when the volcanic activity
ended in AD 79. Not unexpectedly a combination of previous owners and entrepreneurial
ancient looters returned to the scene and removed a great range of public and private artifacts. Increased emphasis on the 'post-depositional' archaeology of Pompeii is beginning to
make clear the extent of that phenomenon. The lack of public sculpture at Pompeii as compared with Herculaneum provides the most vivid illustration of this. It can be assumed that
the ancient looters concentrated on the removal of objects of value, thus seriously distorting
the record that the archaeologists found when they returned to the site from the eighteenth
century onward.

Another major obstacle to applying the Pompeii principle of the perfectly preserved activity areas to Pompeii itself is the increased evidence for what seems to be the massive disrup-
tion of normal activity and traditional spatial use that we tend to associate with the period
between the earthquake of AD 62 and the volcanic destruction of AD 79. Here the researches
of Penelope Allison cited often in this volume is of particular relevance.

Allison and other scholars have demonstrated the potential of the 'archaeology of Pompeian
archives'. The systematic, sophisticated investigation of the more than two hundred years of
excavation records from Pompeii and other Roman sites in the Bay of Naples area can yield
important information on what was found when and where (see now Parslow 1995 for similar archival archaeology at Herculaneum). These records are especially illuminating about the
location of portable material culture finds in various structures. Allison has reconstructed with
great care in which contexts various household objects were actually found by the excavators
during the two centuries of work at the site.

These reconstructed site inventories present a picture of the appearance of Pompeian houses
very different from the common perception of the Pompeian residence as a well ordered
domestic universe sustained by the ancient version of the nineteenth century English butler.
Spaces in both the public and private areas clearly had at least in AD 79 been put to *ad hoc* uses
by ancient owners who had clearly not absorbed the lessons of Vitruvius or Mau.

The reaction to this growing evidence for so much mess and disorder in the domestic sphere
of Pompeii has been to blame it on the earthquake, that disaster which it is argued left so
much of Pompeii a building yard for nearly seventeen years. Not only did the earthquake
produce major social change, but it also disrupted the normal patterns of domestic life and

residential use. A simpler explanation may be that Pompeians did not live the way that modern scholars expected them to live, and that a certain level of chaos and the flexible use of space was a part of their domestic life as it is for a modern Neapolitan house.

The earthquake of AD 62 has, as I have already observed, become a defining event for later Pompeian history and archaeology. It has become a sort of *deus ex terra* that provides the clue for understanding a range of Pompeian historical, social, and archaeological problems. Now new evidence is demonstrating that the interpretation of this earthquake phenomenon must move from simplicity to complexity. The real possibility that the city was struck by multiple earthquakes provides a better explanation of the complex history of restoration at various public and private structures. The various 'messes' in the houses of Pompeii may have been complex combinations of the fluid, flexible lifestyles of the Pompeian élite and continuous expedients used until the interior decorators completed their renovations in the wake of each new tremor.

Much recent research at Pompeii has centered on the macro use of space within the city (Laurence 1994; Robinson in this volume) and the micro-use of space within the house itself (Wallace-Hadrill 1994; Leach in this volume). Both lines of research emphasize the need for an appreciation of complexity and ambiguity in the interpretation of spaces within individual residences. Pompeii has been forced to bear a big burden as the major surviving collective example of 'Roman' domestic architecture. The houses of this small Campanian town have been used to explain everything from the evolution of Roman domestic painting to the political and social rituals of the Roman political élite.

A number of problems arise from this excessive burden. It is probably fair to say that Pompeians were not Romans in the sense that they shared ethnicity or political values with the élite of the capital. It is not clear what was the ethnic composition of the upper classes at Pompeii at the time of destruction. Oscan families certainly survived, and there was clearly a freedman element. As with most Roman colonies, we are not sure of the origins of the average Sullan colonist at Pompeii, but it is fair to say that they were not drawn from the capital's élite.

Pompeii had its own political tradition and political culture. As the rich electoral record makes clear local politics at Pompeii was much more active than it was at Rome. Clearly commerce played a very different role in the life of the Pompeian élite than it did in that of the contemporary Roman élite. Given this dynamic municipal localism, the Pompeian house should be read as a Pompeian house and not as a Roman house. The world of the first century communities of Italy was very different from that of the capital (Dyson 1992).

Examination of the Pompeian house requires not only an appreciation of the importance of local culture, but also close reading of the relation between decoration and spatial use. Recent research like that of Leach in this volume has demonstrated that it is possible to combine pictorial and architectural information to reconstruct the decorative ideology of certain spaces within the Pompeian house. These reflected not only the interests of the owner or decorator, but also the intended function of the spaces used. Within categories of room functions, first style paintings had a very different distribution from those of the fourth style.

However, this emphasis on continuous redecoration and the ideological associations of styles with spaces must raise disturbing questions about the use of the classic four Pompeian styles as chronological indicators. That these changing decorative schemes grew out of an original stylistic evolution with distinct chronological parameters seems clear from the archaeo-logical evidence both from Rome and the Bay of Naples. That the paintings actually preserved on the walls of the houses of Pompeii in AD 79 represented archaeological type fossils which preserved earlier building or decorative phases in the history of a particular house seems increasingly dubious.

The freshness at the time of discovery of certain examples of such archaic painting tech-niques as the first style raises real questions about the relative importance of survival of a painting from a previous generation versus the self-conscious selection of a certain style from the diverse available repertoire for functional or ideological purposes. It is becoming increas-ingly attractive to view the use of Pompeian styles as similar to the modern use of quality wall-paper for purposes of articulating the owner's social status and cultural identity. It makes good sense from what we increasingly know about the approach to self presentation among the Pompeian élite, but it threatens to open a Pandora's Box in the area of reconstruction of house history and the evolution of decorative taste.

It is clear from accounts of the excavations discussed in this volume that the greatest new frontier in Pompeian studies lies in the exploration of layers below the AD 62–79 surfaces. This archaeological research will require sophisticated methodologies, careful consideration of post-depositional processes, and imaginative new archaeologically based models of socio-economic development. The reconstruction of the earlier phases of occupation at Pompeii will require much more in the way of careful and imaginative excavation and the recovery and interpretation of a greater range of archaeological features and artifact types, from postholes and beaten earth floors to environmental, faunal and floral remains. The report by Richardson, Thompson and Genovese in this volume provides tantalizing insights into the type of envi-ronmental evidence that can be recovered and the information that can be extracted from it.

The report on the excavations by Carafa and his colleagues demonstrates clearly the time depth of occupation at Pompeii. The eruption of Vesuvius destroyed a settlement where occupation went back to the Bronze Age. That and other papers in this volume on recent excavations at the site make plain the extent to which that earlier archaeological record has been disturbed. Macro-events like the bombing of the city in World War II are spectacular instances of that disturbance, but more common and insidious are the hundreds, even thou-sands of disruptions in the subsoil caused by centuries of reuse and rebuilding in a densely inhabited area.

The density of surviving remains at Pompeii and the unlikelihood of any extensive removal of structures from the last phase of Roman occupation will limit the potential for major open area excavations which will lay bare in a systematic and carefully controlled stratigraphic manner extended sectors of the buildings of the earlier community. Such excavations will be largely confined to places that were gardens or open areas in AD 79. These may or may not have had a history of different use in earlier periods. However, the most densely built and used zones will mainly be the domain of key-hole archaeology, with all of the technical and conceptual limitations which that type of excavation imposes. There is an adage in archaeology that the quality of field technique is often in inverse relationship to the quality of the finds. The errors and atrocities committed in the long history of clearing first century AD Pompeii would seem sadly to confirm that folk wisdom. Clearly the recovery of the disturbed, fragmentary, yet highly complex remains of early Pompeii will challenge the best of contemporary field methodology.

It will also require a more sophisticated social archaeology that moves beyond the Roman history textbook to a combination of the detailed analysis of material culture, the placement of that information in the wider context of cultural change in Campania from the later Bronze Age to the Roman conquest, and application of models of interpretation developed by archaeologists researching later prehistoric Europe. The arguments advanced by Carafa and his colleagues that early Pompeii can best be understood in the context of evolving hill fort communities of Iron Age Samnium rings true. That may not give comfort to classicists who want to stress Pompeii's close association with the Etruscan, Greek and Roman high cultures of the Mediterranean.

I opened this essay by focusing on the surety of knowledge of the past that Pompeii seemed to provide to the eighteenth and nineteenth century investigators. The richness of the information unearthed at the site has multiplied well beyond the dreams of those early explorers. However, that quantitative increase in information and the growing sophistication of the questions asked of that information has bred complexity and ambiguity. Each year we know more and also know less about Pompeii. The old certainties are crumbling. This is good, for not only will that uncertainty foster the types of diverse and ambitious research represented by these papers, but also stimulate the hard questioning that will lead to newer and more valid models of interpretation of this most important of archaeological sites. The combination of a new generation of imaginative Pompeian archaeologists and the presence of an Italian archaeological administration very supportive of new lines of research means that research at the archaeological site that in the eighteenth century provided many of the foundations of our discipline is now entering a new Golden Age.

References

Allison, P., 1992. Artefact assemblages: not 'the Pompeii Premise', in E. Herring, R. Whitehouse and J. Wilkins (eds.), *Papers of the Fourth Conference of Italian Archaeology* (Accordia Research Centre: London): 49–56.

Andreau, J., 1973. Histoire des séismes et histoire économique: le tremblement de terre de Pompéi (62 ap.J.C.), *Annales Economies Societés Civilisations* 28: 369–395.

Binford, L., 1972. *An Archaeological Perspective* (Academic Press: New York).

Binford, L., 1981. Behavioral archaeology and the 'Pompeii Premise', *Journal of Anthropological Research* 37: 195–208.

Castrén, P., 1975. *Ordo Populusque Pompeianus: Polity and Society in Roman Pompeii*. Acta Instituti Romani Finlandiae 8 (Rome).

Dyson, S.L., 1981. A Classical Archaeologist's response to the New Archaeology, *Bulletin of the American School of Oriental Research* 242: 7–13.

Dyson, S.L., 1992. *Community and Society in Roman Italy* (Johns Hopkins University Press: Baltimore).

Dyson, S.L., 1993. From New to New Age Archaeology: archaeological theory and classical archaeology – a 1990s perspective, *American Journal of Archaeology* 97: 195–206.

Etienne, R., 1992. *Pompeii. The Day a City Died* (Thames & Hudson: London).

Jenkyns, R., 1980. *The Victorians and Ancient Greece* (Blackwell: Oxford).

Laurence, R., 1994. *Roman Pompeii: Space and Society* (Routledge: London).

Leppman, W., 1966. *Pompeji. Eine Stadt in Literatur und Leben* (Munich).

Mau, A., 1882. *Geschicte der decorativen Wandmalerei in Pompeji* (Berlin).

Parslow, C., 1995. *Rediscovering Antiquity: Karl Weber and the Excavation of Herculaneum, Pompeii and Stabiae* (Cambridge University Press: Cambridge).

Richardson, L., 1988. *Pompeii. An Architectural History* (Johns Hopkins University Press: Baltimore).

Schiffer, M.B., 1985. Is there a 'Pompeii Premise' in archaeology?, *Journal of Anthropological Research* 41: 18–41.

Swanson, V., 1977. *Sir Lawrence Alma-Tadema. The Painter of the Victorian Vision of the Ancient World* (Ash and Grant: London).

Tomlinson, R., 1991. *The Athens of Alma Tadema* (Alan Sutton: Gloucester).

Wallace-Hadrill, A., 1994. *Houses and Society in Pompeii and Herculaneum* (Princeton University Press: Princeton).